Building
Object-Oriented
Software

Building
Object-Oriented
Software

Stephen L. Montgomery

McGraw-Hill, Inc.

New York • San Francisco • Washington, D.C. • Auckland • Bogotá
Caracas • Lisbon • London • Madrid • Mexico City • Milan
Montreal • New Delhi • San Juan • Singapore
Sydney • Tokyo • Toronto

1 2 3 4 5 6 7 8 9 0   DOC/DOC   9 0 3 2 1 0 9 8

ISBN 0-07-043196-5

The sponsoring editor for this book was Simon Yates, and the production supervisor was Tina Cameron. It was set in New Century Schoolbook by Multiscience Press, Inc.

Printed and bound by R.R. Donnelley and Sons.

McGraw-Hill books are available at special quantity discounts to use as premiums and sales promotions, or for use in corporate training programs. For more information, please write to the Director of Special Sales, McGraw-Hill, 11 West 19th Street, New York, NY 10011. Or contact your local bookstore.

 This book is printed on recycled, acid-free paper containing a minimum of 50% recycled deinked fiber.

For Sarah

Contents

Introduction

Organizations today are becoming exceedingly complex, placing great demands upon the information systems that support them. These organizations require:

- More timely access to information whenever and wherever their business and technical personnel require it
- Information in useful formats that can be easily understood and adapted
- Accurate and consistent data throughout each area of the organization
- A high degree of responsiveness to changing business conditions
- A high degree of information sharing across an organization

Unfortunately, high-quality information systems to support these needs do not come easily. Rather, they require a high degree of planning and careful implementation and maintenance. As with the planning and construction of buildings or other engineered products, enterprise architectures require careful planning and skillful construction.

Enterprise Architecture Planning

Enterprise architecture planning, as viewed by John Zachman, results in a high-level blueprint of data, applications, and technology that is a cost-effective, long-term solution; not a quick fix. Enterprise architecture planning can be labeled as business-driven or data-driven, because (Spewak, p. xxi, Preface):

- A stable business model (independent of organizational boundaries, systems, and procedures) is the foundation for the architectures.

- Data are defined before applications.

- Data dependency determines the sequence for implementing application systems.

This author wholeheartedly agrees with this statement, but would extend the data and application concepts to objects. Whereas traditional information systems development began with a discussion of processes and programs and then evolved to a discussion of processes and data accessed by programs, modern information systems tend to deal with systems of interconnected, communicating objects.

The momentum for proliferation of enterprise architecture planning has increased with computer-aided software engineering (CASE), use of information engineering methods and techniques, the trend toward down-sizing of organizations and their systems, business process re-engineering, and advancement of various information systems technologies that encourage information sharing (see Montgomery 1990, 1991, and 1994 for discussions). Most information systems managers recognize that a comprehensive enterprise-wide plan is necessary (indeed, essential) for achieving success with information technology. This book aims to support the concept of enterprise architecture planning and implementation using object concepts, techniques, and tools.

Enterprise architecture planning is defined by Spewak as:

"the process of defining architectures for the use of information in support of the business and the plan for implementing those architectures"

Architectures in this context consist of data architecture, application architecture, and technology architecture. They serve the same function in information systems development as do the blueprints, drawings, and models of the construction and engineering disciplines. Enterprise architecture defines a business and its architectures, but does not aim to define the systems, database, or network designs. Architectures define what business support is needed (in terms of definitions, standards, and ideas), while the plans define when the architectures will be implemented. When dealing with enterprise architecture planning, we need to be able to answer how to:

- Access data in a useful format, when and where needed

- Adapt to changing business needs

- Provide accurate and consistent information

- Share information across an organization

- Contain costs

What, you may ask, is different about enterprise architecture planning with respect to traditional information systems planning? The differences may be boiled down to:

- Architectures are founded on a functional business model.

- Data (objects) are defined before applications.

- Object dependencies are used to determine implementation plans.

- Both the short-term operational focus and the long-term strategic focus are based on use of information and technology to support an organization.

This probably seems obvious, but this author never ceases to be amazed at the number of times that organizations fail to plan adequately for systems integration, so the so-called "islands of automation" continue to be built and maintained (at very high cost to the organizations). At times throughout this book the reader may get the idea he or she is being preached at, and that may indeed be the case. It should be understood that this author is very committed to building effective information systems that, because they are based on solid architectural principles, will endure over time and may be more easily evolved to adapt to business change rather than being repeatedly replaced in their entirety.

Why We Need Object Technology

The main benefits of object-oriented systems development are improved reliability and enhanced developer productivity. Reliability can be improved because each object is simply a "black box" to external objects that it must communicate with. Internal data structures and methods can be refined without impacting other parts of a system. Traditional systems, on the other hand, often exhibit unanticipated side effects when a section of code is modified. Object technology helps developers deal with complexity in systems development.

Developer productivity can be enhanced because classes of objects can be made reusable such that each subclass or instance of an object can use the same program code for the class. Developer productivity is also enhanced due to a more natural association between system objects and real-world objects. Application development becomes shortened once the object paradigm has been learned. Object models of the world are more natural because data and programs are stored together, hierarchical model structures are possible, and successive layers can express increasing levels of detail. This all adds up to make object analysis models and systems designs easier to understand, enhancing system maintenance.

David A. Taylor (pp. 103–107) discusses these benefits of object modeling and development:

1. Faster development

2. Higher quality

3. Easier maintenance

4. Reduced cost

5. Increased scalability

6. Better information structures

7. Increased adaptability

Taylor (pp. 108–113) goes on to discuss some potential concerns we should have when evaluating object technology at the present time:

1. Maturity of the technology

2. Need for standards

3. Need for better tools

4. Speed of execution

5. Availability of qualified personnel

6. Cost of conversion

7. Support for large-scale modularity

Improved Systems Development

Today, business organizations find themselves confronted with a serious dilemma. They are becoming increasingly dependent on information processing to handle almost every aspect of their operations. Their ability to handle information is failing to keep up because the volume of information is increasing faster than the capacity to handle it. The problem is not due to computing platforms—hardware and operating systems software. Rather, the failure to keep up with information processing demands lies in the inability of software developers to capitalize on the potential benefits. The main problem here is the need to maintain mountains of outdated software programs and databases.

This gap between computing power and the ability of software to adapt to the computing platforms gets wider all the time. Although everyone who uses computers is affected, large organizations with hundreds of thousands of lines of software code are most affected. It is a rare occasion when a major information systems development project is completed on time and within budget. What is worse is that the systems that are built are usually so full of flaws and so rigidly constructed that it can be impossible to enhance them with essential changes without major redesign and redevelopment.

The rate of change in global business and political environments exacerbates the problem to the point that many organizations are on the verge of a crisis in information management. Important organization-wide information systems can be obsolete even before they are delivered. Even when they are delivered they are not capable of evolving to address future organizational needs. Some studies indicate that as little as 5 percent of all systems development projects create working systems and the rest are rejected and result in reconstruction, abandonment after completion, or are never completed. In order to resolve this crisis in software development, we need a radically new way to approach the analysis, design, and development of information systems.

Modular programming, structured programming, CASE, and fourth-generation languages each have attempted to address the development problem. They have had some degree of success. Despite all the efforts to date to discover better ways to build systems, the development crisis is getting worse with the passage of time. We still build systems largely by hand. Better construction methods have been developed but tend not to work well on large projects. Current methods tend to produce systems of erratic quality that are difficult to modify and maintain. Object technology can meet these challenges. The rest of this book discusses how object technology can address many of the problems the software crisis presents us with.

Assembling Systems from Components

Object technology has become an established way to build quality software at reasonable cost. Some reasons for this are that object technology is an excellent way to deliver systems based on reusable components. Also, objects provide solutions to business problems such that they better support adaptable and flexible business organizations. They do this while at the same time increasing the productivity of developers and users of the systems. It is becoming increasingly necessary to develop information systems that can deliver extensible, tailorable, modular components, and do this without becoming overly complex.

Object technology can be more productive than traditional technologies because it has the potential to reuse existing components via their specifications, often referred to as their contracts. Class libraries (for business models, design specifications, or application code) provide reuse repositories. Components may be tailored as required using inheritance. Object systems provide greater productivity during development due to their richer modeling content, which is more imperative than procedural in nature.

Hardware is assembled from pretested components, which are used repetitively to design and build even larger assemblies, which are themselves reusable. The quality at each level of design is ensured by pretesting system components. Error-free assembly is ensured by interface standards that focus on the functionality and behavior of each system component at its interface. The same concepts can and are being applied in software development via object technology. Tools are available that support object-oriented design, analysis, and system construction. Special libraries of reusable components are readily available, especially for graphical user interfaces. In addition, object database management systems are becoming more widely used.

Today, much of the conventional software is written largely from scratch. Because such software is usually written to solve very specific problems, it can often be easier to write new systems than to convert existing ones. Objects, on the other hand, are general-purpose building blocks that closely reflect real-world entities, not special-purpose processing tasks. Objects can be made useful for subsequent application projects, even if the purposes of the new systems are different. As more and more object classes are constructed, they can be accumulated into an enterprise-wide systems building block library. Then development can shift from creating new object classes to assembling existing ones in new and innovative ways. It is possible that experienced object system developers can spend as little as 20 percent of their time creating new classes, instead of assembling proven system components into new, powerful, and reliable systems.

Unlike conventional programming languages and designs, whose abstractions are of computer constructs, object systems are abstractions of real-world concepts. Object abstractions (the objects themselves) contain data, just as files and tables in conventional systems do, but they also contain behaviors (procedures). This is equivalent to having files and tables contain programs. Much in the same way that relational tables can be designed to "normalize" data to minimize data redundancy, objects provide normalization of procedures, which can be defined in one place and accessed from elsewhere using messages to the objects that contain the procedures.

Object-oriented analysis and design provide even greater benefits than object-oriented programming, because they tend to create models and patterns that are readily extended. We can add an object or group of objects to a system without having to take the system off-line, recompile, and retest it because of the reusable structures identified earlier in the life cycle. Inheritance provides even greater benefits of reuse, available through libraries of objects that can be purchased or constructed in-house. This means that we can more easily assemble systems from reusable components.

Support for User-Interface Designs

One important way that object orientation will affect many business organizations is in the development of event-driven, graphical user interfaces. These interfaces are driven by business events rather than by computer events, but can be costly to design and build using conventional techniques. Object-oriented languages designed for user-interface development allow user interfaces to be constructed using very few lines of program code. Because object languages help programmers to model user concepts, the user interfaces they are used to build will be more intuitive and easy to use. Objects encapsulate information about their visual forms, so programmers don't need to embed knowledge as fixed procedures. If every user-interface object is also a program object, the mapping from user-interface objects to business objects to database objects becomes more intuitive, and thus easier to build and maintain. Object systems are models of objects in a business and the processes in which they can participate, which we model by message passing.

Support for Client/Server Computing

Object technology supports development of client/server systems, helping users by placing more power on the desktop so that systems interfaces can respond better to user needs. Object-oriented interfaces enhance usability by allowing object-action (rather than the traditional action-object) dialogs. These interfaces encourage a user to point to an object and then decide what action to take upon the object. We could point to a file and indicate that we wish to transfer the file to a different network location. This style of user/system interaction supports event-driven computing. Client/server computing supports better interfaces to multiple, distributed information resources and places computing power where it is needed most. Object models and components make this flexibility easier than ever to achieve.

Basic Object Concepts

The idea of an object that combines both static data structure and dynamic processing behavior fits well with the way we view objects in the real world (at least with objects that move or create or manipulate information). Although experts may disagree on how the term object should be used, for our purposes an object is a single thing or concept as distinguished from other things or concepts. Strictly speaking, we should refer to a kind of an object (such as a person) as an object type and a specific occurrence of that kind of object (such as John Jones) as an object instance. In this book we refer to an object type as an object class and an object occurrence as an object instance.

An object class describes a set of object instances that have similar:

- Data characteristics

- Behavior

- Relationships to other objects

- Real-world meaning

A person may have a name, address, phone number, age, and many other attributes. He or she may perform certain tasks as part of his or her job, report to managers and be reported to by other employees, and be known to play the role of a certain type of worker. Thus a specific person is an instance of the person object class, as well as an instance of the employee object class. Objects can be identified in a description of a system (in this case, a business) by nouns in sentences. The tasks performed by objects (the object behavior, or operations) can be identified as verbs in these same sentences.

Objects that are members of an object class share some attribute types and behavior types. Individual object instances can be distinguished from other instances by differences in the actual values of the attributes and by associations with other object classes and object instances. Object instances that are members of the same class share a common real-world meaning in addition to their shared attributes and relationships.

Abstraction

Abstraction allows for easier management of complex ideas. A description of a real-world object, situation, or process can be simplified in an abstracted model to emphasize aspects that are important to a user of a model. Other details not needed for understanding are suppressed and displayed only in more detailed models. The idea of abstraction in object-oriented development models is to separate the essence of a problem area in order that it can be understood and used independently of the way in which the solution is actually implemented.

For our use in building models of systems of objects, an abstract model emphasizes the external view of an object, with the implementation details hidden inside the boundaries of the object (see the next section on encapsulation). The external interface of an object describes only the essential behavior of an object. Classification (see Chapters 3 and 4) provides a way of building levels of abstraction into object models. Seidewitz and Stark (1986, mentioned in Booch 1991, p. 40) speak of kinds of abstractions useful in building models of objects:

Entity abstraction	Represents a model of a problem-domain entity
Action abstraction	Provides a generalized set of operations, all of which perform the same kind of function
Virtual machine abstraction	Groups together operations that are all used by some superior level of control, or operations that all use some junior-level set of operations
Coincidental abstraction	Packages a set of operations that have no relation to each other

These kinds of abstraction provide the same kind of logical groupings as the various kinds of module coupling found in structured systems design (see Montgomery 1991, p. 201). Object abstractions are used in analysis and design models to represent more naturally the concepts and vocabulary used in the particular problem domain that we are modeling. A problem domain might be the customer support area of a business, or product research, or product engineering design and development.

Later in this book I speak of clients that request the services of an object. Abstraction may be used to model systems of objects as networks of clients and servers. Using analysis and design models of the external characteristics of objects allows us to model only the interactions between clients and servers, not the details of how these interactions will be implemented. Implementation specifics will be covered in detailed object design and implementation models (Chapters 6 and 7).

Encapsulation

In object modeling, as in traditional structured analysis and design, abstraction precedes the implementation details. Only the minimum of details required to enhance understanding of an object should be used to represent that object in an abstract model. Abstraction leads us naturally to the concept of encapsulation (known as information hiding in structured design).

Encapsulation provides a conceptual barrier around an object, preventing clients of an object from viewing its internal details. Thus encapsulation can provide appropriate barriers for various levels of abstraction in a system model. In relational database design that uses Structured Query Language (SQL) to implement that design, application programs define what data they need to do their jobs, not how to navigate through relational tables. The logical view of a database is all that is required to access data within a relational database using SQL. Object databases can go to even higher levels of abstraction by accessing classes of objects using only the external protocol defined by encapsulation. Only the name of the object(s) being accessed and the operations to be performed on the object(s) are required to process object data. Higher levels of object abstraction are shielded from the encapsulated details of lower-level abstractions.

Each object class, then, must have an external interface defining the outside view of the class and an implementation that defines the mechanisms that provide the behaviors that the object must exhibit.

Hierarchies and Inheritance

Objects and their organization can provide the extra benefit of reusability of data and code. Programming procedures implemented in one object can be used in another object through a system of classes, hierarchies, and inheritance. A business could have a consumer and a commercial customer. The consumer would inherit the behaviors of a customer object: the ability to maintain a name, address, and account number. The consumer object would also have specific characteristics of a consumer customer as opposed to those of a commercial customer.

The consumer object does not need to have all characteristics rewritten for it. It simply inherits the data structures and code for all customers. This assists programmers in keeping applications current. If another class of customers is needed, a new subclass could be built to inherit all of the data and procedures of the common customer class. The data and procedures that are inherited are already designed, implemented, and tested. This easy management of changes in a business environment makes object-oriented applications much more maintainable than they otherwise might be. A developer can be more productive when he or she does not have to rewrite all details of a new business object and its associated functions. Productivity is improved by eliminating the need to design, implement, and test key parts of a system.

Encapsulation helps manage complex system models by hiding details at lower levels of abstraction. Still, we often need more help in managing abstractions. We can simplify object models by defining hierarchies of data structures. Two common kinds of data hierarchy are generalization ("kind of," or class structure) and aggregation ("part of," or object structure).

Generalization. This kind of hierarchy defines a relationship among classes. One class shares the structures and behaviors defined in one class (single inheritance) or in more than one class (multiple inheritance). A subclass inherits characteristics from one or more superclasses and can refine the definition of the superclass(es). A general definition of a motor vehicle superclass can be refined by more specific definitions of the subclasses: automobile, truck, and bus.

Aggregation. Aggregation relationships depict "part of" hierarchies. An automobile is build up of subobjects: engine, body, and chassis. The engine, in turn, is composed of fuel, cooling, and ignition systems. Each of these systems is composed of subsystems and/or discrete parts. The higher-level abstractions are generalized, while the lower levels are specialized. An automobile is modeled at a higher level of abstraction than any one of its component classes.

Association

An association defines a conceptual connection between object classes with common structures and semantics. All the connections between object instances that an association represents connect objects from the same classes. An association describes a set of object instance connections in much the same manner that a class defines a set of object instances.

Associations are bidirectional in that a connection may be traversed in either direction from one object to another. In structured analysis, entity types are connected via relationship types in much the same manner that object classes are connected via associations in object modeling. Associations may be binary, ternary, or higher order, but in practice most are binary. Higher-order associations are difficult to model and build, so it may be better to try to work with associations that can be decomposed into sets of binary relationships. Object modeling in the future will likely consist of some form of extended entity-relationship modeling with much richer semantics than the various forms of data modeling in wide use today incorporate, but entity-relationship modeling is still a good place to get started.

The concept of association (or relationships) is not new but is not supported at present within many implementation languages or databases. Still, associations can be very useful for modeling relationships between object classes. Associations provide a way to depict information that is not unique to a single class but that depends on two or more classes.

Messages

When objects have been encapsulated to insulate the outside world from the details of the object structures and behaviors, there needs to be a way to interact with these structures and behaviors. Messages provide this mechanism.

A message is composed of the name of an operation to perform on object data and any necessary parameters to qualify the operation. When a client object sends a message to another object (a server), the client is asking the server to perform some operation and perhaps to return some information to the client. When a receiver of a message processes that message, it performs an operation in any way it can. The sender of the message does not (indeed, should not) know how the operation will be performed. Because of encapsulation, the details of how an object performs an operation are hidden from view of outsiders.

The total set of messages that an object can respond to comprises the behavior of that object. Some messages might be internal ones that are not part of the object's public interface. An object could send a message to itself to perform recursive operations, for instance. If a program is needed to print the contents of a file, regardless of the type of the file, a PRINT message could be sent to the file object, causing the file to print. The details of how that print operation is performed are hidden from the calling program's view. An EDIT operation, and subsequent COMPILE and LINK operations, could be performed on a program module with the actual implementations of each message hidden from view of the user or calling program. A PRINT message sent to another file of a different type would cause a similar action to take place by the other object (see the next section on polymorphism).

Polymorphism

Polymorphism is the ability of two or more object classes to respond to the same message, but in different ways. The meaning of the commands that are passed between objects is packaged with the objects, so a client object does not need to be aware of which server object its message is being sent to. Polymorphism allows the similarities between different object classes to be exploited. Since it is possible to have different responses to the same message, the sender of a message can simply transmit it without regard to the class of the message's receiver. A PRINT, EDIT, COMPILE, or LINK message could be sent to a program file with no regard to the language the source program is written in or the type or version of editor or other tool the file invokes in order to respond to the message.

Implementing printer support in an object-oriented environment allows you to define a general printing interface that defines the way to communicate with that interface. A print message could be responded to by a plain-text file, a bit-mapped graphics file, a vector-mapped graphics file, or a formatted report file. Each type of file is implemented as an object with a print method to respond to a print message, perhaps in conjunction with a set of optional parameters unique to each file type or the associated tools (print spooler, print queue, file formatter, printer, plotter, etc.) used for the print operation.

Polymorphism allows objects to communicate without knowing how other objects perform their functions. A customer invoice object could obtain customer data from the customer object without having to include procedures for making the calculations upon customer data. Thus object-oriented software can be made to better represent business objects and functions and helps make applications more understandable for future modification and tuning.

Summary

This book aims to show some of the many possibilities for improved systems development, integration, and evolution using object concepts, especially in a distributed computing environment. We begin by describing how a business and its objects and processes can be modeled using object concepts. Our approach is an event-driven one, using the increasingly popular concept of a business event in business process analysis and, at the system interface, the concept of a "use case." The book starts with a business focus and moves increasingly into the technical world of design and programming. Key concepts in the area of object technology are covered, with emphasis on industry standards and evolving adaptations of object concepts to system testing, metrics, and quality assurance.

References

Booch, G. *Object-Oriented Design with Applications.* Menlo Park, CA: Benjamin/Cummings, 1991.

Montgomery, S. L. *Object-Oriented Information Engineering.* Boston: AP Professional, 1994.

———. *AD/Cycle: IBM's Framework for Application Development and CASE.* New York: Van Nostrand Reinhold, 1991.

———. *Relational Database Design and Implementation Using DB2.* New York: Van Nostrand Reinhold, 1990.

Seidewitz, E., and Stark, M. "Towards a General Object-Oriented Software Development Methodology," In *Proceedings of the First International Conference on Ada Programming Language Applications for the NASA Space Station.* NASA Lyndon B. Johnson Space Center, TX: NASA (1986): p. D.4.6.4.

Spewak, S. H. *Enterprise Architecture Planning: Developing a Blueprint for Data, Applications, and Technology.* Boston: QED Publishing Group, 1993.

Taylor, D. A. *Object-Oriented Technology: A Manager's Guide.* Reading, MA: Addison-Wesley, 1990.

Define Scope and Model Events

Model the Business Context

Business process modeling often begins with the building of a model of the business environment. The process flows from business process analysis, if already completed, can be used to select a business process to examine further (see Figure 1.1). We call the model of the environment of a business process the business context model (Graham refers to it as an external context model). A common context modeling technique with structured analysis or information engineering is to use a level-0 data flow diagram for this purpose (see Figure 1.2). We can use this basic approach on object-oriented projects, but we need to change the way that we interpret the models. The information gathering techniques are the same, but workshop facilitators and business analysts need to focus on objects (perhaps process objects) instead of business functions. Thus a simple data flow orientation is not sufficient.

We are better off viewing interactions between a system (an object) and actors (external objects) as message flows rather than data flows. Using this approach, an actor is a person, an external system or device,

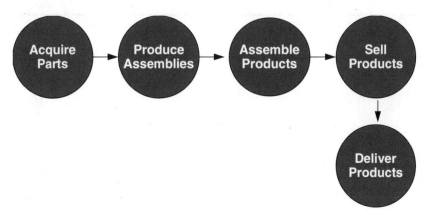

Figure 1.1   A business process flow diagram.

or an organization that interacts with the business (the business area) being studied. Initially, we can view this model in pure business terms, with no regard to automated or manual objects and their operations. Once we begin to discuss the automated portion of the business system, we can refer to our model as a system context model (Graham's internal context model).

A context model, whether a business context model or a system context model, depicts the passing of messages into and out of a context (the business area or automated system, respectively). Messages carry information in both directions, whereas data flows carry information in one direction only. We draw message request arrows from the requester to the server, but a return from the request is assumed. A data flow shows the physical direction that information flows in. A message im-

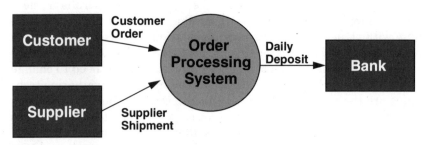

Figure 1.2   A data flow context diagram.

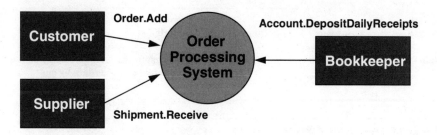

Figure 1.3   A business context model diagram describing messages.

plies a commitment and some sort of return value type (even if that return type is void). Also, a message flow is named as a verb phrase to represent a request for service, whereas a data flow is named using a noun phrase to represent only the information contained in the flow. Figure 1.3 shows an example business context model diagram that describes message flows.

Business activities are triggered by some business event. Business process modeling allows us to examine the activity flows resulting from these events. To get started, we can use a business context diagram that depicts events that imply messages. This seems to be a more natural way to describe business activities than messages, even though systems analysts can more readily incorporate messages into a system design. A business context that describes event flows is shown in Figure 1.4.

We can list business events using a structured format (see Figure 1.5), or list messages flowing into and out of the model context (see Figure 1.6).

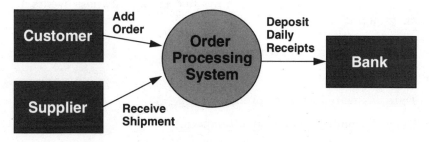

Figure 1.4   A business context diagram describing business events.

Event Name	Source	Target	Expected Result	Purpose
Add Order	Customer	Order	New customer order created	Enable entry of orders by customers

Figure 1.5   A structured business event list.

Message Name	Triggering Event	Agent	Event Type	Information inputs	Expected Result	Goal
Receive Shipment	Shipment arrives on receiving dock	Supplier	External	Packing slip information	Shipment receipt recorded	Record receipts as soon as possible after arrival

Figure 1.6   A structured context message flow table.

Group Business Events

We can perhaps best serve our business clients by grouping business events into useful categories, each of which may be described more fully at a later time. Some convenient ways to organize business events include grouping them by:

- Process or functional area

- Actor

- Data associated with the event

- Type of event (i.e., external or temporal)

We can choose to group events by business process, provided that we have described to some extent the business processes during business process analysis. These business events can then be modeled using a context diagram that shows key interactions between an actor and the system. Usually, this is done in detail only for the system context, but is equally applicable for describing the business context. We can begin by using an activity flow diagram from business process analysis. If we focus on one of these business processes, we can identify events that pertain to this business process.

Model the System Context

The system context represents the scope and boundary of an automated system. The business context model captures requirements for a business process that include manual and automated activities. The system context model describes only those activities and objects that are part of an automation portion of the overall business process. Another refinement that the system context model often provides is a description of actors in specific system user roles. The business events from the business context model can be represented in the system context model as use cases and, in system design, as transactions. A system context model may remove references to external objects that do not communicate directly with the system being modeled. A sales clerk, for instance, may actually interact with the sytsem on behalf of a customer, so the clerk becomes the agent for some transactions in the system context model. The customer object appears in the system context model only if it interacts with the system directly.

In the business context model, we represented actor/system interactions as business events. In the system context model, we represent these interactions as system events (or, for interactive systems, as use cases) or as messages. Message flows are related to events. For actors, we only model events that flow into or out of the model context by way of messages. A message is sent in order to perform some work, which involves performance of some task. A message sent from one point to another is initiated by a triggering event, which has a goal to achieve. Some information is sent from the requester to the server to indicate that a particular task should be performed. The message is complete when a reply of the correct type is received (although we could have a return type of void), so a message models a transaction in a simple kind of way. When we model message flows in detail, we can describe in a richer manner the transaction that results from a message. Figure 1.7 shows a use case diagram for depicting external business events as use cases, while Figure 1.8 shows how actor/system interactions are modeled as messages.

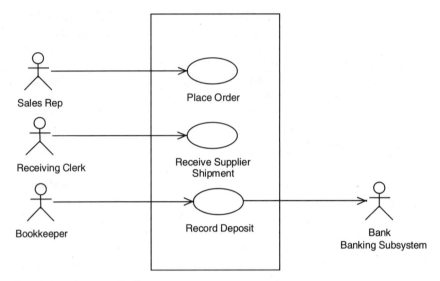

Figure 1.7   A use case diagram.

Along with our context diagram, a system context model needs to have some information about the messages: We can describe some of the details of each message using a message table (from Graham), whose format is shown in Figure 1.9.

This table should have one message row for each message interaction described on a context diagram. Each message represents an im-

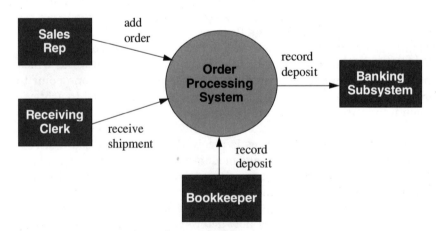

Figure 1.8   A context message flow diagram.

Message Name	Trig-gering Event	Sender	Receiver	Infor-mation Inputs	Expected Result	Goal

Figure 1.9   A message table.

plicit closed loop between the sender and receiver. Initially, we care about capturing the fact that an agent interacts with our business or automated system, so we can describe a group of messages as if they were one message. This simplifies the table and context diagram, because only one message interaction need be drawn on the context diagram to get started. Later, as analysis proceeds, we can divide these composite message flows into their components. For a simple system, it may seem easier just to draw all the known messages and record them in the message table. However, for all but the smallest systems we will find that the context diagram gets busy very quickly.

We can often make a useful distinction between external events and temporal events, based on how the event is triggered. Thus we have three major types of events:

- External

- Control

- Temporal

If an external actor triggers the event, it is an external event. If the event is triggered by a process detecting some condition (a state) of some portion of the system, this is a control event. Finally, if the event is triggered by a process checking for a certain date and time, it is a temporal event. A temporal event is really just a special kind of control event, because of the values of date and time properties being examined.

Identify Actors

In order to begin describing interactions between business personnel (or other systems) and a system being studied, you need to identify the specific actors (or the categories of actors) for which we need to develop use cases. Actors may be individual business users of a system, organizations that interact with the system, or other systems external to the one being studied. Once actors have been identified, you have a starting point for defining the scope and boundaries of the system. Describe actors using a template similar to this:

Name   A business identification for the actor

Description The purpose and function of the actor

Scenarios   Names of major scenarios (use cases) performed by the actor

Contact   Person to contact for further information about the actor

Identifying human actors can be as simple as answering "Who are the people that the system will support?" It can be more difficult to identify all of the external systems that need to interact with the system under study. Once you have identified the actors for the system, you can begin to build a system context diagram to graphically depict the scope and boundaries of the automated portion of the business system. Draw a system boundary (a box or circle) and place the actors around the perimeter of the system boundary. Then draw lines from/to the actors to depict the message flows.

Identify Use Cases (Task Scenarios)

Begin identifying use cases by focusing on typical interactions with a system. Leave the details of less typical interactions and handling of business error conditions for later. Try to ensure that each use case identified is significantly different from other use cases. Minor differences between similar use cases can be noted within the text of the distinct use cases.

For each actor identified earlier, list use cases for that actor. Each use case should identify and describe a specific way of using the system, representing a compete sequence of events that can occur in an application as part of the functionality of the system. A complete collection of use cases for an actor specifies all of the ways that the system can be used by that actor. By extension, the collection of all use cases for all actors describes the complete external functioning of the system.

Develop Use Case Scripts (Task Scenarios)

Use cases should be recorded initially using simple text narratives. Since actors perform use cases, we can begin by examining each role of each actor and identify ways that each actor interacts with the system. Use case details can often be extracted from requirements specifications, but the best way to develop use case scripts is through direct interaction with human actors or personnel directly responsible for the interaction between an external system and the system under study. Jacobson et al. (1992) list some questions to use to develop use case scripts:

- What are the main tasks of each user?
- Will the user have to read/write/change any of the system information?
- Will the user have to inform the system about outside changes?
- Does the user wish to be informed about unexpected changes?

For each incoming message flow in the context model, you should establish what the actor would normally expect to happen, perhaps in the form of a stated goal and a script beginning with an event. For example, when a "request to raise invoice" event occurs, the actor generating this event might expect the system to check the credit limit, and, if it is OK, print the invoice, send it to the client, file a copy, and send a confirmation message. This is all the detail needed at this stage of analysis, and it probably suffices to have a "produce invoice" operation attached to an object that is responsible for invoice processing.

For each goal mentioned in the system's statement of purpose, there should be a use case script. Ideally, this script is written as a single sentence of the form Subject + Verb + Direct.object [Preposition Indirect.object]. Example use cases:

- A trader enters counterparty details.
- A system manager changes the trader's authorization.
- A customer requests account information.

Each use case script describes what the system is normally expected to do. To emphasize exceptions, try to record "side-scripts" correspond-

---

1. The case worker logs on to the system.
2. The case worker identifies a specific date when the case should be reviewed and why.
3. The case worker requests the ability to set a follow-up notification.
4. The case worker sets a follow-up notification.

Figure 1.10   A simple use case script.

ing to exceptional conditions. We can reduce the number of scripts we need to deal with by classifying them and linking them to their associated use case scripts. The sections below describe how to do this. See Figure 1.10 for an example use case script.

You may discover that several use cases may be very similar in their described functions; others may contain completely distinct functionality. Although it can be difficult at first to decide between a variant of an existing use case and a different one, it can be helpful to think of a basic course of action and alternative courses. Consider a basic course to be a use case that best describes the typical course of operation and provides the best understanding of an actor's requirements. Variations or error-handling situations represent alternatives of this basic course.

Use case scripts may be classified, just as objects are. A script for "capture equity trade" may inherit features from "capture trade" and add new features specific to equities. Subclassifications of this kind are sometimes called "subscripts." Scripts may have attributes and associated tasks. Associated tasks are those that are similar. We can characterize use case scripts this way (from Graham 1995):

- Scripts may be one sentence or an essay.

- Use case/task analysis should be used to decompose complex scripts into component scripts.

- Atomic scripts should be in *Subject Verb Direct.object [Preposition Direct.object]* form.

- There may be side-scripts that deal with exceptions.

- Textual analysis can be used to find objects and operations.

- Use case/task attributes and associations should be recorded, if known.

USE CASE

ROLE	Submit Application	Evaluate Case	Initiate Case Management
Underwriter	Participant	Owner	Owner
Medical Consultant		Participant	
Agent	Owner		

Figure 1.11   Role/use case matrix.

Refine Business Events/Use Cases

Once we have a reasonably large set of business events (we'll call them use cases after Jacobson), we can begin to refine our view of events by examining the relationships between events:

- Define role/use case relationships.
- Define use case–to–use case relationships.
- Create use case decomposition.
- Create use case specialization.

We can define role/use case relationships using a simple matrix to map an actor role to the use cases that correspond to that particular actor role (see Figure 1.11).

It can also be useful to map use cases to other use cases, perhaps for the purpose of identifying reusable use case definitions or sequences of use cases (see Figure 1.12).

USE CASE

USE CASE	Set Reminder	Send out Status Letter
Change to new role	Extends	
Set reminder to review a case	Extends	May result in

Figure 1.12   Use case/use case matrix.

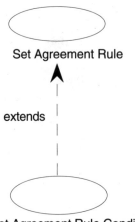

Set Agreement Rule

extends

Set Agreement Rule Condition

Figure 1.13   An extends relationship between use cases.

Complex use cases may be decomposed into their component use cases using what Jacobson calls an "extends" relationship, as illustrated in Figure 1.13. Use cases may also be classified into general and specific types of use cases using Jacobson's "uses" relationship, as illustrated in Figure 1.14.

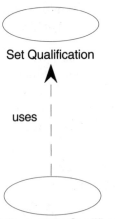

Set Qualification

uses

Set Agreement Qualification

Figure 1.14   A uses relationship between use cases.

We develop use cases during systems analysis to describe, in business terms and concepts, interactions with a system (use cases) from which the objects and classes, events, and internal interactions may be discovered. To develop use cases, we usually meet with business personnel in a requirements workshop or through interviewing or informal meetings.

Extend Use Cases

Use cases may be structured using an "extend" mechanism (see Jacobson et al. 1992). This mechanism depicts how one use case may be inserted into another to "extend" its functionality with more details. Each use case should be independent of others and can be developed without referring to another use case. Use the *extend* mechanism to model:

• Optional parts of a system

• Complex and alternative courses that seldom occur

• The fact that several different use cases can be inserted into a special use case

An *extending* use case describes the point in the original use case where it is to be inserted for extension. When a new use case is inserted, the original use case executes normally until it reaches the point where an *extend* use case has been inserted. At the point of insertion, the *extend* use case begins to execute and runs to completion. Then control passes back to the original use case, which continues to run from the point of extension, acting as if no extended functionally had been inserted. See Figure 1.13 for an example of an *extends* relationship between use cases.

Generalize Use Cases

Another way that use case functionality may be reused across a set of use cases is via the "uses" mechanism (again, see Jacobson et al. 1992). This mechanism models how one use case may inherit common functions from a more general use case. Essentially, the *uses* relationship represents an inheritance relationship in the same way that a subclass

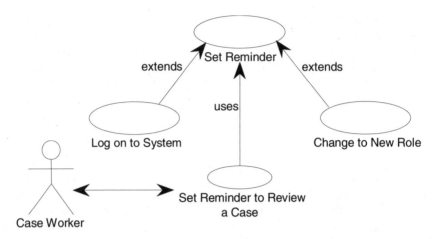

Figure 1.15   A combination of use case relationships.

may inherit from a superclass via an inheritance relationship. Incorporating *uses* relationships into use case models is normally done after basic and alternative courses have been modeled.

The reason why we would use the *uses* or *extends* relationships to refine a use case model is to maximize reuse and reduce redundancy in the system requirements. The basic way that use cases are refined is to identify similar parts of a use case and extract from it the parts that are similar across multiple use cases. The idea is to describe system requirements only once. See Figure 1.14 for an example of a *uses* relationship between use cases and Figure 1.15 for a combination of use case relationships.

Identify Operations

Use cases have proven useful for identifying operations in a system, describing a trace of events and responses. Event traces should depict interactions involved in fulfilling system responsibilities. Use cases can be developed for different subsystem responsibilities and should be developed for different situations that the system is required to handle. We use an event-trace diagram to describe how the use case functions are supported in the classes and objects in a system.

An event-trace diagram (also called a message sequence or object interaction diagram) shows the flow of messages from one object to an-

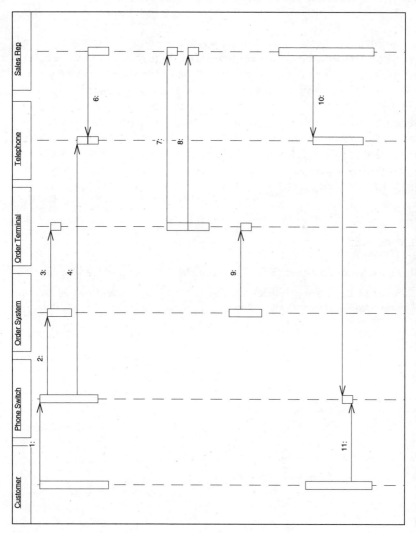

Figure 1.16   An event-trace (object interaction) diagram for an order entry system.

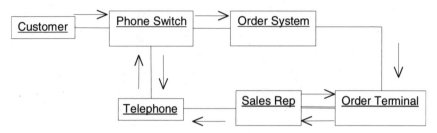

Figure 1.17   A collaboration diagram for an order entry system.

other across the horizontal access, with the sequence of steps shown down the vertical access (see Figure 1.16). Figure 1.17 shows a collaboration diagram for an order entry system. Often, the business scenarios developed during business analysis are used to describe the steps down the left side of the event-trace diagram. Sometimes, designers and programmers will use this same diagram with the messages annotated with their programming names and parameters either on the diagram itself or along the right side of the diagram. This provides an easy way to map programming constructs back to the business requirements that they support.

References

Graham, I. *Migrating to Object Technology*. Wokingham, England: Addison-Wesley, 1995.

Jacobson, I., M. Christerson, P. Johnsson, and G. Overgaard. *Object-Oriented Software Engineering: A Use Case Driven Approach*. Reading, MA: Addison-Wesley, 1992.

2

Redesigning Existing Systems for the Future

Existing Systems

We cannot simply scrap the multitude of systems we have built using older technologies. For perhaps decades our newer, cleanly designed systems must coexist with the older, mostly successful systems in use today. The older systems are getting more and more expensive to maintain but will have their maintenance greatly enhanced as CASE tools, techniques, and repositories are more widely used.

Because so much has been inverted in existing information systems that do an adequate job of supporting business requirements (although at a higher maintenance cost than newer systems require), there is an economic incentive to give serious consideration to upgrading systems to new architectures. Some of the many reasons to upgrade existing systems include:

- Maintenance and enhancement of current systems can be continued.

- Changes can be implemented quicker.

- New systems can be developed faster.

- System quality can be improved.

- Migration to new information systems architectures and tools can be accomplished.

One of the greatest advantages of systems composed of objects is that development can make use of standard, reusable objects, similar to use of standard, reusable product components. Standardization in software can be achieved because the actual production of the components is fairly easy. Once object classes are defined, all instances of a class are guaranteed to be identical. Objects can be produced in quantity, are immediately available, and there are no production costs. The challenge of applying standardization to software system construction lies not in production but in design. System designers must define classes that are universally applicable and easily reusable. While not easy to achieve at first, the potential savings in production are immense.

There are a number of ways in which an object-oriented system should coexist with existing systems, including those listed in Figure 2.1 (from Graham, pp. 42–43).

To get the most out of object-oriented development, build working models of a part of an enterprise's operations, build up the model to the enterprise logical model, and, finally, build the logical model up to the

---

- The evolutionary migration of an existing system to a future object-oriented implementation, where parts of the old system will remain temporarily in use

- The evolution of systems that already exist and are important and too large or complex to rewrite at a stroke, and where part or all of the old system may continue to exist indefinitely

- The reuse of highly specialized or optimized routines, embedded expert systems, and hardware-specific systems

- Exploiting the best of existing relational databases for one part of an application in concert with the use of an object-oriented programming language and/or object-oriented database for another

- The construction of graphical front ends to existing systems

- The need to build on existing "package" solutions

- Cooperative processing and blackboard architectures may involve agents that already exist working with newly defined objects

- The need to cooperate with existing systems across telecommunications and local area networks

Figure 2.1   Ways in which object and nonobject systems should coexist.

enterprise planning model. By doing this, a large inventory of reusable objects can be built. All higher-level objects can be reused in future projects. Solutions built on the enterprise planning and logical models are more flexible than solutions based directly on low-level objects. If your organization's operations change, you can change the business models without making changes to the high-level classes that implement specific solutions. Sure, it takes a lot of time, energy, and foresight to build enterprise models than it does to craft specialized solutions, but these specialized solutions cause major problems in organizations when these solutions do not integrate well together.

Object-oriented development, with its emphasis on growth and adaptation to change, may allow production of far more sophisticated systems than is possible using today's conventional analysis and design techniques. It makes sense to invest the time and energy to evolve existing systems to an object architecture.

Numerous critical systems exist in business organizations around the world today (legacy systems), and we have a very tough job ahead of us if we want to build an integrated set of information systems within an enterprise (and sometimes ones that will span enterprises). We need to make sure that the new set of cleanly designed systems fits in well with our old world of legacy systems. By judicious use of object technology, we can sometimes encapsulate an old system with a "wrapper" that defines the old system as a class with a public interface for receiving and sending object messages from/to external systems.

Today, many organizations are beginning to replace nongraphical user interfaces with graphical, object-oriented user interfaces. This is a simple example of how an old, traditional system can be wrapped with object technology. More extensive use of workstation capabilities dictates moving key parts of an application's programs and databases to the workstation in a client/server architecture, but using a newer graphical user interface (GUI) that is based on objects helps make the move to a more powerful architecture of intercommunicating objects.

Assess Impact on Systems and Their Components

In order to move systems from a traditional environment to an object-oriented one, you first must identify all systems and their components that are affected by the migration:

- Databases and files
- Programs and modules

- Interfaces
- Documentation
- Manual procedures
- Hardware
- Network components

Impact analysis of this sort should be conducted from the top down, viewing the most general requirements first. Then it should move down to the strategic and detailed designs. Finally the details of the implementation are examined. Review all information sources including repositories, technical documentation, and user documentation in order to provide insights into the effects of changes on:

- Inputs
- Outputs
- Processes
- Manual procedures
- Stored data
- Programs
- Other systems
- Hardware
- Personnel

Consider following these steps when analyzing impacts of reengineering systems—determine the impact on each of the following:

- Interfaces
- Requirements
- Database/file designs
- Process designs
- Procedural code
- Documentation

The various system models discussed in this book can be used to perform a wide range of maintenance functions. They help to understand and confirm a change request, conduct impact analysis, and plan and implement a system enhancement. Other uses of models are to establish and test assumptions about errors, improve designs, and conduct corrective maintenance. These models serve as valuable inputs into the systems enhancement process. They also provide a foundation for planning and implementing the desired changes.

Logical models of a current system provide an initial point of reference for adding or changing processes, stored or flowing data, and data relationships to build an initial model of the target system. Physical models represent the design into which enhancements must be built. In order to assess properly to which conceptual level a reverse-engineering effort should be directed, consider these analysis and design steps:

1. Review and update the business information requirements.

2. Review and update the business system requirements.

3. Review and update the preliminary systems design.

4. Review and update the detailed systems design.

Business Process Reengineering

Michael Hammer (1990) states that the usual methods for boosting business performance—process rationalization and automation—haven't yielded the dramatic improvements organizations need. Heavy investments in information technology have provided disappointing results largely because organizations tend to use technology to mechanize old ways of doing business. Simple reengineering of existing processes—leaving processes intact and using computer technology only to speed processes up—cannot address fundamental process performance deficiencies. It is important that any information system reengineering project examine closely whether the supported business processes need reengineering themselves. Reengineering existing systems can often "pave the cow paths" when what is needed is a "total redesign of the transportation infrastructure."

Many business job designs, workflows, control mechanisms, and organization structures were developed in an older business environment—even before computer automation—and emphasize efficiency and control. What is really needed today is innovation and speed, service and quality. Hammer lists the following principles of business re-engineering that aim to avoid automation of old business rules:

- Organize around outcomes, not tasks.

- Subsume information processing work into the real work that produces the information.

- Treat geographically dispersed resources as though they were centralized.

- Link parallel activities instead of integrating their results.

- Put the decision point where the work is performed, and build control into the process.

- Capture information once and at the source.

Once it has been determined that business processes are stable as is and are to be supported with new versions of existing systems, three basic approaches are available for addressing the systems:

1. Do not convert applications but build a bridge to new systems where necessary.

2. Restructure systems but do not rebuild them.

3. Reverse-engineer old systems to conform to formal object models.

Reengineering an old system into a traditional information engineering environment involves a process similar to that shown in Figure 2.2 (adapted from Martin 1990, vol. 3, pp. 428–431).

Identify Candidate File Structures for Subject Databases

If your enterprise has modeled business information requirements using data subjects, you are well positioned to take advantage of object modeling of subject areas as object classes. If not, some help is available. Clustering of data subjects (or, more commonly, data entities) into groups of related data structures according to their use by business processes can be of help, as can affinity analysis.

You might first begin identifying data structures by examining your data dictionary or repository, but, if this information is not available,

1. Structure the code.
2. Enter the restructured code into a CASE tool.
3. Capture the data description of the old system.
4. Convert the data elements.
5. Normalize the data structures to conform to the information engineering models.
6. Convert the file management or database management system.
7. Modify the application to conform to new process models.
8. Adopt new standards.
9. Convert system interfaces.
10. Generate modified data structures.
11. Generate data description code.
12. Convert or enhance reports.
13. Redesign the human interface.
14. Generate new program code and documentation.
15. Use a code optimizer.

Figure 2.2   A process for reengineering information systems.

several reengineering tools can be used to reverse-engineer database and file structures into systems models. The same process can be performed for program module data structures (or data views) and their attributes that reference database and file structures. No matter how data structures are cataloged and modeled, a set of matrices can be built to depict data views that reference database and file structures. Then the data structures can be grouped together. See Figure 2.3 for an example of such a matrix.

The data structure grouping process can begin by grouping file structures that are accessed by module data structures or transactions. A matrix can then be built to show cells where programs create, read, update, or delete file structures. The number of modules and file structures can be large, so an automated matrix modeling tool should be used. Database analysts, programmers, and designers who are familiar with enterprise databases and systems should validate the matrix to ensure that it correctly depicts data/module interactions and that no modules or file structures are missing. A data/module matrix helps highlight problems such as a data structure not created by any module or a module that does not access any data structure. Situations can be identified that might be problems: a data structure that is not updated by any module or one that is created by more than one module.

File Structure   Module

	1	2	3	4
A	Read		Update	
B		Read		Create, Read, Update, Delete
C	Read		Read	
D	Create			Update

Figure 2.3   Matrix mapping modules against file structures.

At a business planning level, an organizational chart can be mapped against functions and data subjects (and/or entities). This tool can be used to check functions against organizational units that perform functions. Data subjects and entities can be mapped against these organizational units. Data access models (create, read, update, delete) can be built from those created using the subject/function or entity/process matrices. This helps modelers to determine how organizational processes and organizational units make use of data structures. (Emphasis should be placed on data structures and how they are used, however, not on the current or future organizational structure. Organizational structures change but organizational functions and processes are more stable. Business information is even more stable.) Such analysis then helps identify key operations on data structures that can later be modeled as object operations (public) and methods (private). Techniques defined in information strategy planning, business systems planning/strategic alignment, and other systems planning methodologies can be used to gather, model, and validate planning information.

If analysis and design models are available in a repository-based CASE tool, these matrices can be built automatically from the models. When missing design information is discovered, this information can either be added to a design model or entered directly on the data/program matrix. Then the program and data object are added to the repository for subsequent modeling. Reengineering tools can populate the repository automatically but often require some tweaking to get the correct results. Still, the process is often much easier than just building the models manually.

Matrix entries can be grouped in a variety of ways. During new systems development and after modeling of existing systems, an analyst or designer can use the matrix to validate models and check them for completeness. Columns and rows can be resequenced and/or hidden from the current user view. A group of programs could be selected for viewing and then sequenced in a certain order for analysis. This group can be examined in detail for completeness. The same can be done from a data structure perspective. Either way, the matrix entries can be validated against diagrams or textual models of system components. It is vital that this matrix be correct before data structures can be forward-engineered into new integrated systems.

Data structures can be mapped to data entities (analysis model), which can be mapped to data subjects (planning model), but this must be done very carefully if the lower-level design model of data structures is not integrated into the views that program modules have of the data structures. On the process side (we are speaking of nonobject systems now), we can map module to programs to application systems at the design level. Design processes such as these can be mapped into business analysis model processes (actually, components of, or groups of, processes). These processes can, in turn, be mapped into business planning model functions.

Data/process matrices can be built for data structures/modules, entities/processes, and data subjects/functions. Once built and validated, these sets of matrices form a solid foundation for modeling and constructing object-oriented systems. We work backwards from design to analysis to planning in our reverse-engineering of models, and then identify data subjects and their components. These data subjects become classes and objects. Classes and objects have operations identified (at the analysis level) that are refined as methods (in design). Forward-engineering becomes object-based, whereas reverse-engineering is largely non-object-based.

In order to group similar entities together by their process usage, a process/entity or function/entity matrix can be built by clustering algorithms. One such algorithm uses a list of functions arranged in the sequence of an entity life cycle and clusters entities that are created by each function. A second algorithm uses affinities among entities as a basis for clustering. Affinities may be provided from an entity-relationship model or computed based on how many processes use both of two entities being examined. (See Martin 1990, vol. 2, for details on these two entity clustering algorithms.)

Model Databases and File Structures as Objects

Databases and file structures, once clustered into classes and objects (at least, at the modeling level), can be encapsulated with procedures. When data structures have been identified and grouped into data subjects, the data subjects become object classes. Components of these classes (entities within data subjects) are subordinate objects (at least, conceptually). The resulting sets of classes and objects (each with its own private data structures) can be modeled as described earlier in this book.

A matrix or set of matrices, along with diagrams and full repository entries, should accompany the descriptions. Mappings need to be maintained between the conventional view of databases and file structures (interacting with programs and application systems) and the newly constructed models of classes and objects interacting with each other and with other systems and subsystems (via public interfaces and formally defined operations accessed through public object interfaces and privately implemented as messages—see the next section). These mappings aid in migrating application systems that access traditional databases to ones that access object-oriented databases, and on to full object-oriented application systems.

Data Management

Object wrapping (see the next section for a discussion) seems to work in some situations but can uncover serious data management problems. When encapsulating (an existing system requires duplication or sharing of data across new and old systems), four data management strategies are possible (Graham, p. 46):

1. Carry a duplicate live copy of the common data in both parts of the system, and keep both copies up to date.

2. Keep all data in the old system and copy them to the new objects as required.

3. Copy the data to the new objects and allow the old system's data to go out of date.

4. Carve out coherent chunks of the database together with related functions.

The first strategy has a problem in that storage requirements could double, and there are real integrity problems with which to be concerned. This strategy is not appropriate for either migration or reuse of commercial systems. This approach requires constant synchronization of updates and retrievals, and only works when there is little or no overlap between data in old and new systems.

With the second strategy, messages to the old system require it to handle updates. This involves borrowing data from the wrapping interface, in a similar fashion to what is done in existing, conventional applications where data are downloaded nightly from a mainframe computer to workstations, and updates are also transmitted in batch.

The third strategy has integrity problems, and the wrapping interface may need to send messages as well as receive and respond to them. This greatly increases system complexity.

The fourth strategy is a difficult one to adopt, requiring solid object analysis to describe the old and new systems, and a translation technique from original systems design documents. With this approach, we must translate a design into an object model. This is easy to accomplish if the old system was developed around critical data structures, which evolve naturally into objects in the new system.

These strategies may be appropriate depending upon whether we are migrating a system to objects, reusing components, extending it, or building an improved front end. If we mean to migrate the old system to objects, the first strategy is flawed for all but the smallest systems, and still there must be little overlap between new and existing components. The second strategy may involve modifications to the old system, and is not usually useful for system migration purposes unless there is an explicit separation between existing functions and new ones. This approach does not allow data to move permanently outward from the old system. This probably means that data must be migrated in one huge step unless a database management system has been used for all data accesses.

Only the third and fourth strategies seem feasible if we need to migrate functions of the old system to a new one; for some systems, none of the strategies seems practical. In some cases, the structure, type, and quality of the system documentation may dictate the approach. The fourth strategy will most often work if the old system can be divided along coherent data sets and if there are some existing data flow models to transform objects from encapsulating data stores. If not, we need to build complex object wrappers using the third strategy, which is far more expensive.

Model System Interfaces as Object Interfaces

Encapsulation

Application systems that interact with other systems can have their interfaces defined as public object interfaces. Messages between systems are processed as operations implemented as methods. These operations are accessible only through the public message interface. In this manner of modeling and building systems, the interface can serve as an object-oriented capsule around a nonobject system. In essence, we build an object capsule or envelope around a conventional system in order to build an object-oriented system package.

The interfaces between portions of an application system may also be defined using object technology. Object-oriented designs do not require an object-oriented programming language in order to implement the designs. Object-oriented implementation requires that we view the world as abstract data types combined with inheritance and methods. While the object-oriented languages make implementation of object designs much easier, traditional languages such as COBOL, PL/I, and FORTRAN can indeed be written in an object-oriented fashion.

Within an object model, an object type may be mapped to an abstract data type record structure just as it is mapped to a class in an object-oriented language. An abstract data type protects its data structures from improper use by outsiders by allowing only certain operations to be performed upon its data. A set of application modules within an application program can be defined in much the same way that operations are defined for classes in an object-oriented language. These languages encapsulate objects with a barrier to shield the objects from improper intervention by outside objects. This same kind of encapsulation cannot be totally enforced using traditional languages, however. Strict standards for programming must be enforced in order to achieve the same clean encapsulation of objects that object-oriented programming languages support.

Inheritance

Object type inheritance allows for reuse of data and procedures through generalization hierarchies, but conventional languages do not support subtypes and supertypes at all. Thus we need to write some program code to get the same benefits that an object-oriented programming language provides. As with traditional code reuse, we have a few options available to us. Martin and Odell (p. 434) mention three basic ways to do this with conventional languages:

1. Physically copy code from supertype modules:

   - copy and paste or use COPYLIB statements

   - control redundant code with proper maintenance procedures

2. Call the routine in supertype modules:

   - call operations from a module to its supertype module

   - works as long as programs are kept up-to-date with what they are supposed to inherit

   - proper maintenance procedures are important

3. Build an inheritance support system:

   - construct an inheritance mechanism external to the programs

   - route requests to their appropriate modules based on object schema and event schema information

   - modules are more stable because no inheritance-related logic needs to be built into programs

   - is model driven instead of hard-coded because it is based on object and event schemata

Methods

To build program components so that we need only specify which operation to apply to one or more objects, we need to have the system choose the method we need for specified inputs. Conventional languages simply do not support operation requests and method selection. Two ways to achieve this using conventional languages are (again from Martin and Odell):

1. Hard-code method selection logic within the requesting routine:

   - works as long as programs are kept up-to-date with all requests and selection criteria

2. Build a method selecting support system:

- first enable modules to make requests for operations without knowledge of where appropriate method is located

- is driven by a table that matches selection criteria with physical code location

- selection mechanism is integrated with inheritance support system (see above) to take advantage of object schema and event schema information

Object Wrapping

One shortcut to full object technology involves covering traditional application systems and their components with a veneer of object-oriented code. You define a very specific and well-conceived interface that defines how systems and programs are to interact with wrapped applications. Wrapping old applications is only a transitional step toward full object orientation, but it can save significant development time and prevent developers having to reinvent numerous application components. The technique is very useful when bridging the gap between mainframe architectures and client/server architectures.

Application wrapping involves defining a small piece of an application that connects to old databases and/or files, or to the user interface. It should be viewed as a temporary solution, but when time and resources permit, you should review each application and rewrite components completely in an object-oriented fashion. As a transition step, wrapping can be a very big time saver. It is possible to create object wrappers around existing code, which can later be replaced. Building object wrappers can protect investments in older systems while new investments are made in object-oriented systems. The wrapper allows interaction between objects and conventional systems by message passing.

One way to allow existing systems to interact with other systems is by replacing menu options with message interfaces so that the wrapped system may respond to messages from other objects. Then, when new functions are required, objects are created and placed behind the interface, and the interface is modified to respond to messages to these new objects. Thus old functions stay as conventional code, while new functions are implemented using objects.

Object wrappers may be large or small but tend to be of coarse granularity. Command-driven systems may have wrappers that consist of a set of operating system batch files or scripts. A form- or screen-based interface may consist of code to read and write data to screens, perhaps using a virtual terminal, specialist software, or an object request broker. All new or replacement functions should be developed by creating new objects with their own encapsulated data structures and methods. Then, if services of the old system are needed, messages may be passed to these services and the output decoded by the wrapper and passed to the requesting application.

Do not be fooled into thinking that implementing object wrappers is easy. One issue is that of object granularity. Small objects tend to be more reusable than large ones, but existing systems tend to be large, with subdividing into smaller objects very difficult. Object request brokers (discussed in Appendix A) are designed to deal with coarse-grained objects. In the absence of such a broker, can we still benefit from using wrappers? Often, coarse-grained objects appear naturally in some problem domains such as geometrical image transformation software.

Wrapping existing systems is not the only way to migrate these systems. Other approaches include:

- Use of object request brokers

- Employing object-oriented databases

- Proceeding in a complete ad hoc manner

The ad hoc approach may be the correct one for many projects, but object request brokers and object-oriented databases often provide a better basis for object development. Using object wrappers seems easy until we need to split object data storage across an old database and some new objects.

The best way to migrate mature systems with significant data management complexity may be to build wrappers around them to support object front ends and to build required new functions within these front ends. We wouldn't do this, however, if existing systems already have coherent data-centered structures that facilitate translation or when migration benefits are great enough to justify building a complex wrapper. If an existing database management system can be wrapped as a whole and maintained for a long time, then wrapped functions may be migrated gradually. At some future point we can move all data at once to an object database and eliminate the database wrapper. This makes sense if you are experiencing adequate performance from existing relational databases.

Serious object systems will be developed only when the pieces of legacy systems are migrated to desktop workstations as parts of client/server systems. Some developers may encapsulate many parts of the existing architecture: SQL statements, data sets, programs, and perhaps entire databases. However you approach application object wrapping, keep in mind that it merely covers up old systems—it does not necessarily improve them in any major way. Adrian Bowles, vice president of New Science Associates, Inc., in Westport, Connecticut, said this about object wrapping (*Computer World*, November 30, 1992, p. 73):

> Object wrapping is sometimes like wrapping fish. It continues to rot inside. So wrapping a system doesn't make it better. It's a lot like coating a pill to make it easier to swallow.

Reuse Existing Components

There are many times when existing systems components or packages need to be reused, with need or intention to rebuild them as objects. An object wrapper that calls a package subroutine or simulates terminal or workstation dialogs can be built. We can also modify packages to export data for manipulation by the new system, but this does not reuse components themselves. Some problems faced when building this kind of object wrapper are listed in Figure 2.4 (from Dietrich 1989).

When dealing with packages, a wrapping approach often will not work because access to the internal workings of the packages is not

---

- The designer is not free to choose the best representations for the problem in terms of objects, since this is already largely decided within the old system.

- The designer must either expose the old system's functions and interface to the user or protect him from possible changes to the old system.

- Where the old system continues to maintain data, the wrapper must preserve the state of these data when it calls internal routines.

- Garbage collection and memory management and compaction (where applicable) must be synchronized between the wrapper and the old system.

- Cross-system invariants, which relate the old and new data sets, must be maintained.

- Building a wrapper often requires very detailed understanding of the old system.

Figure 2.4   Problems faced when wrapping existing components or packages.

available at the level of detail that we require. We may be better off treating a package as a fixed object that offers certain services.

A data-centered translation approach may be the best migration approach when we are mainly concerned with reuse, but borrowing may be viable, also. An existing system that provides adequate functions can be maintained, and we may be able to communicate with it using an object wrapper that calls services of the existing system and provides access to its database.

Using Conventional and Object Databases Together

In most applications of object technology to business information systems that this author has seen, a relational database management system is used, with some existing or planned use of object databases. These databases must be used together to support individual application systems. The interoperation of relational and object programming languages and databases is really just a special case of client/server computing, discussed in Chapter 7.

Increasingly, organizations are considering adapting object databases for processing complex kinds of objects that include bills of materials, documents, and other complex structured objects. Traditional database management systems are too inflexible for handling complex objects, although newer relational database management systems do offer object extensions. For applications that require management of complex objects, a true object database management system can be as much as 100 times faster than a relational database management system, but it still has the flexibility of relational systems. True object database management systems offer support for long transactions and version control. Because most organizations have such a large investment in traditional database technology, that use of object database technology must preserve this investment.

There are two basic ways that objects can be implemented in database: use a pure object database or a relational system extended with object constructs. Several pure object database management systems exist but have not proven themselves mature enough for critical transaction-oriented systems. Some of the existing relational systems are not only mature but can provide very fast join processing. If we continue to use a relational model, we can extend it in various ways. Or, we can try to make object database application interoperate with existing database systems.

The standard relational database management system language, SQL, may be extended with objects, but this approach seems incompatible with objects in at least one aspect: SQL is a nonprocedural query language, while object databases use pointer-based processing. The proposed extension of SQL to objects, known as SQL3, is not only object-oriented (supporting classes and inheritance) but is also a procedural extension of SQL. The question remains regarding what relational systems are supposed to do with messages based on extensions to SQL. Object SQL can never be much more than the carrier of messages, according to Graham. We still must find a way to provide for objects and relations to be used together.

One way to accomplish this is to use an object wrapper written in an object-oriented language to encapsulate a relational database management system. This wrapper would convert messages to and from SQL queries. There are several possibilities for making object components of databases or object models interoperate with the relational part:

- Build object wrappers for the relational system as a whole, treating it as an entire domain model.

- Wrap individual coherent chunks of the database individually.

- Use SQL to communicate with the relational systems.

- Address the relational system through an object request broker.

Wrapping the relational system as a whole offers minimal opportunities to reuse domain objects but may work and still allow the database wrapper to be easily replaced later on. Wrapping chunks of the database could be done using a phased approach. It would use stored procedures and a published object model and would maximize opportunities for reuse. Using SQL to communicate with relational systems means that the new system must be able to generate SQL calls and interpret the resulting tables based on knowledge of the data dictionary and its semantic information. This probably involves use of complex artificial intelligence techniques such as those used in natural language query systems. Use of an object request broker requires that the broker either conforms to CORBA standards (see Chapter 5 and Appendix A) or, an appropriate wrapper is built. An object request broker tends to deal with existing systems as coarse-grained objects, so reuse potential is not as high as when wrapping individual database chunks individually.

Mary Loomis (1991) identifies three problems and three approaches to making objects and relations interoperational. The problems are:

1. Build object-oriented applications that access relational databases.

2. Run existing relationally written applications against an object database.

3. Use a SQL-like query language in an object environment.

The solution approaches are:

1. Convert the applications and databases completely to object ones.

2. Use standard import-export facilities.

3. Access the relational databases from object-oriented programming languages.

The first of Loomis's approaches is complicated and expensive if old functions are to be reused or if migration is gradual. The second approach relies on standards having been defined, which depends on the application. One variation of this approach is to use a database system that supports SQL gateways. The application must provide the mapping between table and object views of data, which can be quite complicated. The third approach implies development of an Object SQL. This might be the best approach, and could use Object Query Language (which is similar to SQL and is discussed at the end of Chapter 5), but few examples of use of this standard are available.

Process Normalization

Whereas both traditional data modeling and object structure modeling build normalized data models, even information engineering does not enforce (but does encourage to a degree) the normalization of processes in a business model. Normalization organizes data into relationships of data elements to reduce data redundancy and enhance data model usability and maintainability. Once a data structure has been properly normalized, each attribute in the model depends upon its entity's key—the whole key and nothing but the key (for a brief discussion of this technique, refer to Montgomery 1990; Finkelstein 1989; or Chris Date's various writings on the subject).

Data normalization has no concise equivalent in process modeling. Object modeling dictates that processes be attached to the normalized data structures that the processes act upon, resulting in process normalization. Information engineering's view of separate data and process models can (and usually does) result in duplication of processes, unless great care is taken to avoid duplication. Traditional systems often were not adequately modeled in the first place, so the processes (and the resulting programs) are likely to be denormalized to a great degree. True structured design and programming encourage the development of procedures into modules that are highly cohesive and that have low coupling between them.

When traditional application structuring is used for modeling and constructing information systems, the requirements for each application are analyzed, modeled, and implemented separately (although the data model can be built to be consistent across all applications). Specifications for many application functions are repeated in more than one place across different applications. In a complex information systems environment, with many applications consisting of many components, it can be very difficult to identify common processing routines. If we can indeed achieve normalized processes as well as data structures, we can achieve a very high degree of reuse and position ourselves for full object systems.

Gearing process modeling around data model components, instead of around application-by-application requirements studies, lets us move significantly toward normalized processes and object operations and methods. William Inmon, in his book on advanced information engineering (Inmon 1989, pp. 103–130), describes ways to link data and process models. His technique uses basic processes that represent the fundamental work in an information system: addition, change, and deletion. These basic operations and their infrastructure must be performed for every data element in an information system. By ensuring that each basic process exists uniquely, we can satisfy one important condition for process normalization.

Inmon states that these three conditions must be met for process normalization:

1. Basic processes and their supporting infrastructure exist once, and only once, throughout the process model.

2. The flow of control from one module to the next is from commonalty to uniqueness.

3. Each function has a high degree of cohesion.

Unique Processes

Basic processes must not exist in more than one place. Changes may exist in multiple locations as long as the change that is occurring in multiple locations is different. For instance, the ADD CUSTOMER basic process should exist in one and only one place (or only once for each geographic location in a distributed system), as shown in Figure 2.5. Within a normalized process model, each basic process must be defined only once. When ADD CUSTOMER or any other basic process has duplicates (as in Figure 2.6), update anomalies can exist, just as is the case with unnormalized (or inadequately normalized) data models. When calls to a uniquely defined, basic process are scattered around a process model, the process infrastructure, not the basic process itself, causes the process model to be unnormalized. This is analogous to having an object operation performed by multiple objects, not the object for which the operation is uniquely defined.

Figure 2.5   A unique process to add a customer.

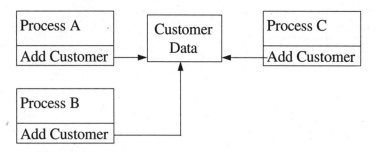

Figure 2.6   Multiple processes to add a customer.

Flow of Control from Common to Unique

The flow of control from one process or program to another must be in the order of common to unique. A more general process calls for a more specialized process. Suppose there were a CUSTOMER process, a BUSINESS CUSTOMER process, and an INDUSTRIAL BUSINESS CUSTOMER process. The CUSTOMER process manages processing for all types of customers, the BUSINESS CUSTOMER process manages processes for business (as opposed to consumer) customers, and the INDUSTRIAL BUSINESS CUSTOMER process manages industrial (as opposed to commercial or nonprofit business) customers (see Figure 2.7). The highest-level CUSTOMER process calls the BUSINESS CUSTOMER process, which in turn calls the INDUSTRIAL BUSINESS CUSTOMER process in order to handle processing for industrial customers.

Notice that this is conceptually the same as what happens in an object system that has the same inheritance tree defined for it (although in object-oriented environments the children have methods defined for them but no implementation, so control passes to the immediate parent—see Figure 2.8). In an unnormalized system, three separate modules are defined for each type of processing, with each one operating independently of the other (a general process does not call a more specialized process). The code to manage general customer data, for instance, is defined at least twice, once in the CUSTOMER process and once in the BUSINESS CUSTOMER process. The code for managing industrial

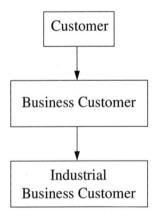

Figure 2.7 Flow of control from common to unique—traditional system.

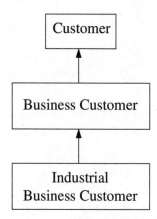

**Figure 2.8   Flow of control from unique
to common—object system.**

business customers is defined in all three processes: CUSTOMER, BUSI-
NESS CUSTOMER, and INDUSTRIAL BUSINESS CUSTOMER.

Module Cohesion

To satisfy the cohesion criterion of process normalization, processes
must be packaged so that each process performs a unique function. The
basic processes DELETE CUSTOMER, DELETE CUSTOMER ORDER, and
DELETE CUSTOMER ACCOUNT should definitely not appear in the same
process but be defined separately and called when needed. The cohesion among the set of processes will then be cohesive, in contrast to the
situation where all three exist in one basic process that is not cohesive
(it performs all three functions, not just one).

   As with the corresponding data model normalization, process normalization is useful for simplifying and structuring a process model.
When a process model is normalized, procedures can be built so that
flow of control is from general to specific. Additions to application requirements should have little or no impact on existing systems. Procedures should be structured for uniqueness of functions, although in
practice some redundancy among processes may be necessary for performance purposes (as with data model denormalization).

   The overall interaction with a database can be controlled by creation
of a standard set of application modules based on a normalized process

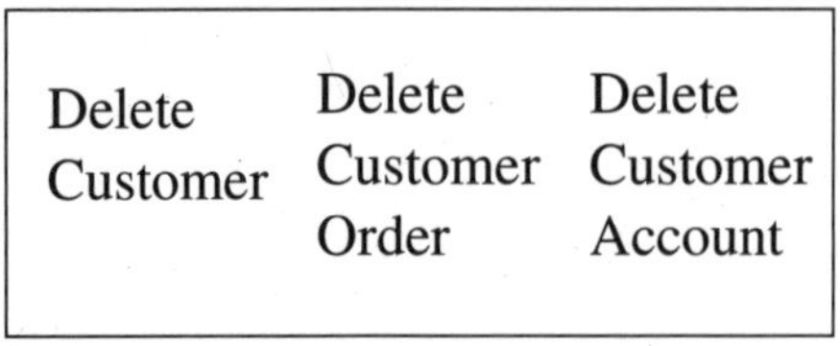

Figure 2.9   Module cohesion.

Figure 2.10   Lack of module cohesion.

model. However, this use of input/output routines does not ensure that the overall process model is normalized. Programs that call these routines may not be normalized. The infrastructure of procedures that surrounds a basic process must be considered when normalizing processes. If only one module calls each add and delete basic process and the procedures surrounding the call of each modify basic process is unique, the set of routines is normalized. For instance, there should exist only one application module to actually create a customer account. But the CREATE CUSTOMER module could be called independently from several application systems.

Each of these applications, prior to calling the CREATE CUSTOMER module, should establish values for the new customer record independently. Figure 2.9 shows module cohesion. In an object system, we have cohesion of this sort, but the routines are distinct methods within the CUSTOMER object, as depicted in Figure 2.10. In this case, the actual message code would exist in the ORDER and ACCOUNT objects. We could either send separate delete messages to the ORDER and ACCOUNT objects, or send one delete message to the CUSTOMER object to accomplish the same results.

Migrating Structured Analysis Models to Object Models

If you have been using information engineering or another structured analysis technique to build process and data models, you have a good

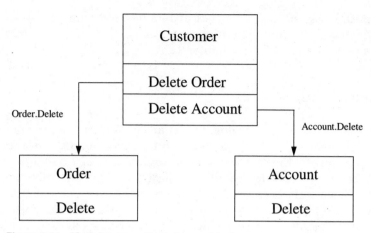

Figure 2.11   Modules as methods in an object.

starting point for migrating systems to object models. While the more traditional analysis models need significant rework to make them object-oriented, it is still much, much easier to manipulate analysis models than it is to work with design or construction models. When preparing to write on the subject of migrating structured analysis models to object models, I came across a paper by Mike Branson, Eric Herness, and Eric Jenney of IBM (1991). Their publication does a good job of describing techniques for migrating models to object orientation. This section briefly discusses their techniques.

The process of converting analysis models involves two steps: identification of candidate objects by dissecting the analysis model and class synthesis and refinement, which takes candidate objects and refines them into a set of abstractions that can be implemented. The conversion process can be summarized as:

1. The conversion process, using the analysis model as input

   • Identify candidate objects

   • Synthesize and refine classes

2. Design language-specific objects and the associated implementation

For our purposes, we are most interested in the first phase of the conversion process. Language-specific design depends upon the language(s) chosen for implementation, which we cannot discuss here due to the wide variety of available options. The following discussion assumes that the analysis model consists of data flow diagrams and process specifications, possibly including context data flow diagrams and event lists (discussed briefly in Chapter 1).

Carve Structured Analysis Models

Data flow diagrams in a traditional model are not object-oriented but do model the essence of a business solution to a problem described in system requirements. Entity-relationship diagrams are also not object-oriented but can prove very useful for object structure analysis and modeling. I do not want to enter into the controversy over whether data flow diagrams or entity-relationship diagrams are useful for object modeling, but recognize that these models exist for many systems and can prove useful for migration to object orientation.

The essential model of structured analysis can be "carved" up into candidate objects. Once this carving has been performed, the candidate objects can be examined to see if they will actually be classes in the final system model. Carving does not remove duplicate objects or duplicate operations, nor does it produce classes, analyze inheritance, or synthesize classes into a hierarchy. These steps must be taken, but only after the initial class identification and refinement have been completed.

Carving uses a complete set of data flow diagrams and process specifications and considers the lowest level of data flow diagrams in detail, but if the objects on the available diagrams are not exploded to a low level they are still used. The process of carving involves:

- Finding certain objects on data flow diagrams

- Dividing operations contained in processes between all objects that the processes touch

The usual types of object on a data flow diagram are derived via the carving: external entity, data store, data flow, and process. The diagram is carved up by associating operations listed in process specifications with only one of these objects. Each process is carved up with its components divided among the objects. Operations should most likely be associated with one object more than others.

Examine external entities. As discussed elsewhere in this book, external entities (sometimes called external agents or terminators) on a data flow diagram represent objects in the real world. They might represent people, organizations, or other systems, but, at the interface with the system being modeled, these external agents represent devices such as printers, display terminals, tape or disk drives, sensors, control pads, and so on. An object should be identified for each external entity in a data flow diagram. The objects that are identified from external entities are used to define classes that hide the messaging protocol and any hardware errors and their handling.

An external entity's class is an abstraction of the object that insulates the system from the detailed operations of the external entity. In addition to the physical devices involved with the external interface of a system, we can discuss classes that may come from the terminal, workstation, menu, or control buttons of the interface. These classes also hide underlying interface details and present the rest of the system with classes such as window, select list, radio button, or menu bar.

Examine data stores. Usually, a data store represents one or more data entities. Initially, each entity within a data store, as well as the store itself, can be viewed as a potential object. Start by identifying a potential object from each data store in a data flow diagram. Draw a line around the store and part of each process that touches it via a data flow (some CASE tools allow you to select all neighbors for a store or other data flow diagram component, so this step is fairly automatic).

Objects identified from data stores are used to define data classes that encapsulate sets of data and the associated operations to manipulate the data. Data classes might include:

- Customer order

- Product

- Employee

- Supplier

Operations for data stores are obtained from the specifications for the processes that touch the data stores. Any operation that manipulates an instance of data in the data store should be included in the list of data store operations. Each statement in a process specification that manipulates data must be associated with one data object.

Examine data flows.   When the data modeled by a data flow are significant to the system, it might become an object. If the flow's data structures are complex, it may be a good candidate for an object. Three types of data flows should be considered:

1. Flows from an external entity to a process (system inputs)

2. Flows from a process to an external entity (system outputs)

3. Flows between processes

Input and output flows are more likely to contain objects than flows between processes. Output flows should be examined to see if they should be objects. If such a flow represents a complex data flow that has a set of operations that must be performed on it, carve it out as a candidate object. Input flows may also represent objects. Examine them to see if they have complex data structures and a set of operations that act on that data. Carve out any such flows as candidate objects. Occasionally, flows between processes can be considered as candidate objects. Examine them to see if they have complex data structures and sets of operations performed on them. Carve out these flows, too.

Classes carved out from data flows tend to be transient data (not persistent, needing to be stored), so they may not become database objects. Examples include:

- Lists of objects passed to a terminal for display, with sorting and merging operations

- Time stamps passed between processes, with formatting and conversion operations

- Control blocks and associated manipulation objects

- Commands issued at terminals and operations to validate parameters and instantiate objects needed to perform functions

- String input from a display passed to the system for manipulation

Examine processes.   Once all other data flow diagram objects have been carved up, some process fragments may remain. These must be dealt with to see if the operations contained within them can be associated with any of the objects already identified. When leftover operations still exist, identify process objects. These tend to be functional objects:

- Essential managers

- Shells

- Sequencers

- Controllers

Process objects tend to use other classes and instantiate and manipulate other system objects. Identify an object for each set of operations not already associated with a class. Draw a line on the data flow diagram to depict carving for these objects. Process objects that are identified really are manipulators of other classes, so later on they will likely become operations of these classes.

Results after carving.   Once carving has been completed, every process in a data flow diagram should be completely accounted for in candidate objects. Process specifications should have been completely partitioned into components associated with candidate objects. The candidate objects and associated objects that result include things such as:

> terminal object
>> read string
>> write string
>
> customer
>> validate
>> update
>> create
>> delete

and so on.

Synthesize Classes

Identify classes.   After carving data flow diagrams, an initial set of objects has been produced. Class synthesis is where object modeling begins. During this process, objects are placed into classes and these classes placed into a class hierarchy. It is assumed that the class hierarchies already exist. Thus, class synthesis is a bottom-up activity that works upward from objects to mid-level and high-level classes.

Candidate objects must be examined to see if they can be put into the same class as other objects identified to be of the same type and to see if they really represent a class. Object classification is performed by associating objects with other objects of the same type. An object represents a single entity but a class represents many such entities. Two objects can be members of the same class if their operations are similar. Objects that belong in the same class may have operations identified that do not appear similar. Look for similar operations not only from their names but also how they act on objects.

Refine classes.   Once classes have been identified, you can begin to refine them. This involves these steps:

1. Split a class into two classes.

2. Combine classes.

3. Refine class operations.

All methods for a class must be defined for the class to be considered complete. You now may need to identify new classes when developing user interfaces. In order to narrow the scope of the interface functions presented to the user, you may need to define one or more application classes to bridge between existing classes and the abstraction needed to present an understandable set of operations to users. Sources for application classes include:

- Entity models

- Context models

- Data classes

- Process objects left over from carving

Relationships between classes in a hierarchy must be defined. Operations on existing and candidate classes must be examined. Look at the class interfaces within class hierarchies, similar operations between candidates, and utility classes (based on abstract data types such as lists, queues, and so forth). Finally, classes should abstract single entities, methods should perform a single action, classes should only have a few methods (say, 20—or classes should be combined), and method implementations should be short (perhaps 25 to 50 lines of code).

Classes should be associated with each event on a business event list. Doing this allows for the tracing of requirements down to the class level. Each event needs to be mapped to the class that implements the event, and this fact should be documented on the event list. Each event may have one or more classes that implements it.

References

Branson, M., E. Herness, and E. Jenney. "Moving Structured Projects to Object Orientation." In *AD/Cycle International User Group Second Annual Conference* (October 1991): 151–170.

Date, C. J. *A Guide to DB2*. Reading, MA: Addison-Wesley, 1985.

Dietrich, W. C., L. R. Hackman, and F. Gracer. "Saving a Legacy with Objects." In *OOPSLA'90 ACM Conference on Object-Oriented Programming Systems, Languages, and Applications*, edited by E. Meyrowitz. Reading, MA: Addison-Wesley, 1989.

Finkelstein, C. *An Introduction to Information Engineering: From Strategic Planning to Information Systems*. Reading, MA: Addison-Wesley, 1989.

Graham, I. *Migrating to Object Technology*. Wokingham, England: Addison-Wesley, 1995.

Hammer, M. "Reengineering Work: Don't Automate, Obliterate." *Harvard Business Review* (July/August 1990): 104–112.

Inmon, W. *Advanced Topics in Information Engineering*. Wellesley, MA: QED, 1989.

Loomis, M. E. S. "Objects and SQL." *Object Magazine* 1(3) (1991): 68–78.

Martin, J. *Information Engineering*. Englewood Cliffs, NJ: Prentice Hall, 1990.

Martin, J., and J. Odell. *Object-Oriented Analysis and Design*. Englewood Cliffs, NJ: Prentice Hall, 1992.

Montgomery, S. L. *Relational Database Design and Implementation Using DB2*. New York: Van Nostrand Reinhold, 1990.

3

Model the Business Object Model

Characterize Object Categories

Object category analysis is a way of defining major groupings of business data objects at a high level. This type of analysis helps to identify all information needed in an organization, in order that this information can be analyzed for its form and manner in which it is used. It also provides a basis for building an information architecture from which business data object analysis activities can be conducted and application projects defined. Example object categories include:

- Products
- Parts
- Customers
- Vendors
- Employees

- Customer orders

- Accounts

Application systems might use more than one subject:

Purchasing
    Parts
    Vendors
    Purchase orders

Invoicing
    Products
    Customers
    Customer orders

Inventory control
    Products
    Purchase orders
    Customer orders
    Vendors

The planning phase of information engineering aims to divide the total set of data structures for an enterprise into manageable units — data subjects. One or more data subjects can be modeled in detail during the analysis phase.

Data subjects are sometimes referred to as object classes. Clustering techniques can be used to group existing data structures into data subjects, if desired. It is necessary to build a high-level model of an enterprise in order to plan what data subjects should exist. Enterprise planning must take into consideration not only data subjects but existing or new files and stand-alone databases for particular applications. Detailed modeling of what constitutes a subject database (derived from an enterprise model data subject) is performed during analysis of business areas. When databases can be quickly implemented based on enterprise model data subjects, application development becomes much more data-driven and, hopefully, fully object-driven.

Object category analysis and modeling can be performed via facilitated group workshop sessions, via a series of interviews, by developing a straw model, or by developing an initial unverified model. The approach you take depends upon your objects for object category analysis and the resources and time you have available.

If at all possible, I would urge you to use a group facilitated sessions approach for analyzing object categories (as well as for analyzing functional and behavioral system requirements). This approach can be very difficult to use, especially if the technical and business team members are unfamiliar with the approach. A good session facilitator that continually challenges a group can quickly build strong ownership and sponsorship. This is definitely the approach to take for analysis and design of a large systems project.

Another approach to conducting object category analysis involves serial interviews. This approach is particularly successful when there exist one or more good object category models. However, if the existing models are not fairly solid, using them can lead to much confusion. Interviews are often used to prepare for intensive group facilitated sessions.

A straw model could be developed by a project team and later reviewed during a group facilitated session. This technique can make effective use of a group's time, but the group may not take ownership of the model because its members did not create the model in the first place.

An initial unverified model developed by a project team in isolation from business experts should be used only if contact with subject matter experts is not possible. Such a model will be inaccurate and may be rejected by subject matter experts. This author participated in such a model building exercise on a large project (out of necessity at first) and we found that extensive rework of the model was needed. Still, the exercise did provide us with a set of questions to ask our subject matter experts once we could begin intensive group facilitated sessions (usually the preferred approach).

Once subject matter experts have given their input (through one or a combination of the above information gathering approaches), you can begin to organize your object categories using an object aggregation diagram. Each object category needs to be agreed upon and defined by all people involved. You also need to define the order and hierarchy of categories and get agreement on these. A technique for getting started identifying object categories is to group them into persons, places, things, or concepts. Identify all object categories that fall into each grouping.

Produce an object aggregation diagram, from object category headings, for visual completeness and consistency checking (see Figure 3.1). The initial categories can be discarded after a complete set of object categories has been identified and defined, but the initial approach helps you get started in managing object category aggregation.

Under a grouping of object categories, the lowest level in the decomposition tends to result in data entities (or discrete objects). However, each level in the hierarchy is a valid subject (and can become a class of

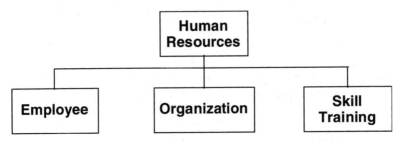

Figure 3.1   A simple object category aggregation.

objects). Object categories and entities are closely related (as are classes and objects), but it is useful to start with higher-level categories than to jump right into detailed lists of entities.

Refine Object Category Classes

An object category can be associated with many other object categories and business functions. An important association is that between functions and object categories. Information strategy planning within a comprehensive information engineering methodology often involves building a matrix of functions that involve object categories (usually called subject areas in traditional information engineering). This matrix can be refined to form a "CRUD" matrix of object category data actions by process (operation): Create, Read, Update, and Delete. See Figure 3.2 for an example object category/business process CRUD matrix. You build a CRUD matrix for object categories in order to:

- Analyze which functions act upon which object categories.

- Determine the priority of object category model and database implementation.

- Record the life cycle of a particular object category.

- Ensure that each function creates or updates at least one object category.

- Provide input into analysis project scoping efforts.

Analysis of object category life cycles can help you to verify a business function model by examining it against targeted object categories.

	Process A	Process B	Process C
Category 1		Read	Create, Read, Update, Delete
Category 2	Create		
Category 3		Update	
Category 4			Read

Figure 3.2   Object category/business process CRUD matrix.

When all data states that an object category can be in have been identified, a function model can be tested for its handling of life cycle states (later on in analysis and design we can use similar techniques for processes/operations and entities/objects and modules and database structures, respectively). When a function-object category CRUD matrix is complete, you should find that:

- Each function reads at least one object category.

- Each function creates, updates, or deletes at least one object category.

- Each category is read by at least one function.

- Each category is created and deleted by only one function (usually) but updated by several functions.

Your purpose in developing an object category CRUD matrix is to be able to identify one function that is responsible for creation of data in each object category. To achieve this goal, you may need to continue to decompose object categories until you have achieved enough detail. At the leaf level of a category aggregation, you will likely find data objects. If you cannot identify one create function for each object category, you need to decide whether you have analyzed the object category in enough detail.

Two key concepts in an object-oriented model of a system are aggregation and generalization/specialization. Object category analysis helps to identify these types of data hierarchies. During this initial analysis of groups of data objects, we are most concerned with identifying classes of data objects. Later on in analysis we can refine our object categories into object hierarchies.

Object categories will ultimately be decomposed into one or more objects. Thus object categories form the basis for partitioning and managing your entire enterprise data object model. You must be sure that the definitions are clear and agreed upon, that boundaries do not overlap, and that object categories are comprehensive. In future analysis efforts you will be glad that you have done your hard work up front during initial object category analysis. Future efforts can leverage off previous analysis models in order to save significant time and effort. A properly architected business object model forms the ideal foundation for change, and the category model is a good starting point. Such a model avoids having organizational or procedural changes impact systems in a major way (as would happen if you modeled functions and processes first and data classes and objects later).

Identify Objects

Identify Candidate Business Objects

At the highest level of data modeling, broad categories of objects (also referred to as data subjects) are identified:

- Customers

- Products

- Customer orders

- Employees

- Sales territories

- Equipment

- Vendors

and so on. Once broad object categories have been identified, we move on to identify specific object types for each object class. An object in the real world is a person, place, event, or other real or conceptual thing about which the enterprise must store information. Object types are used for all object structure modeling of business systems and computerized information systems.

In traditional information engineering, objects (known as entities) are strictly data structures. In object modeling, objects are data structures combined with procedures that manipulate object data structures. Operations for a customer order object might include create, update, and cancel. These operations can only be accessed by sending a message to the customer order object, which activates its own methods to perform the operations. An object must only be manipulated by objects that are defined for that specific object type. Some objects identified from object categories might include:

- Types of customers
  - Residential customer
  - Commercial customer
  - Industrial customer
- Parts of customer orders
  - Customer order
  - Customer order line item
  - Customer invoice
  - Customer payment
  - Customer balance due

Potential objects and classes can often be discovered by examining business descriptions. A natural language description of a business problem can be written out and the nouns and noun phrases identified within the text. These nouns and noun phrases represent potential objects or classes. Obviously, analyzing text in this way is not a precise way to identify objects and classes, because natural languages such as English can be ambiguous at times. Text analysis of this sort is, however, quite helpful in getting started identifying candidate objects and classes. Writing down ideas can help discipline business analysis and modeling and can uncover omissions or inconsistencies in existing documentation. A quick scan over a problem statement can produce a list of candidate objects and classes. Figure 3.3 lists some potential object classes for an electronic filing system (Derr, p. 15); the refined candidate object classes are listed in Figure 3.4 (Derr, p. 17). Other techniques for identifying objects include the scripting of object behavior analysis (Goldberg and Rubin 1992) and the use case modeling of Jacobson (Jacobson et al. 1992). Additional classes that do not directly appear in a problem statement can be identified from knowledge of the problem domain or by implication in the problem domain.

abstract	description	index	system
alphanumeric character	document	junk word	text document
author	document description	keyword	user
content	EFP	number of documents	user-defined keyword
convenient schemes	editor	portion of the document	word processor
conventional	electronic filing system	search	
classifications	filing character set	search criteria	

Figure 3.3   Potential object classes for an electronic filing system.

abstract	keyword
author	line
filing character	page
index	text document
junk word	word

Figure 3.4   A refined list of candidate object classes.

Guidelines for Selecting Object Types

Once object type categories and object types themselves have been identified it is necessary that you attempt to discard unnecessary and incorrect categories. Rumbaugh et al. (pp. 153–156) list the types of situations to examine (see Figure 3.5).

Describe Object Associations

Associations are used to model dependencies (relationships) between classes. An association is a conceptual relationship between instances of an object. Each association can be defined as an ordered list of object instances. Associations describe groups of relationships with common

- *Redundant classes.* When two object categories depict the same information, the most descriptive name should be retained.

- *Irrelevant classes.* When an object class has little or nothing to do with the problem at hand, it should be discarded.

- *Vague classes.* An object class should be specific, not ill-defined boundaries or too broad in scope.

- *Attributes.* If an object type seems to describe another individual object, it probably should be defined as an attribute type, not an object type.

- *Operations.* If an object type describes an operation applied to objects and not manipulated in its own right, it is not an object class.

- *Roles.* The name of an object class should reflect its intrinsic nature and not a role it plays in an association.

- *Implementation constructs.* If a model construct is extraneous to the real world, it should be eliminated from an analysis model. It might be useful later on in design but not during analysis.

Figure 3.5   Situations to examine when modeling objects.

structure and meaning; all instances of an association connect object instances from the same object type category. An association between objects is given a name in both directions so that the relationship name plus the associated object names builds a sentence:

Client	places	Order
	is placed by	

An association may exist between two classes, three classes, or even more than three classes; in practice, though, most associations are between two classes. Although associations are always defined as bidirectional, they do not have to be implemented in both directions. This concept of an optional association is used in some object-oriented languages that implement associations as pointers. Traversal of the associations defined in only one direction may be implemented for performance reasons. Programming languages may implement associations as pointers from one object to another, and various library classes such as sets or dictionaries can be used to build associations.

Associations may be identified, as with object classes, in problem statements using textual analysis. Verbs and verb phrases in the problem statements can be used to list potential associations between object classes. Figures 3.6 through 3.8 list some verb phrases used by Derr to characterize associations for his electronic filing system.

Documents filed in system	EFP retrieves text documents
Documents filed with abstract	EFP stores text documents
Documents filed with author	User prints documents
Documents filed with keyword	User specifies indexable/searchable characters
Documents removed/deleted from system	User specifies junk words
Documents retrievable with convenient schemes	User specifies search criteria
Editor creates document	User views documents
EFP index documents	Word processor creates document

Figure 3.6   Explicit verb phrases for an electronic filing system.

Document referenced by index	Documents retrievable by keyword
Documents created external to EFP	Search criteria has abstract
Documents must be text only	Search criteria has author
Documents retrievable by abstract	Search criteria has keyword
Documents retrievable by author	Scurch criterin has word
Documents retrievable by content	

Figure 3.7   Implicit verb phrases for an electronic filing system.

Abstract describes document	Pages contain lines
Documents contain pages	Text document identified by author
Keyword identifies document	Words contain alphanumeric characters
Lines contain words	

Figure 3.8   Knowledge of problem domain for an electronic filing system.

Cardinality

The cardinality (also referred to as multiplicity), or number of instances of one object type that can be associated with instances of the other object type in an association, is modeled like this:

Client	places	Order
	is placed by	

1   *

This diagram says "a customer places many orders" and "an order is placed by one customer," where the first number on the association, 1, represents the minimum, and the second number, *, represents many. Some modeling techniques (such as that used by Martin) model cardinality (multiplicity) using "crow's feet" or an open or filled circle (Bachman and OMT).

Optionality

The optionality of a relationship ("may" or "must") is modeled as a "0" for optional or a "1" or "*" (placed just inside the cardinality symbol) for mandatory:

Client	places	Order
	is placed by	

1..1   0..*

This diagram says "a customer may place one or many orders" and "an order must be placed by one (and only one) customer." Other modeling techniques may use a solid circle to depict zero or more instances in an association and a hollow circle to indicate zero or one. The basic concept is the same—depicting constraints on an association.

The association modeled above is an example of a fairly simple binary association. More complex associations may include "composed of" (aggregation), inclusiveness and exclusivity, recursiveness, and supertype/subtype (generalization/specialization) associations.

Guidelines for Selecting Associations

Rumbaugh et al. (pp. 158–161) list some issues to be examined when determining which object associations to retain and which to discard. These are listed in Figure 3.9.

- *Associations between eliminated classes (object categories).* If one or more object categories in an association have been eliminated, the association must also be eliminated or restated in terms of other object categories.

- *Irrelevant or implementation associations.* Discard any associations outside the problem domain or that deal with implementation constructs.

- *Actions.* Associations should describe structural properties of an application domain, not transient events.

- *Ternary associations.* Associations among three or more object types can be decomposed into binary associations or phrased as qualified associations.

- *Derived associations.* Eliminate associations that can be defined in terms of other associations because they are redundant. Also eliminate associations defined by conditions on object attributes.

- *Misnamed associations.* Avoid stating how or why a situation occurred; say what it is.

- *Role names.* Add role names to describe roles that an object type in an association plays from the point of view of the other object type.

- *Qualified associations.* A name is usually used to identify an object within some context, but most names are not globally unique. The context combines uniquely with the name to identify an object.

- *Multiplicity.* For multiplicity values of "many," consider whether a qualifier is needed. Also, ask if the objects need to be ordered in some way.

- *Missing associations.* Add any missing associations that are discovered.

Figure 3.9   Issues to be examined when modeling associations

Define Object Attributes

Attributes are properties or characteristics of objects. An attribute describes a single object type although the same attribute name and concept might appear elsewhere in an object structure model to describe other object types. Example attributes for a customer might include:

Name
Street address
City
State or province
Zip or postal code
Country
Home phone
Work phone
Birth date

These attributes describe a customer and are associated only with that object type. Attributes are usually named as nouns (and might be modeled as object types in and of themselves), but their values may appear as adjectives (such as a color or size). During object structure modeling in analysis, we can usually ignore the formal modeling of derived attributes (such as age, which can be derived from birth date and the current date) in order to simplify the model. In design and implementation, we need to take these derived attributes into account using methods to implement the derivation formulae (although we would probably not model these as operations in analysis).

The address might be a separate object type of "customer address" if more than one address is needed (especially if the number of addresses is variable from one to many). The phone numbers also might require a separate object type of "customer phone" if the number of phone numbers is variable (which is becoming more common with people working at multiple locations and using facsimile machines and cellular phones). Object modeling starts with identification of obvious object type categories and object types and progresses to identification of attributes. By examining attributes in detail you will often discover additional object types that must be created to handle situations such as the address and phone number examples.

Guidelines for Selecting Attributes

Before you consider attribute definition complete, consider the guidelines in Figure 3.10 for keeping the right attributes (Rumbaugh et al. pp. 162–163).

Add Specialization

We can add a generalization/specialization relationship to our object models in order to enhance the sharing of attributes and operations. Generalization is a relationship between classes. We can identify general concepts and then specialize upon these in subclasses, or work bottom-up to consolidate general concepts into a superclass. In Figure 3.11, a vehicle superclass is used to contain characteristics common to all vehicle types. Subclasses such as car and bus can be used to characterize specific types of vehicles. Both car and bus inherit all properties of vehicle and can add new properties of their own.

Depending upon the programming language used to implement this kind of model, the subclasses might redefine certain operations in the superclass, thereby overriding those operations inherited from the su-

- *Objects.* If an independent existence of an entity is important, rather than just its value, then it is an object.
- *Qualifiers.* If an attribute's value depends on a particular context, consider restating the attribute as a qualifier.
- *Names.* These are often better modeled as qualifiers rather than object attributes.
- *Identifiers.* Do not list object identifiers in object models—they are implicit in object models. Only list attributes that exist in the application domain.
- *Link attributes.* If a property depends on the existence of a link, the property is an attribute of the link and not of a related object.
- *Internal values.* If an attribute describes the internal state of an object invisible outside the object, eliminate it from analysis.
- *Fine detail.* Omit minor attributes unlikely to affect most operations.
- *Discordant attributes.* If an attribute seems completely different from, and unrelated to, all other attributes, this attribute may be an object class that should be split into two distinct object categories.

Figure 3.10   Guidelines for keeping object attributes.

perclass. In practice, it is quite common to see generalization/specialization hierarchies in business models, followed by inheritance hierarchies in design and implementation. The difference usually is that inheritance hierarchies may define inheritance from superclasses that are not true supertypes but rather classes that are inherited for convenience. For purposes of this chapter, we deal only with supertype/subtype hierarchies that represent generalization/specialization (not superclass/subclass hierarchies that represent implementation inheritance).

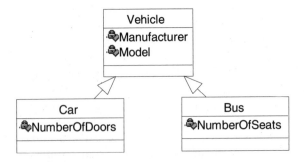

Figure 3.11   A specialization hierarchy.

Navigate Access Paths

Once an object model has been developed to include class diagrams with attributes and associations, the model should be tested for completeness and consistency by tracing access paths through the model. This process of tracing access paths helps validate the model, checking to see that the classes, attributes, operations, and associations needed to implement a system to satisfy system requirements are present and in the correct form. We can validate the model by selecting use cases (scenarios) and tracing the access paths through the model that each use case references.

Use cases, if already developed, help to organize requirements into discrete tasks that need to be accomplished in the system. Execution of each use case against the object model should achieve the expected results implied in the use case scripts. Object interaction diagrams (usually in the form of collaboration diagrams and sequence diagrams) may have been developed from use case scripts and will be very specific as to which messages flow to which objects, referencing specific attributes. If object interactions have not been modeled for complex message exchanges, they can be developed as the use case scripts are executed against the object model. Object interaction models characterize system behavior—beyond the scope of this chapter—and are covered in Chapter 4 and Chapter 7. Chapter 6 describes how to trace messages among objects that support a particular use case.

References

Derr, K. W. *Applying OMT: A Practical Step-by-Step Guide to Using the Object Modeling Technique*. New York: SIGS Books, 1995.

Jacobson, I., M. Christerson, P. Johnnson, and G. Overgaard. *Object-Oriented Software Engineering: A Use Case Driven Approach*. Wokingham, England: Addison-Wesley, 1992.

Martin, J. *Information Engineering*. Englewood Cliffs, NJ: Prentice Hall, 1990.

Rubin, K. S., and A. Goldberg. "Object Behavior Analysis," in *Communications of the ACM* (September 1992): 49–51.

Rumbaugh, J., M. Blaha, W. Premerlani, F. Eddy, and W. Lorensen. *Object-Oriented Modeling and Design*. Englewood Cliffs, NJ: Prentice Hall, 1991.

Model System
Internal Behaviors

Identify and Describe Object States

A good starting point for modeling object behavior is to describe the various states that an object exhibits. States represent object status, phase, situation, or activity. Each object may go through many different states, from object creation until object termination. An object's state is represented by the values that the object's attributes can take on. A change in any attribute's value constitutes a change in the object's state.

There are a number of different ways to discover object states. One way is to observe objects within a system and then to record the observed states. For example, a customer order may be recorded but not filled, filled but not shipped, shipped but still active or inactive. The state of customer orders is recorded by some attribute of the order (and possibly of the individual items on the order as well). The status attribute changes value as the customer order changes state throughout its life.

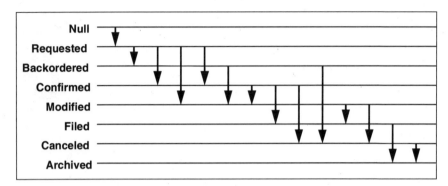

Figure 4.1   An object state diagram—fence notation.

Another way to discover object states is to examine the attributes directly. Each change in an attribute's value reflects a change in the state of the object that owns that attribute. You could first examine the potential values for attributes and then determine whether the system requirements include different behaviors for those possible attribute values. This approach is used by Coad and Yourdon (see Coad and Yourdon 1991).

Processing requirements for an entire system can be described in terms of the behavior of its objects and the corresponding changes in object states. We can describe the behavior of an object over time as a series of state changes. An object state diagram can be used to depict the states that an object can be in over time. This kind of diagram identifies states and transitions from one state to another. Object state diagrams can be drawn using the "fence" notation of Martin and Odell (see Figure 4.1) or a network diagram, with bubbles or boxes for states and lines or arcs for transitions between states (see Figure 4.2). A third notation used to describe object states, and transitions between states, is an object state matrix (see Figure 4.3).

Detailed behaviors and changes in behavior are defined within the specification of each behavior operation (just as the processing logic and data accesses of fundamental processes are specified using minispec action diagrams during business area analysis).

The object state diagram using a network notation represents states by oval bubbles. Each of these bubbles corresponds to a single state of an object. The name of each state is placed inside the state bubble. The arcs connecting the states represent the state transitions and may or may not be labeled, depending upon the needs of a project or upon the methodology being used to model object behavior. It is important to re-

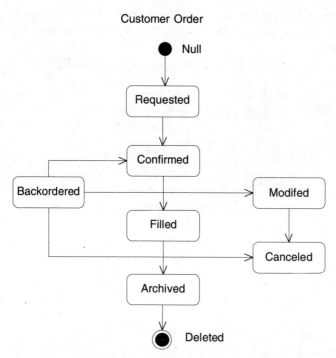

Figure 4.2   **An object state diagram—network notation.**

	A. Null	B. Requested	C. Back- ordered	D. Confirmed	E. Modified	F. Filled	G. Canceled	H. Archived
Record Order	B							
Record Backorder		C						
Confirm Order		D	D					
Modify Order		E	E	E				
Fill Order				F	F			
Cancel Order			G	G	G			
Archive Order						H	H	

Figure 4.3   **An object state matrix.**

member that a state is either on or off at any point in time. A state is on when the object is currently in that state; it is off when the object is in some other state.

Martin and Odell (pp. 320–325) point out that a useful technique for object behavior specifications is the *finite-state machine*, a hypothetical machine that can exist in only one of a finite number of states at any given point in time. Each finite-state machine changes its state and produces output in response to a stimulus from the external environment. This technique is used to depict object state transitions by having each machine describe a single set of objects. External stimuli are responsible for triggering state changes and responses are, in turn, returned to the invoking external environment. Martin and Odell (p. 323) list primary components of a finite-state machine and its interface with the external environment (see Figure 4.4).

In the process of modeling states and their transitions, we need to consider carefully how one state relates to another within the operation of a system. We need to be able to describe expected business events and system conditions that activate a change of object state. The process of moving an object from one state to another is a transition. Events and conditions that activate these transitions are triggers. In our customer order example, the event "receive customer order" becomes the trigger for recording the order. The condition "item out of stock" triggers the recording of a backorder.

An object state diagram should relate triggers and states. When a trigger stimulates an object, the next state depends on the current

---

1. An event in the external environment stimulates or triggers an operation within a machine.

2. Each operation is invoked to change the state of exactly one object.

3. Each operation is specified in terms of object types that must apply to an object before the operation and those that apply after. These prestates and poststates are guaranteed by each operation.

4. Within each finite-state machine, a specific operation is selected on the basis of trigger and state preconditions.

5. Before an operation is invoked, some adaptations of finite-state machines require that a control condition be evaluated. Only if the condition is true will the operation actually be invoked.

6. When the invoked operation is successfully completed (there is a state change), an event occurs.

7. The occurrence of an event indicates that a response should be sent to the external environment.

Figure 4.4   Finite-state machine components and interface.

state as well as the trigger. A change of state caused by a trigger is the transition, performed by an object operation (implemented as a method in design). On a state diagram, the transition is drawn as an arc (or line) with an arrowhead showing the direction of the state change. An object state matrix (see Figure 4.3) depicts explicitly the dependencies between states and the operations that cause transitions to occur. All transitions from a state represent different triggers and thus different operations.

An event or condition causing a state transition operation to occur can be specified on an object state diagram, but we can also use an event scenario diagram for this (see Chapter 7). If an object is in a state, and a trigger identified with one of its possible transitions occurs, the object enters the state on the target end of the transition. This is depicted on an object state matrix as the identifier or name of the target state, placed in the cell at the intersection of the starting state and the operation that performs the transition. If more than one transition leaves a state, the first trigger to occur causes the corresponding operation to execute the transition. If a trigger occurs that has no leaving transition defined for the starting state, the trigger is ignored. A sequence of triggers (events or conditions) can be depicted on an object state diagram as pathways through the network of states.

An object state diagram can be used to describe the behavior of an entire class of objects. By definition, all instances of a class have the same structure and behavior, so they can all share the same state diagram. Each object has its own distinct attribute values (and, therefore, distinct states), so it goes though state transitions uniquely as the different triggers occur.

Identify and Describe Object Life Cycles

In order to build a comprehensive system of interoperating objects, we need to describe completely how an object moves to and from various states. The previous discussion of object state diagrams and object state matrices has given you some idea of how we might model object life cycles.

You could use a formal notation for describing object life cycles (the event schema of Martin and Odell or the state network configuration of Embley et al.) or just document the details within the descriptions that support the diagrams and the method specifications. The actual life cycle of some objects is quite complex. However you document object life cycles, it is important that you examine them in detail.

Subsequent states follow a state transition. Each state could have several follow-on states defined for it (but only one subsequent state is chosen for the next transition), as shown in the object state diagrams and the object state matrix. Prior states precede a state transition. Multiple states may lead to a single state (but not at the same time). Initial transactions activate initial states, those states that exist when an object comes into existence. Initial states have no prior states and have no conditions necessary for placing an object in those states. Common operation names assigned to initial state transitions are: create, record, initiate, and establish. Our state diagrams used a NULL state as a conceptual state for an initial operation to start from when establishing an object.

Final states require no subsequent states. As an operation executes to place an object in a final state, prior states are turned off. When a final state is reached, the object ceases to exist (at least, it is not active in the system but may be archived). Common names for operations that place objects in final states include: cancel, terminate, destroy, finish, close, or end.

Build an Object State Matrix

Begin object life cycle modeling by identifying all known states that an object can be in. Then place these states on an object state diagram. Starting with the NULL state, draw a transition arc or line to the next state. Label the next state and continue mapping transitions from state to state. Be sure to include the final state(s) on the diagram. You may wish to label the transitions using operation names at this time, but be sure that all states are identified and named.

Once the object state diagram is complete, build an object state matrix for those objects whose state networks are fairly complex. Label the columns of the matrix with the states depicted on the object state diagram (I use a letter as an identifier of each row) and the rows with the names of the operations that perform the state transitions (for simplicity you may want to number these rows for subsequent mapping back on the arcs or lines of the object state diagram).

Starting with the NULL state, locate the row that represents the initial state transition operation. In the cell that represents the intersection of the NULL state and the initial operation, place the identifier for the next state that the operation will place the object in, based on the current state (the NULL state, initially). The initial transition from null to the initial state requires no more states, so you can proceed to the initial state and begin defining transitions to subsequent states from that initial state (identify states to place in the cells under the initial state column).

Progress along each column, identifying subsequent states, the operation to make the transition to each of these subsequent states, and the code for the subsequent state that each operation places the object in. Place the subsequent state code (a letter in my example) into the cell that represents that starting state and that transition operation. For each state (column), identify all subsequent states (column codes) and the associated operations (rows) that make the transitions to those states. Indicate the subsequent state codes in the cell for that row and column.

When you have examined all states of the matrix, be sure that each column has at least one cell below it that contains a state code and that each row has at least one cell that contains a state code. Each state may have multiple transitions from it to subsequent states and each operation may have more than one starting state (but only one ending state). Figure 4.3 shows what the finished matrix should look like.

Hierarchies of Object States

Ordinarily, flat state diagrams lack the modeling power needed for large, complex systems. When the system being modeled is very complex, it may become necessary to use layered object state diagrams in the same way that objects are layered in a hierarchy. Each object state diagram in a hierarchy of such diagrams would have one associated object state matrix (if needed). Rumbaugh et al. (pp. 94–98) discuss ways to model object state networks as generalization and aggregation hierarchies. See Figure 4.5 for an example of nested states.

Generalization of object states allows states and events to be arranged into generalization hierarchies with inheritance of common structure and behavior (similar to the inheritance of attributes and operations in classes). Aggregation of object states consists of breaking them into their components as processes are decomposed in a process decomposition hierarchy. Aggregation is equivalent to concurrency among states. Concurrent states can correspond to object aggregations (even entire systems) that have interacting parts.

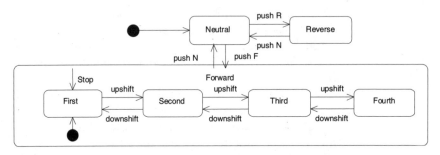

Figure 4.5   Nested object states for an automatic transmission.

Operations in a complex state can be expanded as a lower-level object state diagram, with each state representing one step of the operation. Nested diagrams of this type show input and output transitions, and the set of nested diagrams forms a lattice structure. A nested object state diagram represents a kind of generalization on states, with the generalization being the "or" relationship. An object in a state in a higher-level diagram must be in exactly one of the substates depicted on the child diagram for that state. States on nested child diagrams refine the states in their parent diagrams.

When a customer asks a telephone company to install a new telephone line, a service order is created. From the customer's point of view, the service order is either open or completed, but from the phone company's viewpoint, the service order can be in a multitude of states, one of which is waiting to be installed. The actual installation of the telephone line by the phone company (actions taken during the waiting to be installed state of the service order) places the telephone line in an operational state. This operational state, in turn, consists of substates and operations representing the running of a computerized telephone switch as it manages the telephone line. The computerized telephone switch system is itself a complex system, probably having its own nested object states.

States could have substates that inherit operations from their superstates, as subclasses inherit attributes and operations from their superclasses. Any operation that applies to a state automatically applies to all its substates unless overridden by an equivalent operation on the substate. State transitions of a superstate are inherited by each substate.

Embley et al. (pp. 88–93) discuss ways to interrelate state networks and class generalization/specialization hierarchies using state nets.

Identify Operations Associated with Events

An operation represents what an object does in response to a specific triggering event or condition. Operations are performed in response to a combination of starting object states and the specific trigger that occurs. We need to identify each trigger and any conditions associated with it that may cause a transition operation to execute. Then we need to define the action that takes place during the transition between states. This action may actually be composed of several simpler actions, each of which may or may not execute each time the overall transition operation is triggered. This means that a transition may have multiple threads of execution, each of which must complete before the overall transition is complete. An example of this might be the multiple data accesses required to record information when a customer places an order (read customer record, read product item record, write order header, write order line, etc.).

Many notations may be used to define object operations, but a convenient one might be to use a minispec action diagram. The name of the diagram is the name of the transition operation and the diagram itself describes the overall operation. Conditional logic is easily depicted using condition blocks; repetition blocks depict looping actions. Using an action diagram has the advantage that it is fairly consistent with traditional information engineering techniques, thus providing a workable migration path to full object orientation.

As with more traditional process modeling, a complex object operation may be decomposed into separate operations. A conventional process decomposition diagram could be used to depict levels of operations. The difference between this use of a process decomposition diagram and the traditional way is that object behavior modeling would use a process decomposition within the context of a class, not an entire system (although you could argue that a system is a class, modeling processes at such a high level of abstraction have serious problems).

Once object structures have been modeled and operations identified for class structures within the object model, a process decomposition diagram and the associated minispec action diagrams provide a nice way to both specify object behavior and to migrate from traditional structured analysis models to object models. Within an object model, the decomposition diagram depicts processes within an operation and the minispec action diagrams depict methods to support parts of the overall operation. An operation may affect multiple object state changes via its own methods. These methods (fundamental operation processes) will likely cause one or only a few state changes, and will have specific processing logic defined for making these state changes.

When specifying logic for methods, it is important to avoid building in knowledge of what triggers may cause method execution. Just as an external object must not be aware of how another object implements its methods, those methods must be totally unaware of what external triggers cause their own execution. Also, each method needs to be unaware of what happens after it executes. Methods are, however, aware of their triggers through the parameters passed in from outside. Hiding this information from the inside of a method allows for greater method and operation reuse.

When we need to analyze and model very large, complex systems, consider Figure 4.6, which lists some additional features of object behavior modeling, suggested by Martin and Odell (p. 326).

Operation Scripting

- express how an object's state changes over time with a step-by-step script
- aids experts who are accustomed to starting problems in a sequential manner
- the script entails an orderly sequence of finite-state machines as a way to carry out an operation

Specification Leveling

- compose or decompose each script using levels of process specification
- analysis can proceed from high levels of generality to more detailed ones and vice versa

Operation Reusability

- define operations as processing units
- define kinds of required inputs and outputs
- the same operation can be included within any number of operation scripts—each operation is an object type whose instances are its various invocations

Process Concurrency

- in the real world, processes occur simultaneously
- events can trigger multiple, parallel operations
- parallel operations can simultaneously result in different state changes
- concurrently produced results may require synchronization before invoking further operations

---

Figure 4.6   Features of object behavior modeling (from Martin and Odell).

Model Object Interactions

Model Business Rules

Explicitly stated business rules can determine how to resolve the conflict that occurs when an attribute in a class inherits two different values or can specify whether the default value should be applied before or after inheritance is realized, or before or after a daemon fires. They may specify the relative priorities of inheritance and daemons. Business rules specify information such as dependencies between attributes. Global class invariants and pre- and postconditions that apply to all operations may need to be specified as rules.

A typical business rule in a personnel application, stated in English, might be:

Change vacation entitlement to six weeks when service exceeds five years.

This could be stated as a rule in an employee class (or employee subclass of role). Stating the rule this way helps us cope with business analysis problems where a relational or deductive database with object extensions might be used in the target implementation environment.

We must decide whether rules belong to individual operations (which may be objects themselves) or to an object as a whole. Rules that relate several operations do not belong with those individual operations, and rules that define dependencies between attributes also refer to an object as a whole. On the other hand, rules that concern the encapsulated state of an object belong within one of its operations. An important type of whole object rule is a control rule, which describes object behavior as it participates in structures that it belongs to:

- Default handling

- Multiple inheritance

- Exceptions

- General associations with other objects

Rules may be of several different types. We might, for instance, have triggers, business rules, and control rules. Business rules usually relate two or more attributes, and triggers relate attributes to operations. An example might be:

Business rule:

If service_length > 5 then vacation = 25

Forward trigger:

when salary + salaryIncrement > 20000 run awardCoCar

This business rule could be implemented two different ways. We could place a precondition on *getVacation* that would always check *service_length* before returning its value. Or, we could place a postcondition on *putService_Length* that would detect whether *vacation* should be changed on each anniversary. The first example is lazy evaluation, and the second is eager evaluation. We really shouldn't try to define design and implementation decisions in this manner. A rule-based approach defers such decisions until a later stage of development.

An example of a complex rule set for an insurance salesperson:

If the client is retired and Client.RiskAverse: is FALSE then
    BestProduct: is 'Annuity'
If the client is young and Client.RiskAverse: is FALSE then
    BestProduct: is 'Endowment'
If Client.RiskAverse: is TRUE then
    BestProduct: is 'Bonds'
If Client.Children: > 0 then
    Client.RiskAverse is TRUE

These rules fire when a value for BestProduct is requested from the client object. Some notes:

- Such rules do not violate the encapsulation of client by setting the value of RiskAverse in that object.

- If the value of RiskAverse is already set, these rule do not fire.

- The rules are defined nonprocedurally; the rule that fires first is written last.

- The rule set executes under a backward chaining regime to seek a value for BestProduct.

Control Rules

Control rules are encapsulated within objects; they are not declared globally. These rules may be inherited and overridden. This makes possible local variations in control strategy. The impact of a control structure may be determined on every object. True global rules can be encapsulated in a top-level object and inherited by all objects, where they may be overridden. If a rule is made part of an object's interface, all other objects can see the meaning of the object from its interface alone. Rules can be classified into several, perhaps overlapping, types (Graham 1995):

- Control rules

- Business rules

- Exception-handling rules

- Triggers

Assertions may be attached to each operation and can be inherited. Another way that Graham classifies rules and rule sets is into the six kinds listed in Figure 4.7.

Control rules are concerned with operations and attributes of objects that contain them; they do not reference themselves. They cannot, therefore, assist in determining how to resolve a multiple inheritance conflict between rule sets or some other control strategy problem related to rule sets. This would require a set of metarules to be encapsulated, and these, too, would require a metalanguage. Because this would result in infinite regress, Graham's SOMA method defines that multiple inheritance of rules will not permit conflict resolution. A dot notation is used to resolve any rule sets with the same name. A rule set called "PolicyA" inherited from superclasses X and Y is realized via the separate paths as "X.PolicyA" and "Y.PolicyA," respectively.

It is possible to specify rules (in simple cases) that must be obeyed by all control strategies for multiple inheritance. When objects are identified with only abstract data types, we can use three rules for inheritance:

1. There must be no cycles of the form: x is also known as y is also known as z is also known as x. This eliminates redundant objects.

Rule Type	Comments
Rules that relate attributes to attributes	If service > 5 then vacations = vacations + 1. This could be expressed as a postcondition on put.Service, causing put.Vacations(Vacations + 1) or as a precondition on get.Vacations.
Rules that relate operations to operations	These are naturally expressed as assertions rather than rules.
Rules that relate attributes to operations	These may be expressed as if_needed (pre.get) or if_changed daemons (post.put) or as pre- or postconditions.
Control rules for attributes	Behavior under multiple inheritance conflicts and defaults (preconditions on gets).
Control rules for operations	Behavior under multiple inheritance conflicts (postcondition on gets).
Exception-handling rules	Overheated sensor (invariance or postcondition on temp).

Figure 4.7   Types of rules (adapted from Graham).

2. The bottom of an "also known as" link must be a subtype, and the top must be a subtype or an abstract type (not a printable object; not an attribute).

3. It must be possible to name a subtype of two supertypes. This prevents absurd objects such as "the class of all people who are also toys."

These rules should be checked during design model refinement.

Control rules are not the only rules in a system. Business rules were discussed earlier. In both of these rule types, encapsulating rules in objects makes sense and it enhances reusability and extensibility. System-wide rules belong to the most general objects in a system. These rules are propagated to other parts of the system through inheritance.

Converting Rules to Assertions

The conversion of rules to assertions can be performed rather automatically. First, we need to classify rule types for this purpose. Graham (1995) views rules as falling into the categories listed in Figure 4.8.

Rule Type	Description	Comments
A	Rules that relate attributes to themselves	These are not rules but constraints on attributes. They can be expressed as assertions about the standard put and get methods for each attribute (usually they are preconditions on put).
M	Rules that relate operations (methods) to themselves	These are not rules but assertions concerning operations/methods.
AA	Rules that relate attributes to other attributes	These are expressed as pre- or postconditions on put and get methods associated with one of the attributes.
MM	Rules that relate methods to methods	These usually deal with sequencing and would normally be expressed as pre- or postconditions.
AM	Rules that relate attributes to methods or vice versa	These are triggers or preconditions and could be implemented directly as database triggers or preconditions or indirectly as special code. Rules that relate methods to attributes are invariance or postconditions.
CA	Rules that describe behavior of attributes under global control strategies	These require specific code descriptions in many cases.

Figure 4.8   Rule categories (adapted from Graham).

Rule Type	Description	Comments
CM	Rules that describe behavior of methods under global control strategies	These may require specific code descriptions.
EA	Rules that describe exception handling for attribute values	If the programming language supports exception handling, these map directly to language constructs. Otherwise, purpose-written code is required.
EM	Rules that describe exception handling for methods	If the programming language supports exception handling, these map directly to language constructs. Otherwise, purpose-written code is required.

Figure 4.8   Rule categories (adapted from Graham). *(continued)*

References

Coad, P., and E. Yourdon. *Object-Oriented Analysis*. Englewood Cliffs, NJ: Prentice Hall, 1991.

Embly, D. W., B. D. Kurtz, and S. N. Woodfield. *Object-Oriented Systems Analysis: A Model-Driven Approach*. Englewood Cliffs, NJ: Yourdon Press, 1992.

Graham, I. *Migrating to Object Technology*. Wokingham, England: Addison-Wesley, 1995.

Martin, J., and J. J. Odell. *Object-Oriented Analysis and Design*. Englewood Cliffs, NJ: Prentice Hall, 1992.

Rumbaugh, J., M. Blaha, W. Premerlani, F. Eddy, and W. Lorensen. *Object-Oriented Modeling and Design*. Englewood Cliffs, NJ: Prentice Hall, 1991.

5

Design Databases

Basic Object-Oriented Database Concepts

Object-oriented database management systems are based on a complete object model, the principles of which were covered in earlier chapters. Here we begin with a discussion of basic object concepts and how object database systems support these concepts. Object database systems contain the natural features of object-oriented programming languages, such as C++ or SmallTalk, and add extensions to support database specification and maintenance. These features must be present for a programming language and environment to be considered a database language and system:

- Database structuring policies and mechanisms should provide for forming of data items into meaningful elements such as records or objects.

- Grouping structures into more complex data structures such as lists, relations, sets, bags, and trees should be supported.

- Basic operations must be provided to create, modify, and delete data structures.

- Means to access stored information using powerful query mechanisms must be provided.

Database structuring must represent relationships between data structures within the database schema. These relationships are named structures, which can have their own data components. Relationships support link structures to allow modeling of advanced database semantics. A database also provides persistence and storage for objects. Object database management systems allow objects to be created and persistently stored so that they may be shared by multiple processes or users in a simultaneous fashion. Other features include:

- Data integrity constraints for defining ranges of correct states of data items and their relationships

- Database security

- Database query processing

- Semantic and restricted views of the database

- Data administration support

Object Identity

Object programming and database systems provide a way for any object to be uniquely defined in a system. Each instantiated object in a system is assigned a unique identifier (the object's identity). An object's identity is an invariant value across all possible changes to the object; it acts as a pointer to an item. An object's identity pointer and the object itself are fixed—they cannot change over time if the item is to remain identifiable. The identifier property of an object allows us to either distinguish between two objects that may have the same values for their attributes or determine if two objects are actually equal—they are the same object.

In a relational database, having two tuples in a relation (rows in a table) with the same value is impossible, even if they represent two different real objects. We can fix this problem, however, by adding a key field to provide uniqueness. We then need to provide our own identifier values for the key fields. With an object database, on the other hand, when each object instance is created, it is assigned a unique, unchange-

Parent	Child
Carolyn	Justin
Carolyn	David
Carolyn	Sarah
Steve	David
Steve	Sarah

Figure 5.1   Object identity in a relational database.

able identifier. We can determine if two instances are the same by simply comparing them (comparing their identifiers). If two objects have the same identifier, then they are the same object; otherwise, they are unique objects.

Object identifiers can provide storage and access efficiency. If we wish to add a child tuple to an existing tuple in a relational database, we need to replicate the attribute for the parent in the child (see Figure 5.1). In an object database, we can simply instantiate both the parent and child with each having a pointer to the parent object; the parent object need not be repeated. The object model allows us to easily determine if the objects being pointed to are equal, since this involves a simple object identifier comparison. In a relational database, we must link relationship records and it is more difficult to compare records (although we obviously need the ability to do so).

Inheritance in object databases is more complex. If we need to delete an object in an object database, there may be references to the object that will be left dangling with a simple-minded delete of the instance alone. This is analogous to leaving foreign key attribute references to a deleted primary key record in a relational database. With object inheritance, supertype information is used to further definition or use of subtypes. This dynamic referencing means that the database architecture cannot predetermine all links, and instance deletion is not straightforward. Object databases must, therefore, use concepts to collect objects awaiting deletion until no references remain that point to those objects. When all references have been deleted, an object may be deleted and its memory reclaimed and later reused. This is analogous to the garbage collection techniques used for memory management in object-oriented programming languages.

Database-Wide Object Identification[1]

Inheritance.   As discussed in Chapter 3, inheritance is a characteristic of object models and object software systems that supports reuse of fundamental and constructed object types to be used to define more complex object types. An example of this would occur if an employee (actually, a person employed by an organization) is defined with attributes for name, address, and phone number, with functions to create a new instance of the employee and to access these attributes as instance variables. We could further use this object type definition to specify a type for a special class or refined class of employee, such as a permanent employee or a temporary contract worker. These object subtypes should inherit attributes and operations from the employee supertype (or, ultimately, from the person supertype) in order to avoid repeating the attributes, associations, and operations that are general to all employees (or persons, for that matter).

New object types would each have their own attributes, associations, and operations added to the definition of its specialized subtype. Both would also contain all of the employee type and its associations and operations, so that a permanent employee instance would inherit characteristics of employee to obtain the name, address, and phone number as well as other general employee information and operations. This means that the subtype can access the attributes and operations of its parent type without implementing new code to achieve the same end.

Employee

Employee ID	Name	Address	Phone
59344	Jones	7953 S. 66th Street	459-2288

Contract Employee

Employee ID	Employer ID	Billing Rate
59344	CompuGuys	359.00

Figure 5.2   Joining tables to implement inheritance.

---

1. See Chorafas and Steinman, Ch. 6.

In a relational database system (which most of us use to actually implement our object designs), supertype attributes need to be linked into relations for all subtypes. We can do this by having a reference relation with a tuple for each subtype in the subtype relation that has a reference to an instance in the supertype. For example, to obtain the names and addresses of contract employees, we would join the contract employee relation with the employee relation to create a resultant joined table containing the names and addresses (shown in Figure 5.2). Although this is easy to accomplish in a relational design, it can extract a significant performance penalty.

When used correctly, inheritance is a powerful tool. An object-oriented database system can allow each object to inherit the type "persistent object," thus providing consistent persistent storage of objects and the corresponding maintenance in the database. In a similar fashion, objects can inherit features for:

- Transaction management

- Concurrency control

- Security

- Constraints

- Triggers

- Other database functions

Global characteristics inherited by all objects in a database simplify the building and management of a database system. Object databases have provided this benefit to define basic database management properties as global object classes. More recently, the Object Database Management Group (ODMG) has defined similar functions to be provided in the ODMG-93 extension of the CORBA Persistent Object Service, which defines how to implement a protocol that provides an efficient Persistent Data Service (PDS) for fine-grained objects. This standard uses the Object Management Group's object model as its basis, using an Object Request Broker environment to provide concurrent access to persistent stores that are capable of handling millions of fine-grained objects. The ODMG-93 standard consists of three major components:

1. Object Definition Language

2. Object Query Language

3. C++ and SmallTalk Language Bindings

This ODMG-93 standard is the object database equivalent of Structured Query Language (SQL). It resulted from work done by the Object Database Management Group (ODMG), a consortium of all major object database management system vendors. The ODMG is a working subgroup of the Object Management Group, and its work should allow applications to work with object database management systems from any major vendor. Indeed, most ODMG vendors today are shipping systems that are compliant with large subsets of the specifications, with full compliance in the very near future.

Overloading and Late Binding

Even though inheritance supports reuse of definitions and operations of a supertype within a related subtype object, it does not provide the ability to use the same name or operation for different types or to customize the behavior of inherited operations. Object-oriented programming languages provide the ability to "overload" method names by providing separate implementations of a given method name for each object type specified, as well as to the various implementations. This overloading of method names is also called polymorphism. We can define two basic operations, draw and move, used to perform graphical operations on graphical objects of various types. These basic operations could be inherited by circle and rectangle from the shape supertype (see Figure 5.3 for an illustration).

Each implementation of *draw()* and *move()* in the subtype objects redefines the operation for that subtype. In our example, we need two unique implementations of each operation, using the same name to perform the named operation and possibly providing different input parameter types. This redefinition using the same name is called overloading, or polymorphism. Overloading a function in this way requires that a method name be bound to the correct implementation at the time a program is running. This run-time binding of operations to their implementation is referred to as late binding.

Late binding requires that the run-time system have the ability to resolve differences between input parameter types, matching them to a named operation at run time and locating the correct implementation to support execution of the operation. The usual way to handle this name resolution is to form various implementations into a lattice structure, where types of expected parameters for implementations are used to select which implementation to execute. A dispatcher routine traverses the structure to identify a match between the type parame-

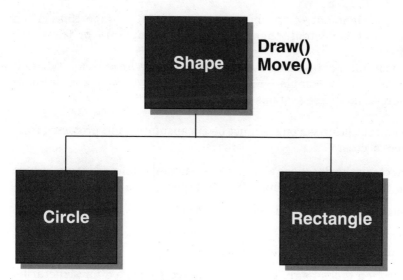

Figure 5.3   Polymorphism via inheritance.

ters provided in the method call and the types in the lattice. This searching continues across the type lattice until the lowest subtype matching the request is located. Programming and database management systems use a variety of data structures to make the search more efficient. One is to form the search space into a tree with subtypes at the leaves; another is to use a directed acyclic graph or hash buckets. This optimization of run-time systems is beyond the scope of this book.

Object Databases

As you would expect, object database systems extend the basic features of object-oriented programming languages—especially in the area of persistence, the property of an object that defines that the object remain in storage (usually on disk) until explicitly deleted. Persistence in object databases must be explicit, extending the basic programming language. Objects may have lifetimes of persistence bounded by events or through various definitions of their attributes and behaviors. Objects may become persistent upon their creation through explicit definition via a persistence property of their classes. Another way to become persistent is for an object to be connected to a subtype of a persistent root object by assignment. Still another way to achieve persistence is assignment of an object to a persistent storage class. If an object is not persistent, then it must be a temporary or transitory object.

Some fundamental features must be present in an object database if its model is to be complete and provide the functionality required of commercial database systems (Fortier, pp. 261–262):

- An object's state variables must be encapsulated and protected from direct access.

- Objects in the database should be persistently defined by a root type and thus reachable through this root type.

- Object instances should know about their type.

- Polymorphism of object operations must be supported, requiring dynamic binding of types for implementation.

- Collection types to group objects must be supported for structuring and queries.

- Relationships between objects should be supported as fundamental components of database structure.

- The object model should support query facilities and versioning.

Representing Objects

Each object's structure consists of valued attributes or references to other objects. These referenced objects describe an object but are not part of its physical implementation. Attribute values are bound to an object structure, but objects are not bound totally to an object's attributes. An object may be referenced and connected to any object, but values are bound to individual objects; they are private to their bound object. Representations for objects in a database should be further supported by collection types:

- Sets

- Bags

- Tuples

- Arrays

- Lists
- Multisets

These object types allow grouping of objects by the same, related, or similar type into extended structures. These extended structures may be queried and optimized for storage, say, to create an object similar to a relational table (a relation). This multiset of objects (the rows of the table) can be refined to have methods for relational manipulation, allowing relational database manipulation.

Inheritance Hierarchy

Type inheritance allows for code reuse, as discussed earlier. Inheritance hierarchies (see Figure 5.4) allow subtypes to specify unique operations, using inherited operations as components of their own operations. The ability to substitute or modify an inherited operation allows a type to substitute operations or values in the subtype for those inherited from the supertype. Some newer object database languages support mutability—the ability of the type of an object to be changed (mutated) through application of a mutator function on that type. This mutator function changes the object's type so that two instances of a type that would otherwise be equal can now be different.

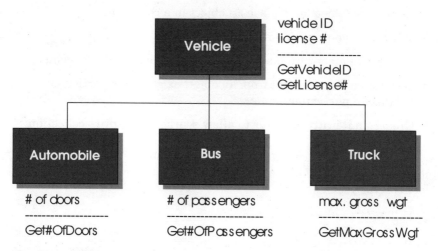

Figure 5.4 An inheritance hierarchy.

Collections

Collections provide a way to group and organize related objects. A collection is itself an object and can have its own attributes and operations defined on the objects being grouped. We can create sets of objects of the same type: a set of customers, a set of suppliers, a set of employees, and so on. Each of these sets has its own embedded operations and share some operations inherited by any supertype set. Objects grouped in a collection must fit the allowable types supported by the operations defined for the collection; we cannot have objects of different types in the collection if these objects need to take action based on the collection's type and its supported operations.

A general supertype collection supports these properties:

cardinality   indicates the number of objects in the collection

empty   indicates that the collection has no objects in it

ordered   indicates whether the collection is structured or unstructured

duplicates   indicates that the collection can hold duplicate objects

All collections support operations to:

• Create, delete, or insert an object in a collection

• Remove an object or replace an object in a collection

• Retrieve an object from a collection

• Select an element from a collection, given some selection criteria

• Determine if an element from an object exists or if a particular object contains a particular element

• Create an iterative pointer to allow search of an entire collection

With the general collection type specification and these operations, more specific collections can be created. Object databases support collection types such as:

• Set

• Bag

- List

- Array

Sets. A set is an unordered collection that does not allow duplicates (Figure 5.5). It can use all collection operations and properties. A set supports creation of a set of a specific type and insertion of elements into the set, without allowing duplicates. Set operations include:

- Union

- Intersect

- Difference

- Copy

- Subset determination

- Proper subset determination

- Superset determination

- Proper superset determination

We can use these operations to take two sets of parts for all automobiles in our product line and perform a union operation on them to get a new set that contains all elements from both sets, with no duplicates.

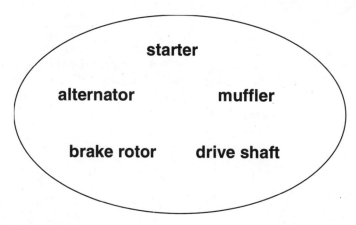

Figure 5.5   A set.

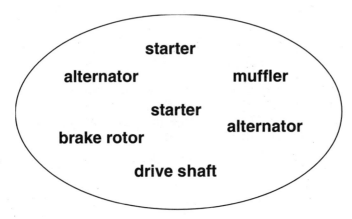

Figure 5.6   A bag.

Bags.   A bag is an unordered collection that is allowed to have duplicates (Figure 5.6). It supports:

- Union
- Intersection
- Difference

operators on compatible sets. We could form a collection of all parts in all automobiles in our product line with a bag type, with some parts duplicated.

Lists.   A list is an ordered group of objects that allows duplicates (Figure 5.7). Ordering of objects within the list is determined by the order in which the objects within the list were inserted into the collection, not by any specific index or sort order. Orderings can be specified by a programmer using operations that allow:

- Insertion
- Removal
- Replacement

alternator ——▶ brake rotor ——▶ drive shaft ——▶ muffler ——▶ starter

Figure 5.7   A list.

of objects in the list. These operations use a location within the list to
determine where the operation should be applied. We could use modifi-
ers to insert a new object before a specific location or to replace an element at a location in the list.

Arrays. Arrays are usually supported in object database models and
systems. An array (Figure 5.8) is a collection of one dimension with a
variable length and can be initialized or changed as the array is popu-
lated with elements or accessed. Arrays allow objects to be organized
and accessed as if they were organized in an indexed list. Arrays support operations to:

- Insert

- Remove

- Replace

- Retrieve

objects at a given location within an array These operations and the
data structures allow a database system to build structures where index values are reserved for specific instances, or, when the array is pop-

1	alternator
2	brake rotor
3	drive shaft
4	muffler
5	starter

Figure 5.8   An array.

ulated, they can be used to index the collection. An array can be searched in one order at a time using a position index as a pointer.

Associations (Relationships)

Associations represent identifiable, named connections between objects. Associations between items in a database are desirable in an object design, but few object database systems support associations directly. An association may be represented as:

• Separate objects that name the connected object instances

• Specific attributes private to the association (if any)

• Constraints on internal attributes and objects involved in the association

An association can be described as a subject (the association object itself) and members of the association (see Figure 5.9).

The simplest association is a one-to-one association between two object instances. Relationships may be:

• One-way

• Symmetric

• Multivalued

One-way associations.   One-way associations are single-valued and involve two objects, with one object pointing to another. Such an association exists in one direction only. To traverse the association in the opposite direction, we need an inverse association.

Figure 5.9   An association object.

Symmetric associations. Symmetric associations imply a corresponding bidirectional association; traversing the association in either direction from one object can return an object in the other direction. Some object systems treat such bidirectional associations as the true associations, with all others referred to as properties.

Multivalued associations. Multivalued associations are the most common ones in data modeling. These associations consist of a collection of object instances that all have the same association to one another.

Associations can be implemented in various ways. One way is to maintain an association as a set or as an extent table, with the extent table representing a list of pointers to objects contained in a similar type structure. We could use such a table to maintain a list of all instances of the employee object type. The table would contain references to all instances of employee, facilitating access and manipulation of these instances. The structure could be used to contain references to related objects and their associated data. This should enable navigation of an association from one end to the other. We should be able to search a tree of associations, starting to navigate an association on employees that includes a link to a parent instance, searching for its parent instance, and so on until we come to the end at the last known link of the association list.

Constraints on Associations

Constraints on associations are used to model business (or other domain) rules regarding data integrity, correctness, and validity. These rules are then used to implement a database that supports these rules. Constraints help provide correctness checking of a database in ways that programming languages do not. Database correctness conditions are "predicates written on the correctness of the state of values and the relationship of these database items' values against each other" (Fortier, p. 271). Data modelers and object structure modelers know these as constraints to check that the type of a data item matches the type of the item's specification or that the data item is within some indicated range of values. Constraints may be specific to a type, such as having a state code be in the list of 50 U.S. state codes.

Other constraints may be more complex, so that rather than being defined to maintain a domain of correct possible values for a data item, they may be set up to restrict the value in one object based on a reference value from another object. These are the referential integrity constraints known to data modelers and relational database designers.

We can also define constraints to restrict values on a collection of objects. An example would be if we wanted to restrict the retail price of all automobiles in our inventory to be less than $100,000, because our dealership does not carry high-priced luxury vehicles. This constraint cannot be written easily into an ordinary automobile object; it would require an upper-level object that can access all of the automobile objects. Another way to implement this constraint is to create a handler object, bound to all instances of the automobile class, catching and checking all updates to the price attribute before these updates are allowed to be executed by an automobile instance's methods. This kind of constraint consists of the constraint rule (a predicate) and a constraint action (the handler). The action will be performed if the constraint is true.

Problems with constraints in object systems. Constraints present certain problems in object systems when we need to check constraints—when do we perform the check? We may need to indicate explicitly when to check a constraint so as not to check it during the completion of a transaction involving cooperation between two or more constrained objects—we may need to perform the check after all updates have been made (but perhaps before the transaction is committed to the database). If we wanted to calculate an across-the-board price increase on all automobiles but still check the total retail value of our inventory for a certain total price ceiling, we would need to update all prices first and then check the total retail value (total price ceiling) at the end of all price updates.

Constraint implementation in object databases. With some object database systems, we define constraints explicitly as components of objects; in other systems constraints are defined as stand-alone objects that refer to other objects when checking constraints. This way of implementing constraints requires the calling of operations from named objects to obtain the values to be used in the constraint checking. Also, there should be operations on the involved objects to correct any detected constraint violations. For an automobile object, a constraint specification requires an operation on the price of the automobile to read the price value and another operation to set the price value by a handler if a violation is detected.

Other constraints can be directly embedded into an object's specification. The values of an attribute or association between multiple attributes of an object can be checked directly via an operation's specification or as a stand-alone operation. The constraint on the value of the domestic attribute for an automobile can be checked to see if it is domestic or foreign. The constraint can be checked whenever the attribute is accessed, only when it is updated, or based on a specified event.

Constraints are a powerful construct in the maintenance of a database, if they are correctly specified. Constraints can be active or passive. An active constraint can check its bound objects when events, time, or other condition is satisfied; a passive constraint is only checked when encountered during execution of an operation. Passive constraints need to be embedded in an object's behavior code, but active constraints do not need to be so embedded.

Queries

Object database systems support an unbounded range of possible data manipulation primitives. These primitives are defined based on how data are used and represented within the system and to application programs. These methods can be changed through object modifications and recompilations, thus becoming basic operations in the database management system.

Query processing in an object database requires some structuring within the database to improve efficiency. Object database systems access data by obtaining object identifiers and using these identifiers to navigate through the database. These systems can support grouping of objects into:

- Collections

- Sets

- Bags

- Lists

- Arrays

as discussed earlier. Object models allow for building of query processing such as that found in relational models. Object properties such as inheritance may make it very difficult to write code that is optimal for some structures. However, if these structures are specified in such a way that the ordering or grouping is done based on object state values, more optimum query processing is possible.

The Object Data Management Group (ODMG) has begun work on an Object Query Language (OQL) to provide functions found in the SQL relational query language. Using OQL, we begin with relational structure and add components to objects to increase the flexibility of manipulations. Using some basic features of object models, we can construct unnamed structures, such as sets of part names and their supplier codes, using the struct operator in the set structure:

```
set (
    struct(name: "Clutch Assembly", supplier: "Centerforce"),
    struct(name: "Y-Pipe", supplier: "The SHO Shop"),
    struct(name: "Muffler", supplier: "Decker Engineering")
)
```

We can make this set persistent and then query it to locate object instances within the set. We could form the same data into a list:

```
list (
    struct(name: "Clutch Assembly", supplier: "Centerforce"),
    struct(name: "Y-Pipe", supplier: "The SHO Shop"),
    struct(name: "Muffler", supplier: "Decker Engineering")
)
```

or as a bag:

```
bag (
    struct(name: "Clutch Assembly", supplier: "Centerforce"),
    struct(name: "Y-Pipe", supplier: "The SHO Shop"),
    struct(name: "Muffler", supplier: "Decker Engineering")
)
```

or as an array:

```
array (
    struct(name: "Clutch Assembly", supplier: "Centerforce"),
    struct(name: "Y-Pipe", supplier: "The SHO Shop"),
    struct(name: "Muffler", supplier: "Decker Engineering")
)
```

We can check for existence using:

```
exists p in Muffler.name : part.name = "Muffler"
```

or test for membership in the structure using:

```
Muffler in SET<T>
```

Other SQL-like operations exist to determine how many objects are contained in a collection and if the collection is ordered and what the ordering is, as well as operations to perform simple manipulations and comparisons on the contents of structures. OQL supports the relational SELECT ... FROM ... WHERE construct found in SQL. Relational query operations can be performed on collections by using binary set expressions, such as:

except	returns objects from a collection that are not named in the except condition
union	takes two collections and creates a new collection, which includes all objects from both collections
intersect	takes two collections of objects and returns objects in both collections

Versions

Object databases support design applications where keeping versions of a design are crucial. Versions provide for access to the history of objects and can be organized in an object model as a collection of objects. Each object in such a collection can have almost all of the same values as the other objects, differing only in the time that the values were recorded. The object model must treat versions of an object as distinct objects, related by a history relationship.

Versioning systems must support query of a collection based on position or values of a given temporal component. Versioning must be able to configure a collection of collections, grouping items having relationships between them into a larger version. An example is the subsystems of an automobile, where each subsystem and its parts may have a separate version. It may be useful to examine the overall collection of subsystems and parts for an automobile or other complex object at certain points in time.

Triggers

Traditional database systems are passive—they do not react to environmental conditions or internal database values. A database can only be manipulated using a data manipulation. If we add active constraint checking and the ability to handle triggers, we can create an active database that reacts to constraint violations by using condition handlers to fire off trigger procedures to handle the violations. With a conventional database, a database's state must be checked by application programs, and actions initiated if necessary. An active database avoids having application programs bear this burden. Triggers in an active database can be aperiodic or periodic and can be based on time intervals, time boundaries, or events. Each trigger is defined as a condition predicate and a triggered action. A trigger actively checks its constraint.

An aperiodic constraint is a one-time trigger that, once activated when conditions are satisfied and completed once, is deactivated. A periodic trigger, on the other hand, once activated will perform its actions and reset itself to be able to test and catch the same constraints again. Triggers are associated with objects and are explicitly activated when the object is created; a trigger is a named object whose identified function is activated by the call. Triggers and their timing constraints can be written across object boundaries to link object activities based on interobject relationships.

Transactions

When considering the need for consistency in database design, we obviously need to consider the degree of overlap between object design and systems design. One useful technique for controlling overlapping and possibly contradictory definitions is to analyze transactions and their performance characteristics; this is outlined in Chapter 6. While examining projected data flows (messages) between active objects in your run-time system, keep in mind that (from Chorafas and Steinman):

- The database is the root of the consistent object space.

- Both default clauses and constraints must be applied in a distributed database sense.

- Every object reachable from this database root must itself be consistent.

This approach should allow database management systems and programming languages to form the basis for database-wide consequence, even if the database system and data structures are heterogeneous.

Instantiation variables should contain the names of all objects serving as roots of consistent object spaces. Only the objects specified in this manner can be shared and accessed via different transactions or queries. A transaction is usually atomic, and its procedures are executed entirely or not at all, as a unit of work. The syntax for working with transactions will differ across even object environments, so a consistency specification is still needed. Presumably, this is easier to implement in an object environment.

With an object system, committing a transaction is achieved by sending a commit message to the system (which must be interpreted in a homogeneous manner, even though differences in syntax lead to heterogeneity). Object technology can help us manage heterogeneity, but there should not be one type of object solution for a transaction environment, another for messages, and still another for handling queries. We also need to be careful to address concurrency control within a given environment. In a distributed database environment, anomalies can develop in database consistency and transaction execution.

Just as with conventional transaction models, an object transaction model supports primitives to:

- Begin transactions

- Prepare transactions for commitment

- Commit transactions

- Abort transactions

Additionally, many object databases support enhanced transaction facilities, such as:

- Partitioned commit

- Partitioned recovery

- Semantic concurrency control

- Other features aimed at greater transaction control flexibility

A new idea for handling transactions in an object database is the concept of nested transactions. With nested transactions, each transaction is composed of subtransactions, which can in turn have nested sub-

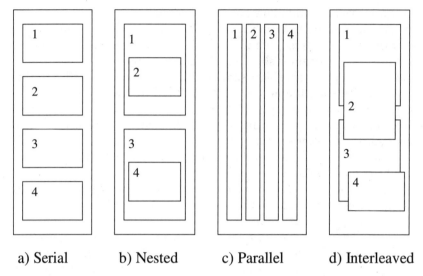

a) Serial   b) Nested   c) Parallel   d) Interleaved

Figure 5.10   Extended transaction models (see Fortier, p. 283, and Orfali et al.).

transactions. For a transaction to commit with this type of design, each of its subtransactions must also commit its work to the database. Other extended transaction models have also been proposed, so that we now have models for:

- Nested
- Serial
- Parallel
- Interleaved transactions

See Figure 5.10 for an illustration of these types of transaction models. The main idea with each of these models is to allow some of the components of a transaction to commit, becoming visible to outside elements, prior to the parent transaction being committed. Building extended transactions involves binding database actions to a transaction code so as to control and coordinate early commit and release of resources of some part of a transaction or provide semantic recovery for these components for correct and consistent execution.

All transactions bound the execution of a transaction with some transaction begin and end primitives, shown here as pseudocode:

```
begin transaction ( )
   ...
   database access code;
   ...
prepare to commit ( )
   ...
commit ( )
or
abort ( );
```

This transaction control also binds all accesses, modifications, creations, and deletions of objects and their components into a unit of execution. Accesses are isolated from other transaction executions and database constraints. An object database transaction includes begin and end delimiters, object operations and user application code, constraint operations, and commit code:

```
begin transaction ( )
   ...
   operation id (oid);
   ...
   operation id (oid);
   ...
prepare to commit ( )
   ...
commit ( )
or
abort ( );
```

An extended transaction model accesses operations for embedded transactions:

```
begin transaction ( )
   ...
   operation id (oid);
   ...
   begin subtransaction ( )
   ...
   operation id (oid);
   ...
   prepare to commit subtransaction ( )
   ...
```

```
   commit subtransaction ( )
   ...
   operation id (oid)
   ...
prepare to commit ( )
   ...
commit ( )
or
abort ( );
```

This model requires that we add extended constraint specifications for preconditions and postconditions on transaction execution. Preconditions must be satisfied before a transaction or subtransaction can begin executing, and postconditions must be satisfied if the commit is allowed at the end of execution. A postcondition constraint is checked during the prepare to commit step. After adding preconditions and postconditions, we have:

```
begin transaction ( )
   precondition check
   ...
   operation id (oid);
   ...
   begin subtransaction ( )
   ...
   precondition check for subtransaction
   ...
   operation id (oid);
   ...
   prepare to commit subtransaction ( )
   ...
       postcondition check for subtransaction ( )
       ...
   commit subtransaction ( )
   ...
   operation id (oid)
   ...
prepare to commit ( )
   ...
   postcondition check
   ...
commit ( )
or
abort ( );
```

More primitives are added for:

- Setting of conditions and procedures for recovery of transactions or subtransactions
- The isolation level of the transaction or subtransaction
- Mode restrictions
- Commit dependencies

Time control over execution may be added in advanced object database systems. These temporal primitives supply transactions with operations to:

- Initiate transactions synchronously or asynchronously
- Begin execution before or after some specified time
- Complete a transaction or subtransaction before or after some specified time
- Create a periodic trigger to initiate this transaction every time period specified until some completion time

Today's database languages, such as SQL2, do not support cooperative execution of transactions or their statements. Transaction synchronization may be specified using preconditions and postconditions on transaction execution; subtransactions may be synchronized with each other or other transactions using preconditions and postconditions. Smaller-grained synchronization requires additional constraint on statements. Time specified may be absolute, relative, or based on event-initiated time. Object databases offer the possibility of added flexibility to allow partitioned commit and control of isolated objects.

Handling long transactions. A long transaction is one that takes more time to complete and address in distributed, perhaps faraway, databases; it is both a concept and a mechanism. Unlike conventional transactions, a long transaction usually involves lengthy interactions with databases spanning minutes, hours, and event days, or covering a wider network topology, often with heterogeneous databases.

Long transactions often include many versions of data, providing the opportunity to use versioning and configuration management to develop applications that have no-conflict concurrency control. Long transaction mechanisms must allow execution across heterogeneous databases. Object orientation is a good way to handle long transactions efficiently. In multidatabase environments, the traditional transaction model has proven to be too restrictive. Multidatabase transactions are often long-running processes. Managing these long-running processes requires extensions to the traditional transaction model, including transaction isolation, ability to handle subtransactions, and sophisticated recovery mechanisms.

With a distributed object database, accesses occur as a long transaction and its subtransactions. Each subtransaction is made up of a sequence of operations performed at the atomic level, but the long transaction in its entirety has practically no time limits on its completion, the database topology, and the number of operations performed in the database. Within a distributed object database environment, a session begins when a client application sends a log-in request. Work on the database is performed within a transaction and its atomic components. All transaction components are performed or none at all. A transaction ends when a commit or abort request is received for the whole transaction. Handling long transactions using objects allows manipulation of a database within a local copy of an object until a transaction ends with a commit, abort, or log-out of the system.

The ODMG-93 Standard

As mentioned earlier in this chapter, ODMG-93 is a standard developed by a group of object database system vendors. This standard defines an object model, a declarative query language, and a C++ and SmallTalk language binding.

This standard extends object languages with these features:

- Persistence

- Transaction management

- Query processing facilities

- Object sharing between concurrently running applications

Programmers can now define new classes independent of language using an Object Definition Language (ODL). This ODL supports basic elements of object models:

- Abstraction

- Encapsulation

- Modularity

- Hierarchy

- Typing

- Persistence

Method implementations must be provided separately in an application language supported by a language binding. OQL allows an application program to access objects based on their state, execute methods on selected objects, and construct new objects. Additionally, objects can be retrieved and navigated via the object hierarchy using pointers (although doing this with a large collection of objects cannot be optimized by the ODMG run-time system). Declarative specifications offer opportunities for optimizing object accesses. The sections that follow were adapted from the *ODMG User Guide, Version 1.0* (C. A. Van den Berg). See the book edited by R. Cattel (1994) for complete coverage of the current standard.

The ODMG-93 Object Definition Language (ODL)

Modularity. An ODL module aggregates and names a collection of related definitions:

- Type

- Constant

- Interface

- Exception

- Module

A module defines a new scope and is used to group functionally related definitions. A module is defined as:

```
module example
{
    (type definitions)
    (interface definitions)
};
```

Abstraction.   An interface definition provides for abstraction, in much the same manner as the class in C++. The state of an object is defined via attribute definitions, its relationship (association) to other objects is defined in relationship definitions, and the object behavior is defined in operation definitions. An interface definition is defined as:

```
interface Person (extent persons) persistent
{
    (constructor definition)
    (attribute definition)
    (relationship definition)
    (operation definition)
};
```

(specializations of Person):

```
interface Department (extent departments key name) persistent
{
    attribute string name;
    attribute Address address;
    relationship Set<Person> people inverse Person::department;
};
interface City (extent cities) persistent
{
    attribute string name;
};
```

Constructor.   A constructor definition is added by ODL. It is used to provide new objects with initial values and to facilitate object creation. A constructor definition example:

```
constructor (in string name, in long date_of_birth);
```

Attributes.   Attributes define the type and name of object properties. For each attribute, a *get_* and *put_* method is generated (in the language binding) for access to the attribute. This increases data independence and allows the same objects to be accessed by different programming languages. Some attribute definition examples:

```
attribute string name;
attribute long date_of_birth;
attribute Sex sex;
attribute Address address;
```

Relationships. Relationship definitions describe one-to-one, one-to-many, or many-to-many relationships (associations) between objects. A relation is, by definition, bidirectional. If an object x has a relation r with an object y, there exists an inverse relation from y to x. The type of the relationship is noted using *bag*, *set*, or *list*. An example of a one-to-many relationship is:

```
relationship Department department inverse Department::people;
```

Operations. Operation definitions describe the signature of a method. A compiler generates a method definition in the target language, and programmers must complement it with an implementation. An example operation definition:

```
int age();
```

Encapsulation. Interface definitions define only the interface of objects. An operation definition specifies the result type of an operation and the input and output types of its parameters. An operation's implementation must be specified in an application programming language. A programmer may access and update object attributes using accessor functions the ODL compiler generates. An example in C++:

```
#include"example.h"
#include <time.h>
int convert_to_date(int date)
{
    return (int) time(0) - date);
}
Student::Student(Ref<Department> dep)
{
    this->department(dep);
}
int Person::age()
{
    return convert_to_date(date_of_birth());
}
```

Hierarchy.   Multiple inheritance is supported in ODL. Interfaces inherit all of their operations, attributes, and relationships, with conflicts from multiple inherited interfaces not allowed. In this example, both *Student* and *Employee* inherit properties from *Person*:

```
interface Student : Person (extent students) persistent
{
    constructor (in Department dep);
    attribute string major;
};
interface Employee : Person (extent employees) persistent
{
    constructor (in Department dep);
    attribute float salary;
};
```

Typing.   In ODL, a distinction is made between objects and values, the difference being that objects can be shared and display behavior. Values might include StateCode or Time. Objects include customer, supplier, part, and so on. Types consist of:

- Atomic types
- Constructed types
- Template types

  Atomic types include:

- Int
- String
- Bool
- Float
- Char

  Complex types can be constructed from atomic types using constructors, such as:

- Struct
- Enum
- Union

Collection types *set*, *bag*, and *list* are used only for object relation-ships. They offer a create_iterator method for sequentially inspecting the contents of a collection and an ODQL method for querying using an OQL expression. Example type definitions:

```
interface City;
interface Department;
typedef struct Address
{
    string street;
    int number;
    City city;
} Address;
typedef enum Sex
{
    Male;
    Female;
} Sex;
```

Persistence.   Interfaces have an extent (an entry point to a set of all created persistent instances) and possibly a collection of key attributes. When an interface is defined as persistent, created objects can outlive a program run-time session (thus they are stored as database objects). By definition, all objects accessible from a persistent object are them-selves persistent, although they are declared to be transient. Both tran-sient and persistent collections can be queried.

The ODMG-93 Query Language (OQL)

Applications can access objects in two ways:

1. By traversing the object hierarchy using relationships or structured types

2. By associative access using OQL, starting from named objects (class extents)

By design, Object Query Language (OQL) is similar to Structured Query Language (SQL), used with relational database management systems. An OQL query can refer to attributes, relationships, and op-erations defined in the ODMG object model; an OQL program has a possibly empty set of query definitions followed by an expression, and the query result may be a literal or an object. A query definition results in a named query, valid only within the scope of an OQL program. Its general form is:

```
select constructor (p1, p2, ..., pn)
from extent list
where condition
```

The constructor determines the type of the result. A set or bag of literals results from a struct or selection of literals, and a set of objects results from a type name or class name. An extent list represents one or more object extents. For each combination of objects in these extents, the condition is evaluated; if the combination of objects satisfied the condition, the constructor is applied and the result returned. The condition is a Boolean expression built from attribute references and method calls. An example OQL expression:

```
select couple(student:x.name, professor:z.name)
from    x in Students,
     y in x.takes,
     z in y.taught
where x.rank = "full professor"
```

C++ OQL binding. Classes are provided for building query expressions, with three aspects considered:

1. Declaration of free variables

2. Specification of a query expression

3. Construction of the result

An example C++ OQL binding is:

```
Var<Students> x;
Var<Courses> y;
Var<Teacher> z;
bind(Couple::student, x.name);
bind(Couple::professor, y.name);
Query<Couple> qry1 = z.rank == "Full Professor" && element(y,
x.takes) && element(y, z.taught);
Set<Couple> result = qry1;
```

References

Cattell, R. G. G. ed., with contributions by T. Atwood, D. Barry, J. Duhl, J. Eastman, G. Ferran, D. Jordan, M. Loomis, and Drew Wade. *The Object Database Standard: ODMG-93, Release 1.2*. San Mateo, CA: Morgan Kaufmann, 1994.

Chorafas, D. N., and H. Steinman. *Object-Oriented Databases*. Englewood Cliffs, NJ: Prentice Hall, 1993.

Fortier, Paul J. *Databases Systems Handbook*. New York: McGraw-Hill, 1997.

Orfali, R., D. Harkey, and J. Edwards. *The Essential Distributed Objects Survival Guide*. New York: John Wiley & Sons, 1996.

Van den Berg, C. A. *ODMG User Guide, Version 1.0*. An introductory paper published on the Internet as http://carol.fwi.uva.nl/~carel/oo/userguide.html, November 9, 1995.

Transform Logical Models
to Physical Models

Transaction Analysis

Transaction analysis describes how data are to be used by individual transactions. We can use a transaction map to answer questions such as:

- Where does the transaction start (what is its entry point)?

- What is the minimum number of objects needed for the transaction?

- What is the flow of the transaction from object to object?

- What type of access is required of the object selected?

Transaction maps have been used for quite some time with structured analysis and design and work quite nicely with object modeling. In fact, they are quite commonly used with several major object methodologies in use today. Many readers will recognize our transaction maps as specialized uses of object interaction diagrams (also called message flow diagrams). These diagrams show the logical order of data access for each transaction, in a qualitative analysis fashion (no load-ing or calculations are done yet).

To determine the entry point or starting object, determine what data you know before you start a transaction. When a transaction starts, you must always enter at some known point and then use the object struc-tures to obtain unknown information. Build a list of attributes needed to satisfy transaction data requirements. You need to determine what data to retrieve and when to retrieve them.

To determine objects required, examine the list of unknown but re-quired attributes. Determine what objects own these attributes. Try to retrieve only the minimal set of objects and attributes. To determine the flow from object to object, retrieve an object only if it has attributes you need to display or modify for the transaction. This should help limit the number of objects accessed. Diagram movement from one object to another by satisfying the required list of attributes. Finally, determine what will be done to the attributes being accessed. Will they be read only or also updated? Indicate the type of access along the message lines:

- Read
- Update
- Create
- Delete
- Load

Building Transaction Maps

Techniques for resolving access path differences build on the results ob-tained thus far and build on them by analyzing each system function and calculating a path for each. When all of these functions have been calculated, we combine results into a composite transaction map.

We begin by building transaction maps for each function by identify-ing some possible functions of an order processing system. The trans-actions (business events or use cases) that have been identified for this system include:

1. Create an order

2. Create an invoice

3. Update backorder

4. Order inquiry

5. Backorder inquiry

6. Product invoice inquiry

7. Product backorder inquiry

8. Product customer inquiry

9. Product order inquiry

Each of these transactions will be mapped. Determine where you want to start by determining known data requirements. Begin with the object that contains the known data and proceed from there to the unknown data required. Determine what objects are needed by obtaining only those objects that contain the attributes needed to satisfy the transaction requirements.

The order entry clerk should know the order number, date, all product/service item numbers, and all item quantities. The transaction needs to create an order from this starting information. The unknown data are the prices and product descriptions. We can use the order object as the starting point. We need additional information to insert an order line item, connecting to the customer object, and inserting backorder information. The map we create is shown in Figure 6.1. The other transactions proceed in a similar fashion, with the resulting maps shown in Figures 6.2 through 6.9.

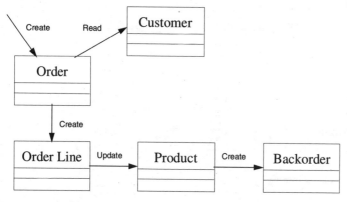

Figure 6.1   Create order.

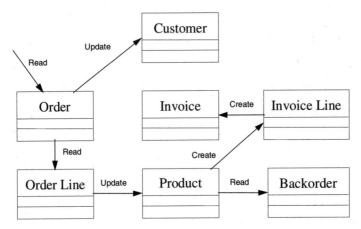

Figure 6.2   Create invoice.

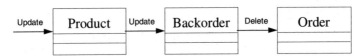

Figure 6.3   Usage map—update backorder.

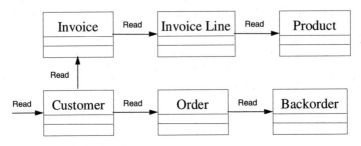

Figure 6.4   Order inquiry.

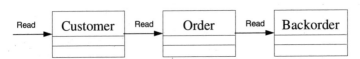

Figure 6.5   Backorder inquiry.

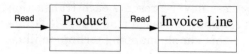

Figure 6.6   Product invoice inquiry.

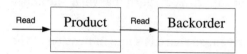

Figure 6.7   Product backorder inquiry.

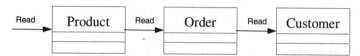

Figure 6.8   Product customer inquiry.

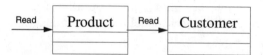

Figure 6.9   Product order inquiry.

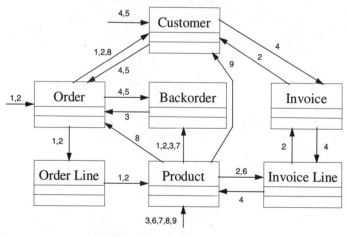

Figure 6.10   Combined transactions.

The transaction mapping process now represents each transaction diagram on an object diagram. A combined usage map would look like that shown in Figure 6.10. Even this simple mapping technique illustrates three key points:

1. The three distinct system entry points provide definite clues as to how data accesses may be optimized (perhaps with database indexes).

2. Each object was used as described, so there is some indication of the validity of the object in the model.

3. Certain paths exhibit a high amount of flow from multiple transactions, meaning that multiple transactions follow the same path.

Creating Overlay Maps

The mapping process can be more useful to designers if it is superimposed over the object diagrams (see Figure 6.11). The resulting diagram can be called a composite overlay map. This map allows us to reconcile any differences between the object model and the transaction

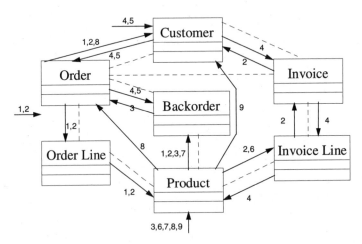

Figure 6.11   Overlay map.

flows. When a usage path does not match the underlying object structure map, an adjustment must be made to either map to eliminate any differences.

Use of an alternative path can lengthen the total path and create additional overhead to any transactions following the path, so all relevant paths should be examined. When an object with an association lacks a transaction path, review the association to see if it is correct. If it is correct, try to determine if the association should be maintained for clarity or future flexibility. If the object could have some future access path added by future requirements, then keep the association. If maintaining the association as a separate object can provide clarity or consistency to a logical structure, construct and maintain such an associative object. Otherwise, keep the association as a many-to-many association only.

The process of creating composite mappings should derive a complete logical structure validated against at least the most important transactions. Once this validation has occurred, you can estimate access loads and then create a finalized object model.

Evaluating Transaction Costs

If we have the time and resources, we can assess the cost of each transaction and then evaluate the cost for an entire system. This cost is determined, for a typical business information system, by quantifying the total input and output activity. The manipulation and conversion of data costs very little compared with the input and output costs. Construction of a loaded object model helps us focus on determining the average number of input and output operations associated with each transaction.

We now need to step through each transaction and record the access path from object to object, the type of access, the average number of times the path is used for that transaction and alternatively for some peak-load time factor. Each access path for a transaction will have a given value for each of these items. When all access paths are complete for a transaction, the total references for that transaction are also recorded. This is done by multiplying the number of paths used by the number of uses for each path.

Analyzing Transaction Paths

A format for capturing transaction load information is shown in Figure 6.12. It consists of transaction identification, path descriptions, and peak-load data. Keep the following rules (from Perkinson) in mind as you capture and analyze transaction path information:

1. On entry, the values for Number, Average and Multiplier, and During One Transaction will always be one.

2. Determine Number by finding the From Object name in the To Object column and putting the During One Transaction number for that path in Number.

3. The value of Multiplier will always be one if you want to use all of the paths.

4. When a specific From Object is desired, or a known number of To Objects are to be accessed, the value of Multiplier is that number divided by Average.

5. Determine the value of During One Transaction by multiplying the Number times the Average times the Multiplier.

6. Obtain Adjusted I/O by multiplying the Access Weight times the During One Transaction number.

7. Total up all the Adjusted I/O fields to give the total number of logical object accesses for the transaction.

Figures 6.13 through 6.18 (adapted from Perkinson) show how these calculations are computed for the order processing example.

Path Description			# of Times Path Occurs		# of Times Path Is Used			
From Object	To Object	Access	On Average	Multiplier	During One transaction	Access Weight	Adjusted Input/Output	During Stress Period

Figure 6.12   Transaction load calculation format.

Path Description			# of Times Path Occurs		# of Times Path Is Used			
From Object	To Object	Access	On Average	Multiplier	During One Transaction	Access Weight	Adjusted Input/Output	During Stress Period
-------	Order	Update	1	1	1	3	3	90
Order	Customer	Read	1	1	1	1	1	30
Order	Order Line	Create	6	1	6	2	12	360
Order Line	Product	Update	1	1	6	3	18	540
Order	Back-order	1	.1	1	.1	2	.2	6

Figure 6.13   Create an order.

Path Description			# of Times Path Occurs		# of Times Path Is Used			
From Object	To Object	Access	On Average	Multiplier	During One Transaction	Access Weight	Adjusted Input/Output	During Stress Period
-------	Order	Read	1	1	1	1	1	30
Order	Customer	Update	1	1	1	3	3	90
Order	Order Line	Read	5	1	5	1	5	130
Order Line	Product	Read	1	1	5	1	5	90
Order	Back-order	Read	.1	1	.1	1	.1	3

Figure 6.14   Create an invoice.

Path Description			# of Times Path Occurs			# of Times Path Is Used		
From Object	To Object	Access	On Average	Multiplier	During One Transaction	Access Weight	Adjusted Input/Output	During Stress Period
-------	Product	Update	1	1	1	3	3	9
Product	Back-order	Update	.5	1	.5	3	1.5	3.5
Back-order	Order	Update	1	1	.5	3	1.5	3.5

Figure 6.15   Update backorder.

Path Description			# of Times Path Occurs			# of Times Path Is Used		
From Object	To Object	Access	On Average	Multiplier	During One Transaction	Access Weight	Adjusted Input/Output	During Stress Period
-------	Customer	Read	1	1	1	1	1	10
Customer	Order	Read	5	1	5	1	5	50
Order	Order Line	Read	5	2	30	1	30	300
Order Line	Product	Read	1	1	30	1	30	300
Order	Back-order	Read	.1	1	.5	1	.5	5
Customer	Invoice	Read	10	1	10	1	10	100
Invoice	Invoice Line	Read	6	1	60	1	60	600

Figure 6.16   Order inquiry.

From Object	Path Description		# of Times Path Occurs		# of Times Path Is Used			
From Object	To Object	Access	On Average	Multiplier	During One Transaction	Access Weight	Adjusted Input/Output	During Stress Period
– – – – – – –	Customer	Read	1	1	1	1	1	5
Order	Back-order	Read	.1	1	.5	1	.5	3
Back-order	Product	Read	1	1	.5	1	.5	3

Figure 6.17   Backorder inquiry.

From Object	Path Description		# of Times Path Occurs		# of Times Path Is Used			
From Object	To Object	Access	On Average	Multiplier	During One Transaction	Access Weight	Adjusted Input/Output	During Stress Period
– – – – – – –	Product	Read	1	1	1	1	1	2
Product	Invoice Line	Read	30	1	30	1	30	60

Figure 6.18   Product invoice inquiry.

Predicting Object Frequency

The steps discussed previously (adapted from Perkinson) vary some-what from the mathematical probability theory approach to load calculation developed by Shaku Atre, who states the following:

> To access segment B from segment A, one needs to know all the segments that have to be touched on the way. One can estimate the number of I/Os

necessary for accessing segment B from segment A if the probabilities of I/Os are known for all intermediate segments.

This approach assumes that the probability than an event will occur is represented by a number between zero and one; zero if the event never occurs and one if the event always occurs. The probability definition (from Cromer) is:

The probability of an event occurring, p, is equal to the ratio between the number of cases that are favorable to this event, a, and the total number of probable cases, c, provided that all cases are mutually symmetric.

Thus,

$$p = \frac{a}{c}$$

The probability of an event not occurring, q, can be determined as

$$p + q = 1$$

or

$$q = 1 - p = 1 - \frac{a}{c}$$

We need to determine a and c. Once designers determine the probability for a particular object type, a mathematical expectation of a particular instance of that type occurring in the database can be determined. Length is always a discrete positive whole integer having some value between one and n, and has a mathematical expectation equal to

$$\sum_{i=1}^{n} vi \bullet pi$$

where v is the variable length and p is the probability. This implies

$$p1 + p2 + p3 + pn = 1$$

Upon substitution of the ration a/c for p, the equation reduces to

$$\frac{\sum_{i=1}^{n} vi \bullet ai}{c}$$

This formula is used by Atre to calculate the average entity (object) length for the distribution of the length of an entity (object).

Building a Load Matrix

We can easily use all data in the load maps to build a table of the data. This load matrix shows:

- The object-to-object count for each transaction
- The combined peak usage for every path
- The ratio of each object involved in a path relationship
- The total of the average number of objects accessed along each path per transaction and per peak-load interval

The completed transaction path analysis is now reviewed to tabulate the usage and loading for the entire system on the matrix. This matrix is a convenient method of showing the contents of transaction analysis on one line in the matrix. This format is used to consolidate the results of transaction path analysis, bringing together key figures into a single line of a load matrix. This provides two benefits:

1. The relative cost in logical accesses for each transaction can now be viewed at a glance, making it easy to determine which transactions are going to be fast and which will be slow.

2. The load matrix provides the ability to examine activity across each path in the system individually. Each individual path is a specific column in the form.

This technique provides access to vital design information regarding relative usage and thus the relative importance of each path. The total accesses for each transaction are the sums of all counts for each path used for the transaction; peak totals are the sums of all paths times peak usage. You can easily construct a full loaded object model and certain paths are identified as high usage. Paths, direction, and volumes are combined in a single structure, which can be examined at the end of object structure analysis. The object model is built by drawing the object diagram and replacing path occurrence numbers with path total figures.

Stress periods are essential to understanding and interpreting response times; they usually must be expressed in short time intervals. You need to know the amount of work to be performed and the time available to do the work. Determining the stress period is an important factor in determining the real loads on the object model.

Implications for Physical Design

Now we need to examine the most frequently used paths and steer the physical design and implementation toward them. In transactions with very high numbers of logical accesses, an inquiry may work better if an intermediate object were created to directly bridge two main objects.

At this point, you need to ask yourself several questions:

- Will a newly created access path object provide greater flexibility in the database structure?

- Are there any attributes of the object other than the identifying one(s)?

- Does creation of the object provide any new information about the logical structure of the model?

- Does the new path provided by the new object provide enough savings to justify its creation?

If you answer one or more of these questions in the affirmative, the new object may be valid and thus needs more than casual analysis. It is important to be willing to change the structure at this point during design in order to produce a better implementation later on.

Object Design for Performance

Object-oriented systems, especially ones using object database management systems, allow structuring of a system for maximum flexibility, but performance may suffer because each object is addressable independently. This is the case when many objects must be combined in a single access request. To minimize performance problems when designing a new system (or modifying an existing one), examine the following (from Andleigh and Gretzinger):

- Class management for managing a large number of objects

- Indexing objects as with relational database tables

- Clustering objects to optimize disk accesses for searches

- Object storage optimization with a copy of methods also stored in the database

- Distributed object management optimizing distributed databases

- Intermediate objects to optimize by maintaining intermediate results in objects

Class Management

We define classes based on generalization and aggregation, with multiple inheritance proving a kind of join class to related classes. Object instances are related to their classes by object types. A class descriptor is provided in some development environments for describing a class itself, listing all attributes and methods for the class. Because object instances are members of a class, object instances of a class can be grouped by class membership. Distribution of instances of a class onto one or more networked servers can be managed using class location descriptors. Another way to manage classes is by using join classes to form redundant associations, providing additional associations designed to reduce disk access for searches.

Often, we need to examine all classes to see if rearranging them can help performance. Some redesign of methods to adjust for different conditions may allow recombination of classes that were separated during early design. Abstracting out common behavior among classes helps restructure classes for more efficient operation, and this is often done naturally by examining class generalization structures for reuse.

Superclasses may be created or updated to contain all common attributes and methods, with subclasses containing only differences.

Indexing Objects

Some object environments provide a collection of generic data structures as predefined class libraries. Among these library classes are arrays, lists, and dictionary classes, which are useful for building indices to object classes. Such indices may be maintained as ordered lists, B-trees, hashed sets, or other data structures. An index is used as a qualified association to speed up accesses. To create a new index, examine each method and determine which associations are traversed and how frequently this occurs. The beginning of this chapter discussed how to do this. All methods (transactions in the earlier discussions) should be listed, and the ones presenting the highest returns from creating index associations should be indexed.

Clustering Objects

During modeling and design, a cluster is a group of classes, associations, and generalizations that can be abstracted to a single object for presentation and management. We called this a class category in the previous chapter. During implementation, clustering involves locating classes, associations (such as aggregations), and generalizations close to each other on disk (perhaps on the same or adjacent disk pages) for efficient access. All methods should be examined to determine the frequency of use of class associations and generalizations to find the optimum clustering patterns. Examining these frequencies of use was the subject of the first few sections of this chapter.

Object Storage Optimization

We can store objects intact, with attributes and methods stored in the same disk area, or in logically organized components. Even though methods are stored only once for each class definition, large amounts of storage space may be required across similar classes. We could separate attributes from methods and use different storage methods and locations for them.

Distributed Object Management

Distributed object management is discussed in Chapter 7. It is important to analyze how applications and processes access certain object classes. We should always try to minimize the number of servers that must be accessed for an application process.

Intermediate Objects

Methods that perform many calculations and intermediate processing steps can be made more efficient if intermediate results are stored in special class libraries during the time that an object is kept in memory. It might by helpful to create intermediate persistent objects.

Object Design for Efficient Access

A nicely constructed analysis model may not perform well when implemented. As with any other design, object-oriented design must consider performance-tuning issues before a system gets placed into production. The analysis conceptual model should always be the first point of reference for design. It captures conceptual information about the system, to which design must add details. Performance tuning helps make a system run faster but can make maintenance difficult, if not a nightmare. Both design clarity and implementation efficiency must be considered.

In analysis, we always try to eliminate redundancy wherever possible to keep the model concise. In design, we need to consider creating or deleting associations between objects. You can often add redundant associations between classes to minimize access costs and maximize overall system convenience. You can also add an additional index to improve query performance. As you analyze the set of associations in an object structure model, examine each operation:

- Examine associations it must traverse; consider implementing one-way traversals as one-way pointers.

- Determine how often an operation is executed and how costly it is to do so.

- Estimate the average number of "many" associations encountered; multiply cardinalities to determine the number of accesses on the last class in a path.

- Determine objects that meet selection criteria and are operated on; for rejected objects, avoid simple nested loops in operation algorithms.

Once you have adjusted your design to handle frequent traversal of associations, seek to optimize operation access algorithms. You can often optimize by eliminating attempted retrievals of unwanted data. To determine all the products supplied by two of our vendors, we may want to narrow the search by retrieving vendor products first and then examining which products we carry. If we carry a large array of products, but each vendor sells us only a few, the performance improvement to answer this query in this manner can be dramatic over that of searching all our products first and then inquiring about vendor products.

Design for Data Management Systems

When preparing to implement database designs, whether flat-file, relational, object-oriented, or some other type, consider both data structures and the operations that act on those structures. Each type of data management system requires a different kind of design. For flat-file systems, define a first-normal form table for each class and its attributes, and for relational systems define third-normal form tables. Consider and test performance issues and adjust your designs accordingly. Measure storage and performance needs and consider denormalizing as necessary. Object-oriented database systems may not need normalization assistance. For a discussion of data normalization, see Montgomery (1990).

Once tables have been defined, add attributes and their operations to each object in the database design. In an object-oriented design, objects need to know how to store and retrieve themselves. With situations that involve multiple inheritance, an attribute and a corresponding storage operation could be defined in the superclass. These would then be inherited by subclasses that need to store objects, as suggested by Coad and Yourdon.

A flat-file system needs to know:

- Which file or files to open
- How to position the file at the correct record
- How to retrieve existing values, if any
- How to update fields with new values

A relational system needs to know:

- Which tables to access
- How to access the correct rows
- How to retrieve existing values, if any
- How to update columns with new values

An object-oriented system does not need to have extra storage attributes and operations added, because it allows objects to know how to store themselves over time. The database management system automatically handles any object marked as needing to be held over time. See Coad and Yourdon for an example of a sensor-monitoring system design. For relational systems, see Rumbaugh et al. (Chapter 17), who discuss ways to implement object structures in relational database management systems.

General Database Design Considerations

Object-Oriented Database Characteristics

While each database application is slightly different from others, there are some fundamental characteristics that an object-oriented database should exhibit, including:

- Support for complex data structures
- Complex relationships
- Retaining unique object identifiers
- Maintaining versions of data structures

A database that supports object-oriented applications should be based on a data model that supports representation of sometimes complex real-world objects as one database object. In this chapter we deal mostly with the modeling aspects of object databases. The physical features that must be addressed in implementation of a database design include the usual services provided by a database management system:

- Recovery

- Security

- Transaction management

- Concurrency control

Modeling of Objects

Most applications require that a database object supports associations with other objects. Database objects might also contain component objects involved in associations. Objects that contain other objects are complex, not like the typical databases or file structures in use today. Complex database objects might include those shown in Figure 6.19.

The last two types of complex objects listed in Figure 6.19 might appear in a systems development environment that coordinates and integrates CASE tools, but they are representative of all kinds of aggregation objects that need to be stored in a database. Complex objects such as these can have their internal structures made invisible to external objects that must access them. A program specification, engineered product component specification, or an entire multiple component document can be defined to have a text-type attribute. This

---

- Documents consisting of sections, subsections, text, graphics, and bit maps
- Hypertext documents that have complex links to other hypertext documents or graphics
- Engineered product specifications, including drawings with subdrawings and component descriptions
- Programs consisting of modules, data structures, statements
- Libraries of programs, modules, and database structures

Figure 6.19   Types of complex objects.

attribute is seen as simple text to an outside object, even though it is itself composed of many other text objects (or even graphics). This approach is simplistic but useful in many applications that do not need to address individual database object components.

When an application needs access to the component objects of a certain database object, we need to allow the structure of an object, its component objects and associations, to be visible through the object's public interface. For a design and programming tool environment, we would need to define programs composed of modules. Common, reusable modules would be stored in a library for public access. Each of these types of objects is complex: Programs are composed of modules, which are composed of other modules, and libraries are composed of some of these same complex modules.

External relationships between different object classes and their associations must be distinguished from the same classes and associations that are internal to an object. Otherwise, if we use only one model for both internal and external object details, our database models are complex from the public view but not complex enough from the internal view. Also, the internal structure of objects is difficult to change when external objects need to know the structural details of each database object.

Some database management systems (the object-oriented ones, but some others as well) are structurally object-oriented (see Dittrich 1986; and King 1989). When the complex structure of database objects is explicitly defined, it is much easier for users and applications to determine which details to focus on while ignoring other aspects of object structure. The database management system can manage the structure and control all integrity issues and application and user views.

Identifying Object Instances

Programming languages, especially the object-oriented ones, provide ways to represent and access database records via properties of the records (by the value of some record field). This can be a problem when object attribute values change over time. Also, associations between objects must be maintained when the value of an attribute used as a foreign key changes (as with relational databases).

Using a unique object identifier for each object that is independent of object attribute values can simplify database designs and applications that use those designs. Attribute values are bound to change, but a system-generated and system-maintained object identifier can serve an object throughout its life. Using unique identifiers for database ob- jets is not a new idea; semantic database models have used the term "surrogates" for this.

User-Definable Database Operations

With traditional database management systems, any operation on complex objects requires that the component parts of those objects be known and stated explicitly. To delete a complex object, delete com- mands must be issued for the components of the object before the par- ent object can be deleted (true, some systems today do support cascading deletes). This requires much effort for program developers and users but also reduces system modularity and information hiding. When the structure of such a complex database object changes, many programs must change. Use of a library module for handling complex deletes is helpful, but does not address the main problem. A better so- lution would be to design in operations that allow creation and deletion of entire complex objects at one time. Object structures can then change but the applications using the more powerful operations are stable.

Operations on database objects should be defined across class struc- tures. Components of higher-level classes need not redefine these oper- ations, and application programs are much simpler. Operations defined across an entire class might include:

- Add to class

- Query class

- Return last update time stamp

- Delete from class

When implementing complex objects in a nonobject database envi- ronment, it makes sense to build and maintain specialized applications for those objects so that functionality and flexibility are high while not sacrificing performance. At any rate, it is reasonable that a database administrator be in charge of maintaining not only database structures but the key operations on those database components. This person must be aware of all key transactions and queries that access each part of a database.

Design for Encapsulation

In earlier chapters we discussed the definition of basic operations on objects, using a CRUD matrix to map create, read, update, and delete operations against operations in application objects that require a database object to perform these operations. We will always implement these operations for any database object. However, complex objects require much more powerful data manipulation operations.

We can combine fundamental operations to perform more complex operations. To remove a complex document and all of its components from a database, we need to check that the document is not in use before attempting the deletion. Then we need to lock the object and all of its components, each of which has a fundamental delete operation defined for it. The high-level delete operation needs only to send a delete message to each component, which in turn communicates with each of its components. Naturally, the higher-level operations are unique to the class for which they are defined but can be made rather simple.

Some database management systems allow object designers to define a set of operations for each complex object type, along with specifications for object structures. This kind of encapsulation makes object database design much easier. If we do not have this luxury, we need to ensure that object data structures are accessible only via special operations defined for those structures. At all times, the implementation of each object should be kept private to the designers and maintainers of that object.

Design for Class Hierarchies

Inheritance can be viewed as a form of *coupling* between superclasses and specialization classes. A high degree of inheritance coupling is desirable. To accomplish this, each subclass should really be a specialization of its more general superclass. A well-defined responsibility should be established for the subclass, without anything that is unnecessary. If a subclass explicitly rejects a lot of the attributes of the superclass, the subclass is only loosely coupled to its superclass. Try to design for inheritance, in which subclasses inherit and use attributes and operations of the superclass.

Attributes and operations should be highly *cohesive* within a class, with no unused components. For each subclass within an inheritance hierarchy, try to ensure that the specialization is a valid one, not arbitrary. If it does not make sense to view the subclass as a type of the superclass, the specialization is not valid. Perhaps the subclass should be placed higher in the hierarchy or within some other place in this or another class structure.

Some object-oriented database systems are based upon class hierarchies, with structural and behavioral inheritance between related classes. Programming languages also have been added to relational databases, and other approaches are available, too. You may need to implement support for inheritance manually.

Estimating System Processing Cost

Estimate system processing costs by estimating the required processing for the system and then multiplying by some factor that represents the cost of one unit of processing power. Main parameters for estimating system processing costs are listed in Figure 6.20.

Major Factors for Determining Processing Requirements

Major types of processing needed:

- Functional calculations
- Input and output to devices
- Accessing of stored information
- Control structure

Estimating Processing Requirements for Data Operations

We determine the processing requirements for the entire system by summing the processing requirement for all data operations (except continuous operations).

Continuous operations.   Continuous operations, including event-detection operations, should have minimum sampling rates estimated. This rate is added to the operation (but if an operation is likely to be allocated to an analog processor, this sampling rate is not appropriate). The

- Event frequencies
- Numbers of instances of objects and relationships
- Storage/instance of objects and relationships
- Number of instances of operations
- Response time for discrete data operations
- Minimum sample frequency for continuous operations
- Processing/activation for data operations
- Maximum transition for state transitions
- Number of instances of agents

Figure 6.20   Main parameters for estimating system processing cost.

calculation is performed as for discrete processes activated with that same event frequency.

Processing/activation. The required processing for one activation of an operation corresponds to the number of machine instructions needed to be performed each time an operation is activated. There are two problems: The first is that the path through the possible instructions will vary depending on run-time values (for conditional selection of logic), so no one fixed value can be used. To handle this situation, either an average over all possible combinations of input parameters may be used, or the worst-case value may be used. The first case is more optimistic and probably more appropriate for most situations. In time-critical systems, the second, more pessimistic, value provides a greater margin for possible problems. The second problem is that the effort involved to estimate processing required by a data operation may approach that of building and testing the operation. Also, the estimate of complexity is required early in development of the system, before all requirements have been agreed upon. This has led to development of techniques for estimating processing requirements from a limited set of key items.

Estimating Processing Requirements for Input/Output

We can estimate the processing requirements for an operation that performs input/output to the external environment by examining event schemata or event-trace diagrams. Flows from an event-response operation to the external environment can be identified immediately. Examine each of these flows and determine these parameters:

- Width in bytes of data
- Number of instances of the agent for outputs
- Expected type of interface

You can estimate the processing requirement for each type of interface used, accounting for these factors. Each type of interface should have a typical processing requirement parameter.

Estimating Processing Requirements for Stored Data Access

A very simple estimate of processing requirements for one activation of a data operation may be calculated as the number of logical accesses/seconds to the stored data. A create, read, update, or delete action on a specific object instance counts as one logical access, as does a create or delete action on a relationship instance.

The processing requirement of match operations is more complex. If a match uses an identifier, then there is at most one instance that satisfies the test. This identifier is likely to be an access mechanism in the production system. This should be handled as a single logical access. For matches that do not use an identifier, the system will require a search or select operation. This processing requirement will often be proportional to the number of instances of the object, with some proportionality constant.

Calculating the Cost of Processing

A single average processing cost can be calculated as instructions/second per unit cost. This factor can be figured as an average over a range of similar systems that have already been constructed, or estimated from first principles. A single factor is used to represent a single homogeneous processing environment. Rather than representing a single processor for the implementation, this factor assumes that when the price/performance curve shows an upturn, the system will be distributed across several processors with roughly the same price/performance ratio.

Estimating System Storage Cost

This should be determined for an entire enterprise rather than for a single project or system, because stored information is a shared resource. The estimating algorithm described below should be used for enterprise systems only. The storage requirement for an information model may be estimated for objects (including associative objects) and for relationships. The storage requirement for relationships is usually significantly less than that for objects and their attributes and depends heavily on the chosen data architecture. The basic procedure for estimating storage costs is:

1. An approximation of the total storage is obtained by estimating storage requirements for each object and adding these together.

2. The storage requirement for one object is obtained by estimating the storage for one instance of the object and multiplying it by the expected number of occurrences of the object.

3. The storage requirement for one object instance is estimated by summing the estimated storage for each attribute.

4. The storage requirement for each attribute is obtained by examining the object type it is derived from.

To calculate the cost of storage, use a single average cost in bytes per monetary unit (say, one U.S. dollar). This factor can be figured as an average over a range of similar systems or estimated from first principles. A single factor represents a single homogeneous storage environment. It does not assume one type of storage medium but rather a characteristic average over all types of storage devices and storage organizations to be used.

Estimating the Cost of System Interfaces

You can estimate the cost of interfaces for an enterprise, but it is not always possible to determine this cost on a system basis, because interface resources are often shared between systems. For systems that are true stand-alone systems, these steps may be useful:

1. Categorize the agents into people and devices.

2. For people, multiply the cost of providing one user interface by the number of instances of the agent.

3. For devices, examine the number of separate signals to and from each device. Categorize these into types of device. Use a typical cost for each device category and estimate the cost to interface to one instance of an agent. Multiply this by the number of instances of the terminator.

Remember to include the costs of cabling, modems, line drivers, cluster controllers, and other devices.

References

Andleigh, P. K., and M. R. Gretzinger. *Distributed Object-Oriented Data-Systems Design*. Englewood Cliffs, NJ: Prentice Hall, 1992.

Atre, S. *Database Structured Techniques for Design Performance and Management*. New York: John Wiley & Sons, 1980.

Coad, P., and E. Yourdon. *Object-Oriented Design*. Englewood Cliffs, NJ: Prentice Hall, 1991.

Cromer, H. *The Elements of Probability Theory and Some of Its Applications*. New York: John Wiley & Sons, 1958.

Dittrich, K. R. "Object-Oriented Database Systems: The Notation and the Issues" (extended extract). In *International Workshop on Object-Oriented Database Systems*, edited by K. R. Dittrich and U. Dayal. New York: IEEE Computer Society Press, September 1986.

King, R. "My Cat Is Object-Oriented." In *Object-Oriented Concepts, Databases and Applications*, edited by W. Kim and F. H. Lochovsky. New York: ACM Press, 1989.

Montgomery, S. L. *Relational Database Design and Implementation Using DB2*. New York: Van Nostrand Reinhold, 1990.

Perkinson, R. *Data Analysis: The Key to Data Base Design*. Wellesley, MA: QED Information Sciences, 1990.

Rumbaugh, J., M. Blaha, W. Premerlani, F. Eddy, and W. Lorensen. *Object-Oriented Modeling and Design*. Englewood Cliffs, NJ: Prentice Hall, 1991.

7

Analysis and Design for Distribution

Today, distributed systems are a reality. Information is stored in multiple locations on rather inexpensive computers, with the trend toward increasingly distributed systems continuing without an end in sight. Thus the need for good design, implementation, and control of distributed systems is becoming more important each day. To avoid chaos, begin thinking early in your design process to incorporate ideas about how your systems and their components should be distributed.

Early on in design, begin to question how database and application objects should be configured across a geographic network of locations. Focus first upon the basic objects themselves, not on the underlying network communications and data storage issues. Determining how objects should be distributed is a complex operation, with many reasons for distribution. Don't focus too early upon network topologies and such. Focus on the analysis and design models built thus far.

Reasons to Distribute or Centralize Objects

The reasons for object distribution are many, but if we borrow some ideas from distributed database design, we can gain some valuable insights. For databases, it may make most sense to store data where they are used. Departmental information is often best kept at the department's location. Martin (vol. 3, p. 345) lists seven properties of data that lead naturally to distribution:

1. Data are used at one peripheral location and rarely or never at other locations.

2. Data accuracy, privacy, and security are a local responsibility.

3. Files are simple and used by one or a few applications.

4. Update rates are too high for a single centralized storage system.

5. Peripheral files are searched or manipulated with query systems that result in alternate search paths (inverted list or secondary key operations).

6. Fourth-generation languages are used that employ a database management system different from that used for the production system.

7. A localized decision-support system is used.

On the other hand, some types of data exhibit characteristics that lead more naturally to centralization (again, from Martin):

1. Data are used by centralized applications.

2. Users in all areas need access to the same data and need the current up-to-the-minute version.

3. Users of the data travel among many separate locations and it is less expensive to centralize data than to use a switched data network.

4. Data as a whole will be searched.

5. Mainframe database software is needed.

6. A high level of security must be maintained over the data.

7. Data are too large to be stored on peripheral storage units.

8. Details are kept of transactions updating certain data, so it is cheaper and more secure to store centrally.

When data are distributed, there can exist some integrity and synchronization problems unless a good design is used. There are many advantages, though. Among them are:

- Reduced transmission costs
- Improved response times
- Increased availability
- Increased survivability (from multiple copies of the same data)
- Organization of databases around the use of data

Problems of distributing include:

- More difficult transaction updates
- Inconsistent views of data
- Increased opportunity for deadlocks
- Increased control overhead
- Increased recovery complexity
- Multiple data representations
- Difficult to audit
- Security and privacy control complexity

Whether or not you think you will need to distribute databases and other objects, it is probably a good idea to begin design by viewing an

---

- Whether or not to distribute
- How to distribute
- Network topology
- Network availability
- Costs of processors and storage devices
- Communications transmissions costs
- Distributed software costs
- Actual decisions on physical locations

Figure 7.1   Technology factors that affect object distribution.

entire system as centralized. Introduce distribution issues later. This way, you can focus on the conceptual semantics of your models without getting into the complexities of the physical world too soon. Also, some technology decisions may not yet be finalized as you begin designing your system (see Figure 7.1).

When you are trying to implement an enterprise-wide architecture for systems and their networks, implementation can take a long time. Therefore, you should try to focus on logical, not physical, mappings of system components. Do collect information about probable distribution situations, but don't model these situations until the centralized versions of the system models are fairly stable.

Mapping Objects to Locations

Often, many organizational units within an organization perform the same tasks; this can be true across locations, too. Each office needs to perform some of the same tasks. The objects (initially, all data and operations) can be mapped against physical locations where the business activities that use the objects are performed (see Figure 7.2). You could also map operations against locations, but the object data structures themselves are most important for placing databases and their components. Instead, you could map high-level business activities against locations (see Figure 7.2), in much the same manner that business functions are mapped to locations. (These high-level activities can be decomposed into separate operations that can be mapped to objects and locations, but hopefully the mapping of operations to objects has been already done in analysis.) The mapping of subject areas and functions

	Location			
Business Activity	1	2	3	4
A		Major	Major	
B	Minor			Minor
C		Minor	Major	
D	Major			Major

Figure 7.2   Degree of business activity involvement at locations.

Location

Object	1	2	3	4
A	Major		Major	Minor
B	Major	Major	Major	
C	Minor		Major	
D	Major			Major

Figure 7.3   Object involvement at locations.

versus locations is a good starting point for building these more detailed matrices.

Once you have mapped out the initial associations between objects and the locations that access them, you can move on to map the basic types of object involvement (Figure 7.3) and types of accesses (Figure 7.4), as well as specific transactions required by each location (Figure 7.5) and the types of accesses (Figure 7.6). This moves you into enough detail that distributed database components can be visualized.

To assess the need to distribute objects to a given location, build an object transaction/view volumes by location matrix (Figure 7.7). This matrix shows how immediate and/or nonimmediate traffic can be projected from a central location to remote locations. A location/perform-

Location

Object	1	2	3	4
A	Create		Update	Read
B	Create	Create Update Delete	Create Read Update Delete	
C	Read		Update	
D	Read	Read Update		Create Read Update Delete

Figure 7.4   Object access types by location.

Object

Location 1 Transactions	A	B	C	D
1	Minor	Major	Minor	Minor
2	Major	Major	Minor	
3		Minor		

Object

Location 2 Transactions	A	B	C	D
1	Major	Minor	Major	
2	Minor	Minor	Major	
3		Major		

Figure 7.5   Object transaction/view involvement at locations.

Object

Location 1 Transactions	A	B	C	D
1	Read	Update	Read	Read
2	Update	Update		
3		Read	Read	

Object

Location 2 Transactions	A	B	C	D
1	Update	Read	Update	
2	Read	Read	Update	
3		Update		

Figure 7.6   Object transaction/view access types by location.

Transaction	Size	Location 1	2	3	Units	Volume
1	195	1250		3400	4650	906K
2	68	750	235		985	67K
3	327	1300	1300	2600	3900	1275
Total	590	3300	1535	6000	9535	2248

Figure 7.7   Transaction/view volumes by location.

ance matrix can then be built to show location/performance combinations that are achieved via a centralized solution as well as those that are not. To depict transactions or user views required at each location, you could build a diagram to depict the overall distributed systems architecture. Each connection between nodes should be described either on the diagram or on a table to describe the connection:

- Distance
- Percentage of processing at central site
- Immediate flow volumes
- Nonimmediate flow volumes

Each node should have described for it:

- Number of users or programs
- Total data volume
- Total update volume
- Names, record sizes, and instance volumes of data storage objects

When this diagram has been built and details collected, you can begin to examine individual transaction and view volumes by individual location. At this point you can really begin to see where individual data storage objects should be placed in the network.

The physical records that you are describing via these matrices will not necessarily be stored at the same location as the procedures that use them, but this is usually what you will want to begin modeling. Client/server systems allow you to separate application processing from database processing in a multitude of ways, but begin by examining the use of data first. When you do begin exploring ways to separate business logic from database logic and user access logic, keep in mind that a good distribution model arranges system functions into clusters such that each cluster has a high level of autonomy (is highly cohesive) and exhibits a low level of interdependence with other clusters (is loosely coupled to other clusters). In order to maximize flexibility while not sacrificing performance, we need to examine traffic patterns between physical locations, nodes, in our communications network.

Estimate Message Traffic between Locations

When computers are very inexpensive, as many personal computers and workstations are today, it seems logical that we would place objects at the same location as the users and application programs that access those objects. Unfortunately, things are just not that simple. Replicated objects would then need to be distributed to each location each time a change to an object is made. If these objects are updated by business activities in multiple locations, and the updates must all be kept current, one copy of the object is easier to maintain (keeping multiple copies of an object is complex, increases message transmission traffic, and requires more elaborate recovery protection from system failures). Maintaining one copy decreases dependencies between locations.

For purposes of calculating message traffic between locations, assume that

U = uses per hour for the data

and

C = changes per hour of the data

and that these activities are spread evenly over N locations. We can define a traffic unit as the data that are transmitted to a location and the response that is sent back. If T = the number of traffic units per hour, then for data centralized at one location the total traffic units per hour can be represented as

$$T_c = (U + C)\frac{N-1}{N}$$

For a totally decentralized configuration, uses of the data do not generate traffic but modifications of the data generate $N - 1$ traffic units. Distributing data results in less traffic if

$$\frac{U}{C} > N - 1$$

When two locations are considered, it becomes better to distribute if

$$\frac{U}{C} > 1$$

With 50 locations, distribute if

$$\frac{U}{C} > 49$$

One change made for every ten uses of data, or

$$\frac{U}{C} > 10$$

results in a break-even point between centralization and decentralization at 11 locations. At more than 11 locations, it is better to centralize. When time is entered into the situation, we have a different situation. Suppose that changes can be applied to data up to H hours after their origination. Every H hours a message could be transmitted to each location, giving changes occurred since the last update. With centralization, this means that we have $(N - 1)/D$ traffic units occurring each hour. With decentralization of data, but updates relayed by the central location, $2(N - 1)/D$ traffic units are needed each hour:

$$T_c = U\frac{(N-1)}{N} + \frac{(N-1)}{H}$$

$$T_d = \frac{2(N-1)}{H}$$

Break-even is at $U = N/D$. When $H = 1.5$ hours and 200 references are generated to data each hour in total, distribute if there are less than 300 locations (1.5×200).

Besides being able to make such calculations, you need to examine the following:

- Operating costs at each location

- Numbers of transactions needed to search all data in their entirety

- Costs to maintain many copies of the data

- Recovery after failures

- Failures during recovery operations

- Type of network architecture

Of course, making such calculations should be viewed as only one way of estimating what the best overall network data placement configuration should be. The best way to configure a network in the end is to describe each and every transaction transmittal and then optimize network traffic patterns, but this can be difficult. The calculations described here help you get a good feel for distribution effects across the entire network and in certain situations can be all that you need. View them as only one tool for deciding upon data placement across locations.

Distributed Database Design

Distributed systems design requires determining how data are to be stored across sites within the system. The first part of this chapter discusses techniques for analyzing distribution patterns. Data distribution must account for the sharing of data among nodes in the network, behavior of access to shared data, and the ability to predict stability of access patterns. Degree of sharing is important for determining information placement and possible partitioning and replication. If information is not shared, it can be placed at the site where it is used. Information accessed by more than one site should be analyzed to determine the site that uses the information most frequently, and at the greatest volume. Site determination should be based on minimized overhead and delays for frequent users or applications, but sometimes it is necessary to create copies of data at some sites to ensure data availability.

Data usage analysis. Another consideration for data placement is the way in which data are used. If data usage patterns are constantly changing, site determination for permanent data storage may change over time as well. When usage patterns are more static, data may be stored at sites of highest data utilization and available storage volume. For most situations, a blend of these simple approaches is required. Data usage changes over time as applications are added or removed from systems and as existing applications are changed with respect to their data usage. Therefore, database mappings may need periodic redesign for optimal efficiency to be maintained.

To develop a data distribution plan, a set of database requirements must be developed and all pertinent information collected on the data to be managed and stored. This process is the same as that for centralized systems. From initial data and requirements we can relate information structures (entities, objects, or files) together to build a global conceptual schema of the database requirements, as well as user or application views of the database. Once we have modeled a centralized database schema, we can incorporate distribution requirements to build a distributed schema. When building the distributed schema, we need to examine applications with regard to their access patterns and sites of allocation. This then leads to study of loading of data and processing loads at each site. Application software may then need to be reallocated to different sites to balance the loading and information flows between sites.

We can begin placing information by analyzing application information requirements and usage patterns. This leads to modeling of initial composite data loads and usage patterns for all sites within a network. To determine a final load, initial loads are analyzed for result data and control flows. This includes examination of the added costs of replication, partitioning, or fragmentation on the normal database functioning. Replication, for instance, improves access times but significantly increases update times.

Once a reasonable logical map is determined, physical database design can begin. This process results in a mapping of the global conceptual schema into local conceptual and physical schemata. When these mappings are complete and the database made operational, it is often necessary to analyze the database designs to optimize them based on statistics of actual use and access.

Partitioning and replication costs. Data partitioning and replication may introduce additional overhead. Partitioning involves one copy of each data item in the database, with data items split up and distributed to separate sites within a network. Replication involves multiple copies of a data item, with copies allocated throughout a network. If data can be partitioned or replicated, the choice of which is better is determined by needs for access speed versus costs of updating data. With partitioned data, costs are increased to read a data item but are decreased to update data. All updates are sent to one site, with no extra coordination required to perform an update. All reads for a data item must be sent to the same location, resulting in added costs for reading. All read accesses incur the cost of transmitting a request and receiving the response.

With data replication, read accesses can be directed to any copy of a data item, reducing overall access costs. Costs are reduced by at least two transfers over the network, one for the request and one for the response. Update costs are greater, however. With replication, costs are introduced to replicate updates at all sites in the network. This involves added communication costs but may increase synchronization costs to coordinate updates.

The choice of replication or partitioning must be based on the costs and usually involves replication, when read accesses are more frequent than update accesses, and partitioning, when update accesses are more frequent than read accesses. Network simulation may be needed to arrive at the right answer.

Other distribution costs.   When there is not enough storage space on a network node, transmission costs are too high, or processing costs are too high, some additional splitting of data structures may be necessary. Fragmentation of structures can be performed at the record level or at the attribute level of a relation or object. This can result in higher costs to process queries that access information in multiple fragments, but this can be an advantage if the fragmentation is done based on usage patterns. We could place only the fragments of a relation or object that a query actually uses at certain nodes in the network. Although fragmentation is not often used for distributed systems, it can be used in specialized situations.

When limited storage space is available on a site for all records that optimally should be stored at the site (based on analysis of use patterns), some alternatives must be examined. Distribution decisions should be made by balancing costs of access, updates refined by storage, processing, and communications. The most workable solution will be based on costs justifiable to the supported applications and users.

Client/Server Architectures

There are, of course, many ways to build and operate a client/server application and database system. Object database systems have many ways in which objects can be stored, and how they can be executed to improve performance. Two basic modes of object storage are available: passive and active object storage. The difference between the two is in how they maintain storage of data and methods for database objects. Three proposed approaches aim to optimize where object management occurs and how object storage is organized and managed:

1. Object/server
2. Page/server
3. File/server

Passive Object Storage

With an object storage approach, objects are separated into object data and object method components (see Figure 7.8). Database storage holds the object data (values of objects within the database), and methods are

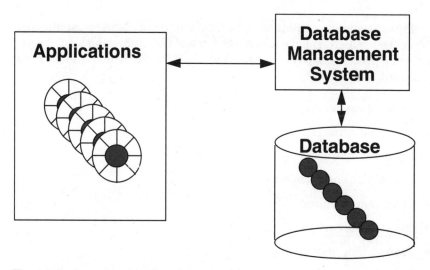

Figure 7.8   A passive object/server architecture.

placed at the sites using them. This approach provides some advantages. Compiled code can be placed near the site where needed. Replicated code can be managed by a single object manager at each site using the objects, or method code can be expanded in-line in application code. The object approach keeps the interface between application and objects consistent, but it requires applications to acquire information from another process (the site object manager). The in-line expansion method does not require additional external access for method code, but it does require interaction with management software to coordinate object data access.

Locating object methods where they will be used helps reduce the message traffic passing between clients and servers. Rather than an entire object needing to be passed between a database and an application, only the object data (data) need be passed. Moving some methods from a database management system to client sites means that client processes are now responsible for assuring correct and consistent object management. This includes services such as:

- Object management

- Transaction management

- Object-level concurrency control

- Copy synchronization

This movement of method code from server to client (or application server) sites helps relieve servers of some of the processing load, freeing up some processing power for servers to better perform database management functions of:

- Lock management

- Recovery management

- Integrity management

- Constraint enforcement

- Condition handling

- Database security enforcement

- Transaction management

- Redundancy maintenance

- Synchronization

Active Object Storage

In the active object approach to distributed object architecture, object data and methods are stored together in an object database. Object method request messages, method results, and possibly entire objects (both data and methods) can be passed between the server and clients. A server can be treated as a central processing location, allowing only messages for method executions; performance of all method requests is performed at an object's storage site and the results transmitted to requesting applications. This approach can result in reduced transmission of information between client and server, but the server ends up performing all method executions. This may lead to a performance bottleneck at the server.

An active object architecture (shown in Figure 7.9) allows objects to be stored anywhere among a network of database servers, with clients unaware of object locations. Only one copy of object methods exists (at the object storage location). Another way to store and manage object data and methods on a centralized server is to allow objects to be transmitted to an application workspace for execution. This policy involves the server acting as a distribution point, receiving requests for method execution, determining the validity and correctness of requests, and transmitting of object data and methods to an application's workspace.

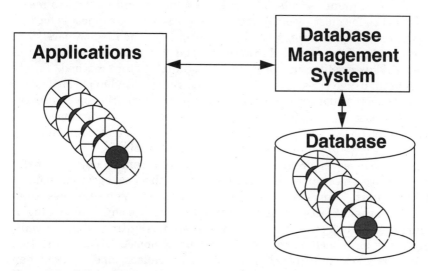

Figure 7.9   Active object architecture.

This policy allows off-loading of method execution from server to applications, freeing servers of executing methods.

Object/Server

With an object/server architecture (Figure 7.10), most database management is still conducted on servers. Services residing on these servers include:

* Transaction management

* Recovery management

* Concurrency management

* Object management

* File and index management

* Page management

* Physical storage and input/output management

Communication between clients and servers is via objects, so both clients and servers must contain object management services for manipulating unique objects. This requires clients and servers to maintain caches for most recently accessed objects. Once an object is located in the cache, by searching the page cache, or in the files on persistent storage, the object is copied into server and client caches for future reference. This architecture provides the ability to store methods for objects at all usage sites. Database systems are required to perform some optimization to determine when best to perform queries on the server or client based on existing data volumes. Also, since all database service actions (other than method invocations) are performed on servers, it is fairly easy to conduct lock management on servers.

An object/server architecture may require a remote object transfer request to a server on each object reference if the local cache cannot fulfill a request. Things get worse when objects are composite ones (composed of other objects). If a client cannot determine object clustering, it must request objects as they are encountered, resulting in higher waiting times for objects than actually executing objects. Also, replication of objects across multiple clients and servers causes, on execution of an object method in an object cache, object managers to cause the same action to occur on other object copies to maintain object consistency. This

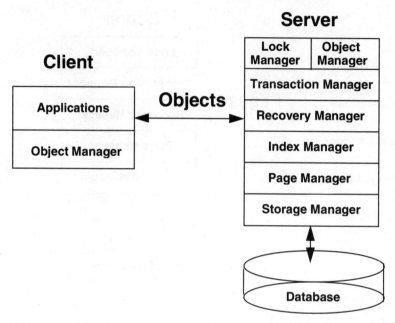

Figure 7.10   Object/server architecture.

consistency maintenance overhead offsets the benefit of distributing object management to clients and also increases the complexity of servers. Servers must support distribution and cooperative servers across sites.

Page/Server

With a page/server architecture (Figure 7.11), storage allocation pages form the interface between client and server. This architecture offloads more services to clients to simplify server storage management. Page, file, and object management are placed at clients, with servers maintaining:

- A physical storage manager
- A copy of the page manager
- A page cache manager
- A log manager

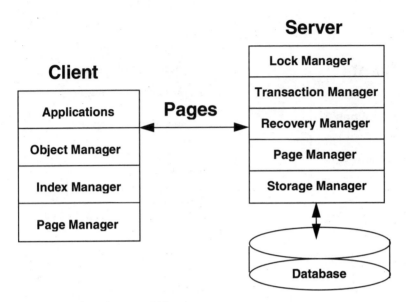

Figure 7.11   Page/server architecture.

- A concurrency control manager
- A recovery manager
- A transaction manager

The interface between clients and servers consists of:

- Page references
- Manipulation requests
- Log records
- Disk data pages

This architecture allows clients to store objects only, pages only, or both, as needed. Database management processing loads are shifted to application processes with this approach. This means that applications can still use object aching for single objects or a small number of objects on a page, but for a larger portion of disk page, a page manager can retrieve a complete page, speeding access. This addresses the problem of complex objects, which can be stored on one or more pages in the client, minimizing repeat requests for objects from the server. Most object processing is performed on clients, so servers are freed up to handle more concurrent clients. However, concurrency management, recovery, and storage management are still centralized. If objects are not clustered by usage patterns, some performance advantage is lost. Also, a distributed update synchronization and concurrency control protocol must be used if object copies are to be maintained. To achieve full advantage with this architecture, applications using it must be structured to fully utilize the partitioning.

File/Server

The file/server architecture places storage management and database management at client sites (see Figure 7.12). This goal is to move all but essential database management synchronization to clients. Most object management services are moved to clients, but some are moved to the storage manager input/output processing. Clients can thus directly read and write database pages via a system-supplied service such as Sun's Network File System. This architecture places concurrency management and log management at the server. Clients must send additional initial lock requests before a read or write can be executed. Some kind of semantic concurrency control or optimistic scheme could be performed on clients to improve on this approach, but this requires that objects individually maintain their own consistency and accuracy.

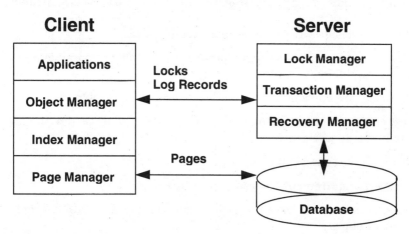

Figure 7.12   File/server architecture.

Distributed Database Systems

Advantages of Database Distribution

Some advantages to distributing databases across a network include:

- Information can be stored at the location where most frequently used.

- Improved performance results from distributed workloads.

- Reduced communications costs result from locating information close to its usage sites.

- Greater reliability is possible.

- Expandability is enhanced.

- Higher data availability can be achieved.

- Local autonomy is maintained.

Disadvantages of Database Distribution

Distributed databases offer many advantages, but distribution of data, control, and resources comes at a cost. Distributed databases are usually much more complicated than centralized database systems. Database control itself is distributed. Security is also harder to achieve. Some advantages and disadvantages of distributing databases include:

- Database design will be much more complicated.

- Distributed query processing increases the number of possible processing strategies.

- Database directory management becomes a global problem.

- Transaction processing and concurrency control must deal with distributed transactions.

- Deadlock detection can occur across remote sites.

- Recovery requirements increase run-time complexity.

- Databases may not have the same structure model (relational, network, or object).

- Remote database sites need to have consistent versions of database software.

Distributed Database Architecture

A distributed database system consists of independent databases connected via a network in such a way that the composite system appears as a comprehensive and centralized information resource management system. Often, a client/server architecture is built, with databases residing in and managed by one or more servers. Multiple clients can run applications that access servers. We can expand our discussion of distributed databases to be one that consists of (in the words of C. J. Date):

> ... a collection of sites connected by a communications network, in which each site is a database system in its own right, but the sites have agreed to cooperate so a user at any site can access data in the network as if the data were stored in the user's own site.

In order that a distributed database presents a single logic view and appears to users and applications as a centralized or local system, a distributed database must have transparency features (Andleigh and Gretzinger):

- Location transparency

- Data partitioning and fragmentation

- Data replication

- Localized failures

Location transparency is a principle of managing a distributed set of database servers with potentially duplicated data and automatically determining how data should be combined from different nodes for a query, or how a distributed update should be processed. With location transparency, users do not know where data objects are stored in a network. Objects are accessed as if they were stored locally, with the actual location transparent to users and applications.

Data partitioning and fragmentation allow elements to be split and spread across a number of servers for efficiency; this fragmentation should be transparent to users and applications. Users should not be aware of fragmentation or how all object components should be accessed. Processes should exist to be able to combine all object components in a transparent manner.

Data replication refers to the idea that multiple copies of objects are replicated in multiple servers in a semipermanent manner to improve performance. A database system needs to guarantee that all replicated copies are maintained synchronously. Synchronization of this sort is complex.

Localized failures refers to a principle by which failure of a node in a distributed system should not affect users. If a node fails, or some database components become inaccessible at a node, other nodes can continue to operate using replicated database copies. Proper and complete resynchronization of databases is required on recovery of failed nodes to ensure that all valid updates made in that node are applied in the proper sequence.

Chris Date's rules for distributed databases.   Chris J. Date has defined 12 rules for distributed database systems, which provide the basis for a variety of distributed systems.

   1.   Local autonomy.   The sites in a distributed system should be autonomous, or independent of each other. A database management system at each node in a distributed network needs to provide its own security, locking, logging, integrity, and recovery. Local operations on database data should use and affect only local resources and not depend on other sites.

   2.   No reliance on the central site.   A distributed database system should not rely on a central site, because a single central site may become a single point of failure affecting the entire system. Also, a central site may become a bottleneck affecting the distributed system's performance and throughput. Each node of a distributed database network must provide its own security, locking, logging, integrity, and recovery, and handle its own data dictionary. Every distributed transaction must not involve a central processing node.

   3.   Continuous operation.   A distributed database system should never require downtime. Such a system should provide on-line backup and recovery and full and incremental archiving. The backup and recovery facilities should be fast enough to be performed on-line with no noticeable effect on the overall system performance.

4. Location transparency and location independence. Users and/or applications should not know or even be aware of where data are physically stored. Rather, users and/or applications should behave as if all data were stored locally. Location transparency can be created by using extended synonyms and making heavy use of a data dictionary. Location independence allows applications to be ported easily from one site in a network to another without modifications.

5. Fragmentation independence. Relational tables in a distributed database network can be divided into fragments and stored at different sites transparent to the users and applications. Users and applications should not be aware of the fact that some data may be stored in a table fragment at a site different from the one where the table itself is stored.

6. Replication independence. Data can be transparently replicated on multiple computer systems across a network. Replication independence is designed to free users from having to know where data are stored. Users and applications should not be aware that replicas of data structures are maintained and synchronized automatically by the distributed database management system.

7. Distributed query processing. The performance of a query should be independent of the site at which the query is submitted. A relational database management system provides a degree of nonnavigational access to data, so such a system should support optimization that not only can select the best access path for a given network node but can also optimize a distributed query's performance with respect to the data location, processor and input/output utilization, and network traffic throughput.

8. Distributed transaction management. A distributed database system should be able to support atomic transactions. Transaction properties of atomicity, consistency, durability, isolation, and serialization should be supported for location transaction and for distributed transactions that can span multiple systems. An example is transaction coordination in distributed two-phase commit processing.

9. Hardware independence. A distributed database system should be able to operate and access data spread across a wide variety of hardware platforms. A distributed database management system should not rely on any particular hardware feature or be limited to certain hardware architectures.

10. Operating system independence. A distributed database system should be operable on different operating systems. Such a system should support function and data distribution across multiple operating systems, including personal computers, workstations, LAN servers, minicomputers, and mainframe computers.

11. Network independence. A distributed database system should be designed to operate without regard to communications protocols and network topologies. Such a system should support function and data distribution across different operating systems independent of the communication method used to interconnect systems. Networks and communication protocols could be mixed to address business, economic, geographical, and other requirements.

12. DBMS independence. A distributed database management system should be able to support interoperability between DBMS systems operating on different nodes, even if these systems are heterogeneous. All components in a distributed database management system should make use of standard interfaces in order to interoperate with each other and participate in distributed processing.

Distributed query processing. One important design issue with any database system is how to access and process information efficiently, based on a user or application request. Query and data manipulation languages specify what data are being requested, but not how these data are to be located and retrieved. Thus the database query processing system must determine how to retrieve requested information based on the data specified in a request. With a centralized database, query processing tries to minimize the cost of access using metrics based on relation size. Queries are processed as input in a host language and then transformed into a low-level execution plan to return a correct result efficiently.

The cost of a given query may be reduced through application of some simple principles, and further cost reductions can be achieved through manipulation of join orderings when multiple joins are to be performed within a query or through reordering of other binary operations. Optimization requires computing cost functions for each ordering and then selection of one that matches the minimal cost function chosen for the optimization criteria. In a distributed system, this optimization process is more complicated. There is the added cost due to distribution of relations over multiple sites. Optimization must now select the best site to process data and determine the order in which processing should be performed across sites.

Query response times become important for remote object access, especially when a complex distributed query requires a combination of objects from several network nodes. With a relational database, this involves joining relations in a specified join order. The complexity of such a join increases by an order of magnitude when performed across multiple database servers. One common way to deal with combining data from different servers is to locate potential elements in each server, returning results of each query to the local system, and then compiling the final result. Unnecessary data are discarded. Another way is to combine the data at each successive server according to the query plan, using the results of one query as one component. Using this approach, each successive result is sent to the next server in sequence and successive operations are performed at the servers. Optimizing a distributed query is complex, requiring careful design of the database and applications.

Query optimization. A primary task in optimizing queries is access path selection for joins and development of an optimal plan for joining multiple relations. The performance of on-line distributed systems depends to a great degree on a query optimizer's sophistication in handling dissimilar queries and remote data. Most systems store access information for each query examined (the query plan) for the future. Obtaining a good understanding of an optimizer's capability helps one to deal better with potential performance issues and in determining how data objects should be distributed across servers.

Query execution plans. A query execution plan describes the internal operations for executing a particular query. It can form a tree, with leaf nodes representing tables and nonleaf nodes representing operations, or it can be in a canonical form (such as in INGRES). Also, the query plan must also account for distribution of data objects among different servers in a network.

With a relational database, reduction of a query to its canonical form allows a query to represent uniquely all equivalent queries, regardless of how the query was written. The number of operations needed to compare a new query with canonical versions of previous queries is smaller. This improves the speed of selecting a query plan.

With an object database, reduction of a query to a canonical form is more difficult. The query plan is less predictable, especially with distributed queries, where the number of possible query plans can increase drastically. Query optimization is still being developed for distributed object databases.

Distributed Transaction Processing

Transactions can be distributed across a network, with costs incurred at the points in a transaction's execution where coordination is needed to guarantee integrity of executing transactions on the database. A transaction is the unit of execution within a database system. Transactions within a distributed database system must operate cooperatively (see Figure 7.13), issuing requests for services to other database managers within the system. During execution of distributed transactions, remote database managers, along with the source database managers, collect and maintain the state of the executing transaction.

As a transaction executes, it requests exclusive access to read or write database records and develops a list of affected database components. When the transaction has completed its read, write, and computation operations and is ready to commit its work to the database, it must send a prepare to commit message to all database management sites affected by the transaction's execution. As sites send the prepare to commit message are ready to commit, they return their states (ready to commit or not prepared) to the coordinating site. The coordinating transaction must determine if all participants are prepared to commit. Once it is safe to commit, the coordinator issues a commit message. Then it waits and collects responses from participants. When all responses have been received, the transaction's processing can be completed.

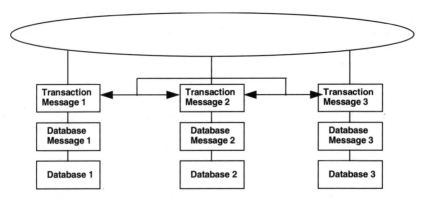

Figure 7.13   Distributed transaction processing.

If an executing transaction fails or aborts during its execution or during commit processing and coordination, the coordinator must issue commands to coordinate each participant's abort processing. Once all abort commands have been issued and responses received, the coordinator can issue the final message that the abort is complete. The coordination of distributed transaction sites requires a sequence of message flows among participants and the transaction coordinator. The added processing cost includes additional coordination messages and control protocol.

Concurrency control. We must be able to ensure that two users or applications do not update the same object at the same time. The first user or application requesting a data object should cause an update lock to be assigned to the object, causing abort of any subsequent update requests by other users or applications during the lock assignment to abort their request. Locking allows concurrent processing of transactions while maintaining database integrity and a consistent view of the database.

With most locking schemes, a transaction requesting update of an object already locked is blocked from further processing, forced to wait until the lock is released. Usually, a two-phase dynamic locking approach is used for this. Locks are requested and applied when records are retrieved for update, and lock releases are deferred until completion of a transaction. In a distributed database system, with many users accessing common database objects, performance may be seriously degraded if lock contention is high. Another approach aborts transactions making conflicting lock requests. These transactions are restarted after a time interval. This removes delays resulting when a transaction must wait for a lock to be released, but it can cause higher network traffic volume. Retries are needed when an update request fails from lock contention. Ideally, the distributed database system can determine the optimum concurrency control method based on the current state of transactions, adapting control methods dynamically.

Commit processing. In order to maintain consistency across a distributed database, transactions must be executed atomically, usually via a two-phase commit or some variation of it. Distributed commit protocols involve successive sequences of message exchanges to guarantee that all parts of a distributed database that must be updated by a transaction in progress are completed. All actions needed for completion of a transaction must be performed in their entirety, or no action is taken at all. When actions are completed successfully, a transaction is committed; otherwise, it is aborted. Distributed functions must account for database and network failures to guarantee that consistency of the database is not affected. Database replication simplifies this process but complicates the process of synchronizing the entire database at all times.

Distributed commits can be implemented as centralized or distributed. With centralization, a single site is designated as the coordinator for all transactions generated in the network and other participating nodes acting as slaves. When the coordinating site completes its processing, it proceeds toward commitment of transactions by executing the commit protocol. With this approach, a coordinating node can become a bottleneck. A decentralized approach is more efficient and fault tolerant, with every transaction origination site acting as the coordinator for a transaction and the remainder of the sites acting as slaves. Each site communicates with all other sites in the network at each step of the protocol to guarantee that the database remains synchronized.

Transaction definition.   In database terms, a transaction is a grouping of database operation predicates (such as SELECT and UPDATE), which must all be applied in the proper sequence at the same time, with no intervening operations. If an entire group cannot be applied as a single logical action, it must be rolled back to the starting point in order to return the database to a consistent state. Transactions can be simple or complex.

In an object database, a transaction involves multiple requests to one or more objects that must execute together as a group (all operations must complete entirely or be rolled back as a unit to their starting point). The effects of each operation become apparent to other users or applications only upon completion of the entire transaction. During the processing of the transaction, all object values remain unchanged until the completion of the transaction.

Distributed processing complicates transaction management, especially when multiple concurrent updates are made to the same object by two or more users or applications. We could disallow multiple concurrent updates, but often such updates do not conflict with each other. Also, performance can degrade if concurrent updates are disallowed.

Updating objects.   Objects are updated whenever some property values are changed. Objects are updated by instance methods or class methods only. A method is invoked on an object, and the object version number is updated. The owner copy of each object must always be updated first, and the owner can then inform all servers with copies of the object that an update has occurred.

Synchronizing local and owner copies of objects is achieved using a well-defined sequence of operations for an update. When a local object server receives a request for an object, it sends the request to the object's owner server. The owner server updates the object and informs the local server, which can then obtain an updated copy. What happens when a client application is informed that an object has been updated? A client that initiates an update knows of the update upon success of the method, but database systems do not usually inform other clients affected by the update. We could allow a user to request notification when an object currently being accessed changes. The points in the update process where update notification to the client application could be (Andleigh and Gretzinger, p. 292) are:

1. After the update request is accepted by the local object server

2. After the update request is accepted by the owner object server

3. After the update is complete and the local server receives a completion notification

4. After the local server receives a copy of the updated object

Selection of one of these options depends upon application synchronization levels and performance requirements.

Transaction management steps. A two-phase commit protocol is most often used to manage transactions in a distributed system (see Figure 7.14).

- Update(TransactionID, ObjectID, Method, ArgumentList)
- PrepareToCommit(TransactionID)
- RequestAccepted(TransactionID)
- RequestDenied(TransactionID)
- CommitObject(TransactionID)
- Rollback(TransactionID)

Figure 7.14   Two-phase commit operations.

The sequence of messages to update all copies of an object involves the local server sending update messages to all owners of objects to be updated. Owners examine requests and verify whether the update can be performed, returning either an update accepted or update rejected message. If an update can be performed, the server copies the object and updates the copy. Upon receipt of an update accepted message, a server must update the object when the prepare to commit message is received. If all owners return a request accepted message, the local server sends a commit object message to complete the transaction. If any object owner returns a request denied message, the local server sends a rollback message to all owners. The rollback message triggers each server to destroy any temporary objects and release any locks for the pending update.

Distributed Transaction Objects

A distributed database system concept for managing distributed transactions was developed by Pons and Vilarem and was adopted and documented by Andleigh and Gretzinger. The latter authors refer to this approach as transaction object management. The following section highlights this approach, which is based on the concept of treating transactions themselves as objects, using features of a base object class to manage complex transactions. The scheme is decentralized in general. A transaction control object (functioning as a transaction manager) is created on the object server that is local to an application.

Transaction object management. A transaction control object serves as a centralized transaction manager. During the first of two phases in which a transaction acts as an object, the transaction reads all data objects to be updated and announces its intent to write to the database. This causes creation of a new version of each object to be updated. The transaction uses these new versions of objects to stage changes to the database. Upon completion of the first phase of transaction processing, the second phase updates the new object versions and marks them as the current versions. This serialized processing avoids lock conflicts and loss of concurrent updates to data objects. Time limits may be placed on processing to avoid excessive waiting to update common data objects.

Use of a centralized transaction manager simplifies two-phase commit processing; the two phases are incorporated into the transaction

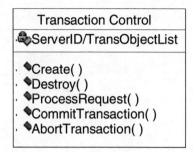

Figure 7.15   A transaction control object.

object. This allows the second transaction phase to proceed directly with updates, without needing update request approval. One potential problem is that a link failure can make a centralized transaction manager ineffective. To address this, we could use a cooperating distributed transaction manager. Transaction manager components operate on each server and communicate constantly using a distributed transaction management protocol for serializing transaction. Link failure may cause failure of transactions managed by the server, which are taken out of service. Other servers and transactions can go about their work. Failed transactions can be restarted on another transaction manager.

Two object types are used to process transactions in our transaction management approach: a transaction control object and a transaction object. The former provides an interface to applications and serves as a control point for transactions. The latter is created by the transaction control object on each server that contains objects updated in the transaction. The transaction object handles each application request within a transaction and handles distributed commits and interactions with

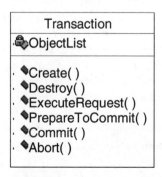

Figure 7.16   A transaction object.

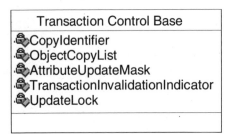

Figure 7.17   A base class for transaction control.

concurrent transactions. Figures 7.15, 7.16, and 7.17 show the structure of a transaction control object, transaction object, and a base object for transaction control.

Creating transactions.   When it receives a request to begin a transaction, a local object server creates a transaction control object, returning an object identifier. As each method in the transaction object is invoked, a remote procedure call is generated and sent to the object server. The contents of this request include:

- Transaction control object ID

- Object class ID

- Object ID

- Method ID

- Argument list

When this request is received by an object server, the transaction control object identifier is examined. If this attribute is null, the request is not part of a transaction and a transaction control object is created, with the transaction executed with the single request. While a transaction is running, each method is executed immediately. Copies of an accessed object are created during transaction execution to ensure that no changes will be visible to other applications. Transaction objects perform transaction requests, and the transaction control object keeps a list of transaction objects for each object server involved in a transaction. Each transaction object is owned by its creating object server.

Committing transactions. When a transaction commit request is received, a two-step process is used to commit the operations formed during the transaction. The transaction object contains a list of all objects on a specific object server affected by the transaction. Transactions commit in the order they are received. If all transaction objects return a success, each transaction object commits the changes by replacing the public version of each updated object with the copies from the transaction execution. Then updates by other transactions are allowed. If any transaction objects return a failure, the transaction control object sends an abort message to each transaction object to cancel the transaction. Upon transaction abort, all object copies are deleted.

Distributed Database Management

Distributed object retrieval. With a distributed system, objects are spread across multiple servers to optimize performance. These distributed objects must be continually tracked to be easily located. Some ways to track distributed objects include central directories, data dictionaries, and name service mechanisms. A distributed object retrieval service that has each object server capable of providing a retrieval service is often used. With this approach, each object class is assigned an object server, which keeps track of all master and copy instances of the class. Object servers maintain lists of all classes and which servers the classes are assigned to.

Information kept on service objects includes a set of attributes describing the status of each object (see Figure 7.18). This class has a data attribute that specifies that data type. To locate an access object, a service object must be located. The structure passed to the method invoked for this purpose receives an object ID and returns a structure

Figure 7.18   Service class attributes.

with the name of an object retrieval list object on the owning server and a list of current locations of the object on all object servers holding copies of the object. When a list of locations of an object on various servers is retrieved, an object can be accessed—from the local server if it resides there; otherwise, it is copied from the owner server.

Distributed system administration. Administering a distributed system of objects is more complicated than with a centralized system and must include:

- Establishing connections among servers

- Authentication of database access and maintenance of data security

- Automatic configuration management

- Backup and archival of data across a network

An object-oriented system provides a way of presenting a simplified and customizable view to users. An object consisting of all files to be backed up can be created to include all procedures needed (see Figure 7.19). Customized obejcts can be created and maintained for each user. All that is needed to administer distributed objects is to invoke a class method that locates all backup objects and executes the correct class method with objects.

Object replication and duplication. Database objects are owned by exactly one object server at any point in time, but objects can be moved around a network of servers as needed. One server owns the object, but

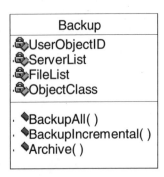

Figure 7.19   A backup object.

many other servers can hold copies of the object; all updates are performed on the owning server. If a copy of an object is needed, a request for it may be sent to the owning server across a network to ensure that the current version is retrieved from the owning server. If a local copy is older, the current version is obtained. Versions can be distinguished by comparison of version numbers stored with the copies. This guarantees that application programs always operate with the most current object version.

To maintain object consistency, all updates must be sent to the owning server for each object; servers with copies must be notified when an object has been updated. Also, whenever an object copy is accessed, the server may send a message to the owning server to verify that the object is current. When only update notification is used, a server may not know about an object update due to failure of update message delivery, but update notification is usually more efficient than version notification. The best situation is to use update notification and version verification in combination.

Object identity.   An object's identity must be assigned upon its creation and never changed. References to objects must include the identification of the server the object resides on, and object attributes should indicate whether this server is an owner or copy server. Each database object must be uniquely distinguishable, and two copies of identical objects must also be uniquely distinguishable. Use of a server prefix to the object identifier can provide uniqueness across multiple object copies.

Name servers and directories.   Across a network of distributed objects, an application may know the location of some objects but will not know exactly where each object is physically located. Locations of objects are determined by connecting to a single object server and depending upon that server to route requests to the appropriate object server. Each server keeps a master index of its owned objects and may have an index of copies of objects owned by other servers. When a request is received for objects not present on a local server, the server must forward the request for processing. Each object server needs to have access to distributed name servers that keep a current map of object locations, or servers for those objects.

Requests for remote objects can be handled by:

- Forwarding the request to a server that has a copy of the object, which processes the request and returns results

- Requesting a copy of the object from the remote server and processing locally

- Forwarding the request to a remote server for processing and requesting that server to send a copy after processing

- Storing version numbers with each object and increment them with each update

Distributed repositories. An object-oriented database must have a way to describe object classes. Distributed repositories describe data types for each attribute and define each method in each object class. In addition, the servers where an object is located and which server methods may be executed are defined. The repositories themselves must either have identical copies on each server, or each server must maintain a repository that only describes that server's components.

References

Andleigh, P. K., and M. R. Gretzinger. *Distributed Object-Oriented Data-Systems Design.* Englewood Cliffs, NJ: Prentice Hall, 1992.

Date, C. J. *A Guide to DB2.* Reading, MA: Addison-Wesley, 1985.

Martin, J. *Information Engineering.* 3 vols. Englewood Cliffs, NJ: Prentice Hall, 1990.

Pons, J.-F., and J.-F. Vilarem. "Dynamic and Integrated Concurring Control for Distributed Databases," in *IEEE Journal on Selected Areas in Communications* (April 1989): 7(3).

8

Performing Quality Checks on Models

You should always strive to check your models for quality. Some ways of doing this are absolutely necessary, while others are only guidelines. Views of a model reference certain system components from different contexts, and, because views overlap one another, we need to ensure that system functions, information, and dynamics fit together so that the model correctly describes the requirements for the system. The major checks on a model should ensure that the model is:

complete	All required views must be present in the model. Each data operation must have a corresponding method specification, and each group of operations must have a corresponding message flow model.
consistent	Because of overlapping views, the possibility exists that two views of a model component are inconsistent.
correct	Even if a model is complete and consistent, it may still fail to represent the requirements for a system.

Checking Model Views

Each view must satisfy rules for its type of modeling construct and must also be checked to ensure that it correctly describes the requirements. Cross-checks of models should be applied as soon as possible after models are built. Consistency checks may be performed as soon as two views to be compared are available, but usually we will defer the actual check until these views are considered stable and complete. Cross-checks should always be applied before a model is considered complete.

If your modeling environment supports it, automated cross-checks should be conducted frequently. The tool used should try to incorporate the minimum information needed to determine what appears on each view. In a manual modeling environment, each view must be logically independent, and checks should be conducted after any change to either view.

Model Completeness

It is important to keep the analysis models minimal, so that the system is not defined to have requirements that are not truly required. There should be no functions other than those required in response to some event. Each function must have a corresponding event to which it is a response.

Single-Instance Views

- There is a statement of purpose.

- There is a single context diagram (or a set of partial context diagrams exist that are equivalent to a single, integrated context diagram).

- There is an event list.

Environmental Completeness

Agents

- Each agent on the context diagram has a corresponding specification.

- Each agent specification has a corresponding agent on the context diagram.

System inputs and outputs

- Each message flow on the context diagram has a corresponding message specification.

- Each event flow on the context diagram has a corresponding specification.

System interfaces

- Each interface on the context diagram has a corresponding specification.

- Each named access on the context diagram has a corresponding specification.

Event specifications

- Each event in the event list has a corresponding event specification.

- Each event specification has a corresponding event in the event list.

Behavioral Completeness

Message flow specifications

- Each message flow on a message flow diagram has a corresponding specification.

- Each message specification has a corresponding message flow on at least one message flow diagram.

- Each object mentioned in a message flow specification has a specification.

Event flow specifications

- Each event flow on an event schema has a corresponding specification.

- Each event flow generated by an operation has a corresponding specification.

- Each event flow generated by a state transition has a corresponding specification.

- Each event flow defined as part of a complex event flow has a corresponding specification.

- Each event flow specification has a corresponding event flow on at least one event schema and is referenced in at least one operation specification or state-transition diagram.

Class specification

- Each class on a message flow diagram has a corresponding specification.

- Each named access flow on a message flow diagram has a corresponding specification.

Event queue specification

- Each event queue on an event schema has a specification.

- Each event queue used by an operation has a corresponding specification.

- Each event queue used by a state transition diagram has a corresponding specification.

- Each event queue specification has a corresponding event queue that appears on at least one event schema.

Operation specification

- Each operation seen on a message flow diagram has a corresponding specification.

- Each message flow diagram (except the context diagram) has an operation group on a higher-level message flow diagram.

- Each operation has at least one corresponding operation on a message flow diagram.

- Each operation has at least one corresponding operation on a message flow diagram.

- Each state transition has a corresponding operation on a message flow diagram

Information Completeness

Classes

- Each class or relationship referenced in an operation must have a corresponding specification.

- If a class is specified as containing another class, the included class must also be specified.

- Each class specification has a corresponding class on a class diagram.

Class and relationship specifications

- Each class on a class diagram that does not appear as an associative entity on any class diagram has a corresponding specification.

- Each associative class on a class diagram has a corresponding specification.

- Each relationship on a class diagram has a corresponding specification.

- Each class specification has a corresponding class on at least one class diagram.

- Each relationship specification has a corresponding relationship on at least one class diagram.

- Each associative class specification has an associative class on at least one class diagram.

State-transition diagrams

- Each class with a state defined in a class specification has a state transition for each state.

- Each state-transition diagram has a corresponding class or associative class on one or more class diagrams.

Model Consistency

A model is usually constructed with overlapping views, so it is possible that two views can be inconsistent. We need to check for consistency for the following reasons:

- Where part of the system requirements appear in two views, this must be stated consistently across both views.
- A component that appears in two different views must be given the same name.
- Components must be used correctly in accordance with their specifications.

Information Consistency

Apply the following rules when information models are complete:

- Each access shown in a state-transition diagram must be allowed by the class specification.
- For any access action in a state-transition diagram, the same access must appear in the class-event table for that event-class combination.
- Each class in a class-entity table has a state-transition diagram showing the event causing that class to be accessed.

Class and relationship creation

- Each class or relationship that the system has *create* access to *require* that the system has all information necessary to check that an instance of the class can be created.
- Each instance of an associative class or relationship being created requires that instances of classes it refers to exist. The system must have *create* or *match* access to these classes. If the access involves only a match, the system checks whether the classes exist before creating an instance of the relationship.
- If an associative class or relationship being created has a rule of association, then the system is responsible for checking that this rule is obeyed before creating the instance. The system must have *read* access to any classes and *match* access to any relationships involved

in this rule of association. If attributes of classes are used in the rule of association, the specification for that class must describe the attribute with a *read* access.

- Any class that participates in a mandatory relationship must have an instance of the relationship created each time an instance of the class is created. The relationship specifications for each entity that the system has *create* access for must be checked to determine these relationships. There must be a corresponding system relationship or associative class specification for this relationship showing the system access as *create*.

Class and relationship deletion

- If the system can delete an instance of a class, then the system must also delete any relationships that refer to these instances. These relationships must have relationship specifications showing the system's access as deleted.

- If the system can delete an instance of a relationship, then the system must also delete any class instances that have mandatory participation in this relationship. These classes must have specifications defining the system's access as deleted.

Environmental Consistency

- Each flow shown as a system input in an event specification or table is an input message flow to the system context.

- Every output message flow on the context diagram must be defined as a system output in the event specification or table for at least one event.

- Each input message flow on the context diagram must be defined as a system input in the event specification or table of at least one operation listed as an event-response or event-detection operation for the event.

- Each event-response operation has as input any system input listed for the event.

- Each event-response operation has no other message flows or flow components (except access flows) than those listed as stimuli or system inputs and outputs on the event-system interface table.

- The only input message flow to an event-response operation is a stimulus on the event-operation table. All other inputs must come from classes.

Behavioral Consistency

Vertical balancing

All inputs and outputs between leveled sets of message flow diagrams must be consistent.

Message flow consistency

For each input data flow to a parent operation, one of the following must be true:

- One or more of the operations on the child diagram must have the same input.
- The message flow is a composite, and all of its elements are input to one or more operations on the child diagram.

Also, for every message flow that is an input to an operation on the child diagram, one of the following must be true:

- The flow must be an output from an operation on the same diagram.
- The flow must appear as an input to the parent operation.
- The flow must be a component of an input to the parent operation.

Each output message flow has equivalent rules.

Event flow consistency

An event flow input or output to one operation is considered an input or output to another if any of the following is true:

- It is seen with the same name.
- It is included in another event flow.
- All of the event flows it includes are input or output.

Class access consistency

Classes are accessed consistently if the classes and relationships they include are accessed consistently, regardless of which classes were used to include them. A class access is consistent if:

- The same class is accessed in exactly the same way.

- The same included class or relationship is accessed exactly the same even if in another class.

- A class including the class is accessed in exactly the same way.

Event queues

- Any event queue updated by an operation group must be updated by at least one child operation.

- Any event queue written to by a child operation must be shown on the parent diagram, unless the queue is only used by operations on this child diagram (on the parent diagram it is shown as being read from).

- Any event queue read by a child operation must be shown on the parent diagram, unless the queue is only used by operations on this child diagram.

Triggered operations

- If a parent operation is triggered, no child control operation may enable a child operation (but it can have a control operation that triggers other operations in a group).

- If a parent operation is triggered, no operation of the child diagram may generate a continuous flow.

- If a parent operation is triggered, no operation of the child diagram may access an event queue that does not appear on the parent diagram with an access to another operation, other than the parent operation.

Message flow diagram and operation specification consistency

- A continuous operation may be shown as enabled and disabled on a message flow diagram, but it is not allowed to trigger it.

- A continuous control operation that has state behavior must be specified with a state transition diagram or with state transition and action tables.

- A discrete control process must be specified with an operation specification.

Operation/operation specification consistency

- An object that is an input to an operation on a message flow diagram must also be an input of its operation specification.

- An object that is an input to an operation specification must be an output from its operation.

- An object that is an output of an operation must also be an output of its operation specification.

- An object that is an output of an operation specification must be an output from its operation.

- If there is an access message flow from a class to an operation, there must be a create, delete, or modify action on a class or relationship contained in that class by the operation specification.

- If there is an access to a class from an operation, there must be a match or read of a class (or relationship) contained in that class by the operation specification.

- If an operation specification reads or matches a class (or relationship), there must be an access message flow from the operation to a class containing that class (or relationship).

- If an operation specification creates, deletes, or modifies a class (or relationship), there must be an access to the operation from a class containing that class (or relationship).

- Any event queue initialized by an operation specification must be written to by the operation that is being specified.

- Any event queue written to by an operation that is specified by an operation specification must be initialized or signaled to by that specification.

- Any event flow output from an operation that is specified by an operation specification must be generated in that specification.

- Any event flow generated in an operation specification must be an output from the operation that it specifies.

Data conservation

- Any input to an operation should be used by that operation to derive an output.

- It should be possible to derive all outputs of an operation from its inputs.

Control operation/state-transition diagram consistency

- For any operation triggered by an operation specification or state-transition diagram, or enabled/disabled by a state-transition diagram, there is an operation with the same name on the message flow diagram that contains the control operation being specified.

- Any event flow input to a control operation must be used at least once within a condition on the state-transition diagram or by the specification for that control operation.

- Any discrete event flow output from a control operation must be signaled from its state-transition diagram or operation specification.

- Any continuous event flow output from a control operation must be raised or lowered at least once by the state-transition diagram or operation specification.

- Any operation triggered by a control operation must be triggered by its state-transition diagram or operation specification.

- Any operation enabled or disabled by a control operation must be enabled or disabled by its state-transition diagram or operation specification.

- Any operation triggered by a state-transition diagram or operation specification must be triggered by its control operation.

- Any operation enabled or disabled by a state-transition diagram or operation specification must be enabled or disabled by its control operation.

- Any signal by a state-transition diagram or operation specification must be a discrete event flow output from its parent control operation.

- Any continuous event flow raised or lowered by a state-transition diagram or operation specification must be a continuous event flow output from its parent control operation.

Activation consistency

- Every operation on a message flow diagram must either:

  — be explicitly enabled and disabled by a control operation

  — be explicitly triggered by a control operation

  — be permanently able to run and have a stimulus that will cause it to run.

- If a control operation triggers an operation group, all operations in the group have an *activation* mechanism or *trigger.*

- If a control operation enables or disables a process group, no process in the group may have an activation mechanism of *permanent.*

Other consistency rules

- There is no more than one control operation on any message flow diagram.

- An event queue must have at least one signal access and one wait access.

Consistency between Environment and Information Views

- If there is a class or relationship on the function-class table that is not created by the system, it either must be accessed by the system and by a create access by an agent or the creation must be added to the function class, class or relationship specification, and class-event table.

- If there is a class or relationship that is only created or only deleted by the system, but never matched, updated, or read, an agent has an input access to a class that includes the class or relationship.

- Each data access on the class-event table should be in at least one data operation that detects or responds to that event.

- Each data access by an event-response process must be under that event on the class-event table.

- Each data access by an event-detection operation must be under that event in the class-event table.

- Each operation creating an instance of a class, associative class, or relationship must ensure that the relationship meets all rules of association.

- Each operation accessing a class instance must validate to ensure that the instance is in the proper state for that event/access combination.

- Each operation deleting a relationship must validate that no classes that must participate in that relationship exist or must also delete those instances.

- Each operation deleting a class instance must validate that no relationships referring to that instance exist or must also delete those relationship instances.

- Each operation creating a class instance that must participate in a relationship must also create the instance of that relationship.

Model Correctness

To ensure that a model represents the system:

Correct Scope

- Each output from the system context must exist to satisfy a responsibility listed in the statement of purpose.

- Each responsibility listed in the statement of purpose must be associated with one or more inputs and/or outputs to the system context.

- Each event detected by the system must be able to meet one or more responsibilities in the statement of purpose.

- Every class the system uses must be needed to support a responsibility in the statement of purpose.

- All classes and relationships specifically mentioned in the statement of purpose should appear on the class relationship diagram(s).

Correct Policy

- To ensure that the system will actually perform as required, each operation specification should be reviewed by two independent subject matter experts. Given the same test information, they should be capable of determining the same outputs, using only the operation specifications and manual calculation. Two subject matter experts should derive the same resulting outputs.

- Each state-transition diagram must be verified as describing the required sequence of system behavior.

Object-Oriented Testing

Object modeling and development should lead to process and product improvement that is vastly superior to that which exists in traditional systems. Object-oriented approaches encourage iterative development, which does allow for early and frequent feedback from system users and subject matter experts. However, when complex subject areas are tackled for analysis and system design and development, defects can and will occur in the final system. Traditional development approaches have included a testing phase at the end of development.

With object-oriented development, we sometimes need to include an explicit testing phase just to be safe, but we prefer to capture defects, omissions, or inconsistencies in our systems as we analyze and develop them. This chapter covers testing from an object perspective. With the advent of formal specification languages and techniques, the concepts of assertions and exceptions will be built into specifications at analysis time, avoiding many headaches usually present when trying to test complex systems. Also, projects that make heavy use of use case modeling tied to object interaction models will benefit greatly from identification of key test cases (the use cases themselves) early.

Types of Test Suites

Conditional Test Suite

Test classes using a conditional test method and accompanying:

- Assertions
- Exceptions
- Concurrent test operations
- Message polling scripts

Hierarchical Incremental Test Suite

Test foundation components using various test models and scripts:

- State-transition test model
  - Model the dynamic behavior of classes as states and transitions
  - Test objects are transaction flows
- Transaction flow test model
  - Model the dynamic behavior of classes as black box transactions
  - Test objects are life cycle flows through the model
- Exception test model
  - Model exception behavior of classes
- Control flow test model
  - Model the dynamic behavior of methods as a flow of control through a method
  - Test object is a single flow through the model
- Data flow test model

Integration Test Suite

Test combinations of foundation components using hierarchical models with scripts that use all components.

System Test Suite

Test foundation components and systems.

Each object has its own optimization approach details. Operational objectives for each object constitute the test standards for that object.

The following chart shows different classes of test model, test object, and corresponding test scripts or reviews.

Test Model	Test Object	Description	Review or Test Script
Requirements Model	Use case	A series of actions that comprise a single requirement at the system level	Requirements review
Object Model	Generalization/ specialization hierarchy	A hierarchy of classes from the object model	Classification review
Object Model	Composition hierarchy	A hierarchy of classes from the object model	Aggregation review
Dynamic Model	State-transition cycle	A sequence of states and transitions from the dynamic model of a class (its life cycle)	State-transition test script
Domain Model	Domain partition	A partitioning of the inputs and outputs of a method	Domain test script
Exception Model	Exception condition	A collection of conditions that will raise an exception when you send a particular message to an object	Exception test script
Control Flow Model	Control flow	A sequence of linked control nodes that models the flow of control through a method	Control flow test script
Transaction Flow Model	Transaction flow	A sequence of linked control nodes that models an object through its life cycle	Transaction flow test script

Test Model	Test Object	Description	Review or Test Script
Data Flow Model	Data flow	A sequence of linked control nodes annotated with data that model the flow of data through a method	Data flow test script
Condition Model	Error condition	A rule that, if violated, asserts that the object is not valid	Assertion
Condition Model	Exception condition	A continuously monitored rule that, if violated, raises an exception from a method	Exception
Condition Model	Concurrent error condition	A continuously monitored logical predicate within an object that, if false, asserts that the object is not valid	Concurrent test operation
Design-Interface Model	Protocol	Definition of message structure for a class method	Interface and protocol test script
Design Concurrency Model	Concurrent operations	Sequences of object behavior operating concurrently in separate objects that require synchronization	Synchronization test script
Exception Model	Exception handler	Sequences of object behavior following the raising of an exception	Exception test script
Design User-Interface Model	User-interface bitmap	Together with event timing, represents expected outcome of a series of input GUI events	True-time test script
Design User-Interface Model	Style-independent bitmap	Specifies elements such as object location and font style as irrelevant	Character recognition test script
Design User-Interface Model	User-interface widget	For a sequence of events associated with a GUI object, represents expected outcome of a set of input events	Widget playback test script

Test Model	Test Object	Description	Review or Test Script
Requirements Model	Use case	The relationship between the finished system and the use case(s)	System validation test script
Requirements Model	System resource	A thing that the system consumes during processing	System stress test model
Requirements Model	System performance 333requirement	A use case that specifies required system performance	System performance test script
Requirements Model	System configuration	Logical and physical devices upon which the system depends	System configuration test script
Requirements Model	System malfunction	A failure in the software or hardware upon which the system depends	System recovery test script
System Security Model	System vulnerability	A system weakness	System security test script

Test Suites

Hierarchical-Incremental Test Suite

Corresponds to test models based on object, dynamic, and functional test models:

- State-transition test scripts
- Transaction flow test scripts
- Exception test scripts
- Control flow test scripts
- Data flow test scripts

Because the hierarchical incremental test suite is the most complex of the test suites, it is discussed in a separate section starting on page 198.

Conditional Test Suite

Tests classes using the conditional test model and its accompanying assertions, exceptions, concurrent test operations, and message polling test scripts.

Integration Test Suite

Tests combinations of foundation components using the hierarchical incremental models with scripts that use all the components.

System Test Suite

Tests systems of foundation components using system test models.

Regression Test Suite

Tests foundation components and systems.

Hierarchical-Incremental Test Suite

The essence of this kind of test suite is the inheritance between classes. When you test a class, you also test its parent classes and construct a test you can later reuse to test subclasses. Each class is the result of combining the structure and behavior of the parent class or classes with new attributes and methods. We can distinguish three kinds of methods (see Harrold and McGregor 1992):

New methods	Methods defined in subclasses, including ones with the same name as methods in a superclass but with different parameters.
Recursive methods	Methods defined in a superclass that you don't override or overload in the subclass.
Redefined methods	Methods defined in a superclass that you override or overload in the subclass.

Each of these different method types has a different testing requirement in the context of the class:

New methods	Complete testing
Recursive methods	Limited retesting if the method interacts with new or redefined member functions; only retest test objects relating to the interaction.
Redefined methods	Retesting with reuse of test models and objects developed from specifications rather than from internal control logic.

Hierarchical-incremental testing covers a range of test models. Two structural models apply to methods:

Control Flow Model	Models the class as a series of control flow graphs deriving from the method implementation.
Data Flow Model	Models the class as a series of control flow graphs with data annotations showing the flow of data values through the method implementation.

Three functional models apply to classes:

State-Transition Model	Models states and transitions for a class with regard to its position and inheritance hierarchy. Consists of a set of state-transition path test objects.
Transaction Flow Model	Models the object life cycle as a transaction. May be derived from the functional model (processes) or the requirements model (use cases).
Exception Model	Specifies what methods raise what exceptions under what conditions. Involves both exception-raising test objects and test objects not resulting in exceptions.

Steps

1. List both abstract and concrete classes that comprise the set of classes being tested in the suite.

2. For each class, build an appropriate series of test models or adapt the set of models.

3. For each test model, derive a set of test objects.

4. For each test object, develop a test script in the appropriate format.

5. Build the test scripts into an automated test suite using the test framework appropriate for the test scripts.

6. Build any test data required by scripts into the test repository.

Class-Object Test Script

Four specific subclasses of the class-object test (which all operate through the conditional test suite):

Assertion	A program statement that aborts the program during debugging upon a condition that evaluates to false.
Exception	A program statement that raises an exception in a method upon a condition that evaluates to true.
Concurrent Test Operations	A program statement that tests for valid conditions and takes appropriate action during execution of a method.
Message Polling Test Script	A program statement that is part of a set of such statements that validate the status of an object of the class at any time.

Control Flow Test Model

This model represents the control structure of a method and is a structural model of a class. There are two subclasses of this model:

Data Flow Test Model	Adds data flows to the control flows.
Transaction Flow Model	Models an entire class with control flows based on use cases.

Guidelines

• Ensure that the test suite includes requirements-based, functional test models.

• Choose paths through the system representing sensible paths likely to be taken.

• Develop equivalence classes of variations on the initial paths.

• If all sensible paths have been selected and branch coverage has not been achieved, look for control flow problems, absurd situations, or inaccessible procedure code in the method.

Data Flow Test Model

This is a kind of control flow test model annotated with data elements that shows what happens to data moving through a method during execution. The model describes the same control information for a method as does the control flow model and includes several kinds of data elements:

Global variables	Variables outside the scope of any class.
Class variables	Data members of a class with a value shared between all object of the class to which the method belongs.
Object variables	Data members of the class with separate values for each object of the class.
Parameters	Values of the classes passed to the method by value or by reference, making the outside value visible inside the method, regardless of its defining scope.
Local variables	Variables the method defines that exist only when the method executes.

Guidelines

The testing objects are the different paths through the graph (control flows). Look for data anomalies in these flows:

- A sequence of two definitions for the same variable
- A destruction immediately following a definition
- A destruction following a destruction
- A use following a destruction
- A destruction by itself
- A use by itself
- A definition by itself

Look for problematic data situations:

- An array use that uses an uninitialized or out-of-bound element
- A variable use as a consequence of a variable use
- Use of data of an unknown type
- Assumptions about data that may not be true

Method design guidelines (from Beizer 1990):

- Avoid modifying variables you pass into a method (pass by value, not by reference).
- Keep data construction and destruction at the same level.
- Avoid strong typing.
- Always initialize data members and other data elements.

State-Transition Test Model

This model tests behavior at a level beyond an individual task or activity. Use cases specify requirements that translate into a sequence of activities, so they can provide input into state-transition testing. Rules for checking state-transition models include (from Beizer):

1. Verify that states represent the true set of states. Make sure that there is one state for each possible (or equivalent) value of the underlying state variables.
2. Check that the model accounts for all possible events that you require the class to acknowledge. There should be a transition from each state for every method in a class.
3. Check that there is exactly one transition for each event-state combination. Build a matrix showing all possible combination of states and events.
4. Check for unreachable and dead states.
5. Check for invalid actions, including methods that don't exist or methods that do not satisfy requirements for the transition.

Transaction Flow Test Model

This is a kind of control flow test model that applies to a class as a whole rather than to just one method of the class. This model scales up the control logic to deal with object life cycles rather than with method life cycles. It is a functional rather than structural model; it deals only with the testable behavior of the object, not with internal logic and structure.

Build a transaction flow model from requirements use cases, focusing on the sequence of control decisions that affect the object. This is a functional model, with no direct relationship to the underlying implementation. Start building the model by using a traceability matrix associated with the class being tested. Otherwise, start with use cases directly and build transaction flow models for all classes involved.

Steps

Build the model in a series of iterations:

* Eliminate any external references (i.e., databases, files, or methods in other classes).

* Simplify the model where possible. Combine methods into a single process.

* Review any remaining use case references that don't appear in the class design.

* Review any public methods that don't appear in the model with the designers.

Exception Test Model

This model makes explicit certain kinds of behavior that might not be evident in other functional models. An exception is an anomaly in an executing system, which must be handled in an appropriate way. This model should help you answer:

Does the base model support the specification of exceptions?

Do programs raise exceptions in some special way or does the model handle them?

The exception test model consists of the object model and a listing of exceptions that each method can raise. During the building of an exception test model, consider all the system exceptions for each class method. Examine overloaded methods or situations that occur only within the context of a subclass. To test exceptions, create a situation that causes a method to raise the exception. The test object for the exception test mode is the individual exception for a method.

Conditional Test Suite

A conditional test suite is a collection of test scripts based on conditional models of a class. The model describes the logical contract of the class to its clients. The models range from simple assertions for variable values at certain points in method execution to a complete model of the behavior of a class through a decision table or other logical model.

Four types of test scripts may be used in a conditional test suite:

Assertions	Program statements that abort the program if a condition fails.
Exceptions	Program statements that raise an exception if a condition exists.
Concurrent test operations	Language statements that monitor a condition continuously and handle the situation when the condition exists.
Message polling test scripts	Program statement that evaluate a condition on demand from a client of the class.

Steps

1. Create a conditional test model for a class and its methods.

2. Derive the individual test objects from the model.

3. Translate the test objects into the appropriate format for a test script, and place the script in the appropriate place. Where possible, combine individual test scripts into aggregate ones.

4. Document the test object.

Conditional Test Model

This model describes the contract of a class for services to its clients. It may consist of logical sentences constructed of a series of constants related by logical operators:

AND

OR

NOT

IF-THEN

IF-AND-ONLY-IF

Start with the attributes of a class and include any other data visible to the class. Build up a sentence from individual attributes and logical operators. Don't try to model every aspect of a class through conditional logic, just the parts that ensure that the class will fulfill its contract for services to its clients. Model the following types of conditions:

Class invariant	A condition that must be true if the class if valid.
Precondition	A condition that must be true when you execute a method.
Postcondition	A condition that must be true when a method finishes executing.
Loop invariant	A condition that must be true at all times during execution of a loop.

Steps

1. Examine data attributes and class requirements for the class to which a model applies.

2. Work out any logical conditions that apply to the class at all times (class invariants).

3. Ensure that the expression applies only to this class and its subclasses. If not, move it up the hierarchy until that is true.

4. For each method in the class, work out the preconditions and postconditions.

5. Determine which data come from outside, which are purely internal, and variables that get exported back to clients.

6. Create preconditions for the outside variables and postconditions for the exported variables. Ensure that purely internal variables with data flow test scripts are properly initialized or set.

7. For each loop in each method in a class, work out the invariant conditions. Examine the data objects that a loop uses to see what happens if the value changes during the course of an iteration through the loop.

Assertion

An assertion is a program statement that evaluates an expression to true or false and then takes some well-defined action if the expression evaluates to false. Assertions use a programming language to express the condition, so you can use variable names; constants; expressions; and relational, logical, and arithmetic operators. The assertion assumes a conditional test: If an expression is false, then abort the procedure. Assertions are an effective way to embed conditional tests into programs to aid class testing. If you need to test a condition and enforce it at execution time, use exceptions.

Exception

An exception is a programming language statement that evaluates a condition and raises an exception if the condition is true. Unlike assertions, the program raises an exception during execution as well as during testing. Whereas an assertion tests a class, an exception validates it. Exceptions may be used to handle validation in constructor functions, which cannot return data to the client (in C++). Exceptions thus form the only mechanism for handling errors in a constructor function, and condition validation is one set of such errors.

Concurrent Test Operation

A concurrent test operation is a program statement that continuously validates a condition. This allows recovery, or at least permits graceful failure. The operation runs in both production and testing as an exception. Instead of passing control to another routine, a concurrent test operation handles the problem immediately.

A common use of a concurrent test operation is a test for a null pointer (in C++). The test script also can monitor critical hardware failure situations and other vital conditions. Unlike an exception that implies some risk of program failure, a concurrent test operation guarantees that you retain as much control as possible given a failure. One downside to using concurrent test operations is the overhead—a condition evaluates continuously, consuming some resources. Assertions and exceptions offer better performance at the expense of graceful recovery from an error.

Message Polling Test Script

This kind of test script is a program statement that is part of a set of such statements that validate the states of an object of a class at any time. These scripts can be packaged in a class method (often called verify or assertValid), and clients call the method to validate the status of the class on demand. Message polling evaluates class-invariant conditions, which are true at all times for all objects of a class. It is an approach to validating a class that has two disadvantages. First, an object relies on a client to inquire about problems; it does not do this automatically. Second, if you return information from the encapsulated data in the class, encapsulation is violated.

Integration Test Suite

An integration test suite consists of a series of tests against an integration component or cluster of components. Tests in the suite usually each test a specific component and its integration with other components comprising the cluster. A specific integration test suite usually relates to a specific software component, though it may need to execute or use components from other systems to test primary components fully.

The integration test suite is a concrete class, with two specialized test suites:

Functional Test Suite	Tests the vertical integration of a cluster of components.
Abstraction Test Suite	Tests the horizontal integration of a cluster of components.

Make sure that individual classes are safe by putting them and their components through thorough requirements and design reviews and then through full suites of hierarchical-incremental and conditional tests. Once you have established a solid basis for further testing, you can begin to test clusters of classes.

Two abstract categories of tests check more than one class at a time, focusing attention on integration risks as opposed to requirements, design, and coding risks:

Class-to-Class Test Script	Tests the interactions between two classes based on a message relationship. This includes protocol-interface tests, synchronization tests, and exception-handling tests.
User-Interface Test Script	Tests the user-interface components of clusters of components and the components on which they depend. This includes true-time tests, character-recognition tests, and widget-playback tests.

Integration testing finds these messaging errors:

- Failure to meet requirements
- Message sent to the wrong receiver
- Wrong type of message sent
- Incorrect message priority
- Incompatible message and method in the sender and receiver
- Incorrect event timing between object actions
- Incorrect initialization of objects with respect to other objects
- Incorrect destruction of objects with respect to other objects

Integration testing finds these user-interface errors:

- A given sequence of user actions does not have the desired effect on the component
- The timing of event received from the user results in the incorrect functioning of a component
- Failure to meet functional requirements
- Failure to meet performance requirements of a component

Functional Test Suite

You can partition a system for testing purposes to focus on a specific function of the system. Functions may be defined by use cases or scenarios from system requirements. Classes in a system support parts of the total function, and a functional test suite focuses on how well the system implements requirements stated in use cases that the script tests. Test scripts must construct appropriate objects, call indicated methods, and compare the results to expected results according to the use cases or other requirements. This kind of test suite could be called a vertical integration test suite, referring to a vertical path through the containment hierarchy of the system of objects involved in a use case.

Abstraction Test Suite

This kind of test suite verifies the services of an abstract layer of a system. The abstraction is horizontal, referring to the abstraction of a service layer or application programming interface (API) from an underlying set of objects or functions. It may be referred to as horizontal, because it deals with a horizontal line through the containment hierarchy of a system representing the application programming interface. It tests the integration of the API layer with underlying classes and functions that it abstracts. Test scripts must construct the required objects, call methods indicated by the use cases in requirements, and then destroy the objects.

Class-to-Class Test Script

This kind of testing checks the computability of classes by focusing on the messages between objects. The test script here is an abstract class that tests the internal interface between any two classes, including primary interfaces that other systems call (the system application programming interface). Message-related integration tests are two-class tests: a message has a sender and a receiver. The sender and receiver may be objects of the same class.

Interface and protocol test script. This script tests the messages sent from objects of one class to objects of another class for compatibility and validity. One class may interact with other classes in the system through messages in many ways. Interface testing examines the ways they actually do interact. To develop these test scripts, you must know how one class calls other classes and you must build test scripts based on this to test compatibility of the actual message with the method of the receiver.

The protocol test examines the contract between classes. Here, we focus on the service that the receiving class provides to a specific sender and whether that service fulfills the contract. The contract should be defined in design and requirements use cases. A contract consists both of the relationship between classes and the requirements for the service that the receiver performs.

You need to ensure that objects create and destroy the appropriate nested objects by sending the correct constructor and destructor messages. A common problem is failure to initialize an object properly. Another is to fail to destroy objects at the appropriate time. Ideally, all construction and destruction should be verified under all situations.

Synchronization test script. A synchronization test script tests concurrent behavior. Concurrency permits interacting objects to act simultaneously. A common form of synchronized behavior is the interaction of several clients accessing a database at the same time. Transaction processing provides logic for the timing of read and write access to data. If a class implements transaction processing, or depends on some other processing for it, you should test this function.

A special kind of asynchronous behavior is an event or interrupt. This could be a hardware or a software event. Timing conflicts between multiple devices or processes can disrupt a running program. You need to test the timing of events and interrupts by carefully analyzing the requirements use cases for timing requirements and then test these requirements through a synchronization test script.

Exception test script. This kind of script tests the raising and handling of an exception between two classes. An exception is an explicit or implicit instruction to transfer control during execution of a method. The method raised the exception, and then control transfers to an exception handler defined for that exception. There are different models of exception handling, the most common of which handles the exception through the nearest handler (the most recently registered by a calling object). The handler executes its statements and resumes execution. An exception may be an object itself with attributes and methods.

Exception testing, in this context, does not test the raising of the exception (which is local to the class) but the handling of the exception. A component under test is a message sent to the receiver that raises an exception, transferring control to the nearest handler. This ensures that the correct behavior occurs in the handler and that the exception object contains the correct attributes given the sender and receiver.

User-Interface Test Script

User-interface testing examines how users interact with a system. These test scripts apply only to systems that actually allow direct user interaction. It tests a specific user-interface component and the components of the underlying system with which it interacts. An automated integration environment runs the test script to verify the integrated behavior of the system and to validate the implementation against requirements use cases. A user-interface test script is an abstract class with three subclasses:

True-Time Test Script	Verifies exact behavior in the user interface.
Character-Recognition Test Script	Verifies behavior allowing for specific differences such as fonts or relative pixel location.
Widget-Playback Test Script	Verifies behavior of objects rather than collections of pixels.

True-time test script. A true-time test script examines keyboard and mouse events exactly as they are recorded. The script assumes a fixed set of pixel images on the screen; if anything at all changes from the recording, the script regards it as an error. The strengths of this test are the timing test and focus on external events. Use it to test very specific drawing requirements. The weakness of the test: If you are mostly interested in application behavior rather than external events, timing, or external output, the test becomes unusable very quickly with application changes.

Character-recognition test script. This test script manipulates areas of a screen without requiring an exact match between a recorded sequence of events and outputs and the actual test results. It deals with characters rather than groupings of pixels and handles a wide variety of character font and location changes without creating a failure. The advantage of this type of script is that it is better for basic application testing than for exact pixel testing. If screen objects appear in different locations or with different fonts, it is particularly useful. Still, this approach is quite limited; change the interface too much and the script becomes useless.

Widget-playback test script. This script focuses completely on the application behavior of a system. It refers to external events only as abstract instructions that drive application behavior, ignoring the display images. It can name user-interface objects and place some indirection between an object and the screen. Use this kind of testing to test the user interface solely as a driver for the underlying application. It works best when the application behavior does not require further display in the user interface. With this type of script you can build scripts that are portable across various user-interface platforms.

System Component Test Suite

System component test suites can reuse previously developed test suites, use cases, and scripts. Testing begins and progresses parallel to requirements gathering and analysis. High-level use cases are developed to model systems requirements during requirements gathering, and details are added to reflect feedback from future users of the system. Use case review and refinement parallels and enhances development of a final set of requirements. A complete set of use cases should represent a set of test scenarios that defines and covers the entire set of system requirements. This set of use cases also represents a set of acceptance criteria for testing your system. As system development proceeds, development of the system test suite proceeds. Test suite development involves design of executable test scenarios, coding of input data, and documentation for execution of test scripts and evaluating output.

System testing may be divided into two broad test suites:

System Acceptance Test Suite	Derived from the set of use cases covering the system requirements.
User Options Test Suite	Based on the probable usage patterns of the features and functions delivered with the system. It is designed to simulate ways that end users may combine discrete system features and functions to synthesize new and different usage patterns.

Specific test scripts must be included for the system test, including scripts for:

Functionality	The basic features and functions of the requirements.
Reliability	Supports the reliability requirement stated and verified with system test scenarios.
Availability	May include beta system testing, recovery testing, and simulation. May involve maintainability.
Security	Designed and executed to attempt to compromise the security of a system.
Performance	Includes stress testing and volume testing.
Configuration	Includes hardware and software variations, compatibility requirements, and installation tests.
Usability	Includes user interface, help information, user documents, and flexibility.

References

Beizer, B. *Software Testing Techniques*. 2d ed. New York: Van Nostrand Reinhold, 1990.

Harrold, M. J., and J. D. McGregor. "Incremental Testing of Object-Oriented Class Structures." In the *Proceedings of the 14th International Conference on Software Engineering*, 1992.

10

Object-Oriented Metrics

Product and Process Metrics

Forecasting costs for system production and/or maintenance drives the development of a cost estimation model, although system production tends to be emphasized. It is possible to evaluate likely trade-offs in cost factors. The most basic trade-off involves the balance between system development costs and maintenance costs: When development costs are cut short, maintenance costs rise (if project scope is not reduced to maintain quality). With respect to the development process, the unit costs for fixing an error in maintenance are significantly higher than if the same correction is made earlier in the development process.

Process metrics are used not only to measure the software development process, but also to use the development process as a predictor of future development costs. Some development cost estimation techniques are based on modules such as COCOMO, SLIM, and PAMELA. Other process metrics focus on performance and state of completion.

Some challenges are presented to us as we attempt to apply process metrics. We would like to be able to estimate costs for projects during their concept stages, but there are few (if any) cost estimation models that are widely applicable and reasonably accurate for this purpose. Another challenge is that no two projects are identical, requiring some research and customization to be embedded within the development process for any new project. This research and customization can be extremely difficult to forecast. Estimating costs later in the life cycle gets easier since some costs are already known. Thus any cost estimate made early in the development process must have a significant adjustment for error; this error adjustment becomes less significant as development progresses.

Process measures address the entire project life cycle by describing the dynamic variation of properties such as staff allocation or by summing over the life cycle. A snapshot taken of the process at a given point in time can describe static characteristics. Static properties are known as product metrics and should be specific to a particular life cycle phase. For example, distinct individual measures are used for design and development.

To use a process metric in the past, a reference had been made to the size (a product metric) of a system being constructed. This has required a measure of team productivity that is unique to an organization. Size is one of the easiest product measures to construct but is only available (reliably) late in the development process. This has led to a focus in product metrics on estimating size.

A more complete analysis of product metrics suggests that complexity, not size, is more appropriate for measuring and estimating software systems. Complexity, for purposes of this discussion, is that characteristic of software that causes us to allocate resources for design, research, or development. Product or structural complexity can be measured by module metrics and intermodule metrics. *Modularity metrics* focus at the individual module level and can measure the procedural complexity of a module in terms of size, data structure, or logic structure, as well as the external specification of the module. *Intermodule metrics* measure systems design complexity by describing connections between modules (thus describing system-level complexity).

Product Metrics

In an object-oriented system, a measure of interactions between classes in an important concept. The term coupling has traditionally related to the strength of data coupling and the structural intermodule coupling between modules. Data coupling examines input and output variables entering or leaving a module, whereas structural intermodule coupling examines control coupling in subroutine calls or message passing.

Intermodule Metrics

Intermodule metrics are used to assess the complexity of a system design. Some recommendations for properties of system design complexity metrics include (from Tsai et al. 1986; Zuse 1990; as summarized by Sheetz et al. 1991):

1. A measure of both the structure of the data and of the process must be included.

2. The measures must demonstrate consistency (i.e., if a structure is contained within another structure, the containing structure is computed to be at least as complex as the contained structure).

3. The measures must be capable of representing at least a weak order (i.e., they must be at least on an ordinal scale).

4. Measures must be additive (i.e., if two independent structures are put into sequence, then the total complexity of the combined structures is simply the sum of the complexities of the independent structures).

5. It must be possible to automate the measures.

Structural intermodule coupling.   Structural coupling between modules has been used in the past as the fan-in-fan-out metric. This metric measures fan-in as the number of locations from which control is passed into a module plus the number of global data. Fan-out measures the number of other modules required plus the number of data structures updated by the module being measured. These couplings can be determined during system specification and used across the project life cycle.

Many measures incorporate fan-in and fan-out. Card and Glass (1990) propose:

$$\text{structural intermodule coupling} = \sum\nolimits^{n}(\text{fan-out})^2 / n$$

A family of information flow metrics (Henry and Kafura 1981):

1. fan-in * fan-out
2. $(\text{fan-in} * \text{fan-out})^2$
3. module size (in LOC) * $(\text{fan-in} * \text{fan-out})^2$

where LOC represents lines of source code being estimated.

Minimizing module complexity. A minimum complexity can be determined for a single module:

$$\text{Module complexity} = (\text{fan-in} * \text{fan-out})^2 + \frac{I_O}{(\text{fan-out} + 1)}$$

In many applications, low fan-out is preferable. (One recommendation might be to eliminate any unnecessary fan-out, and then minimize fan-out across encapsulation boundaries by maximizing it within encapsulation boundaries.)

Object applications. During design (and subsequent code evaluations on modules), intermodule coupling is measured by the number of relationships between classes or between subsystems. Connectivity between classes is usually a binary state for any pair of classes. This contrasts with implementation, where a single connection of the design may be expanded to show multiple message paths when several services of a class or object are used by the same client class or object.

Class coupling needs to be minimized by constructing autonomous modules. However, this conflicts with the aim of a weakly coupled system and close coupling exhibited by class/superclass relationships. Without any coupling, the system becomes useless. For any given implementation, there exists a baseline or required coupling level; we wish to eliminate extraneous coupling. Unnecessary coupling needlessly decreases the reusability of classes.

There are some who advocate increased use of polymorphism to reduce complexity (Sharble and Cohen 1993). It has been shown (by Tegarden et al. 1992) that use of either inheritance or polymorphism reduces the counts of standard metrics, but tight coupling of inheritance provides potential complexity not foreseen by traditional metrics. Subclasses can access a superclass's internal data and methods, violating hidden information. Complexity is also increased when hierarchies become deep and compounded when methods are overridden in subclasses.

During modeling, the number of association and aggregation relationships and the argument lists can be counted. Still, these will be poorly defined early in the modeling and design process. If two classes are coupled early in modeling, it is likely that later on this will expand to several connections, as well as the addition of message arguments not foreseen earlier.

We can measure the fan-in and fan-out of classes. Low fan-out is desirable, since a high fan-out results from a large number of classes needed by a particular class under study. However, high fan-ins can represent good object designs and a high level of reuse. It seems impractical to maintain a high fan-in and a low fan-out together across an entire system.

Module Metrics—Semantic Complexity

Semantic cohesion is a module-focused measure that is distinct from the internal module measures discussed earlier.

Object applications. According to Myers (1978), a module possessing good informational strength has multiple entry points, each of which perform as a single specific function, and all conceptually related, data-related and resource-related functions are hidden within the module.

This focus on an extended interface and information hiding is more a syntactic than semantic focus. Semantic cohesion remains a subjective measure, assessing whether an abstraction represented by a module (a class) can be treated as a whole. Booch (1991) describes cohesion as supporting the behavior of an external world concept and adds the criteria of sufficiency, completeness, and primitiveness. Sufficiency requires a class to capture sufficient characteristics to be identical and meaningful. Completeness requires a class to capture all meaningful characteristics. A primitive operation can be efficiently implemented only if given access to the underlying representation of the class.

Module Metrics—Procedural Complexity

Size and complexity metrics are the most common metrics, but generally they can only be obtained from program code; thus they are inappropriate for analysis and design.

Size metrics. The most common size metrics are:

- Lines of source code

- Tokens

- Function points

- Feature points

Lines of source code. *Lines of source code* (SLOC or LOC) is perhaps the oldest method of measuring software. This metric may be interpreted differently for different programming languages. A line of source code can be considered as any line of program text that is not a comment or blank line.

In spite of its limitations, lines of code remains one the major metric tools being used today. One feature lacking in the metric that limits its usefulness is the ability to account for complexity of a line of code. Inclusion of code from libraries and other projects in the metric also creates problems.

Tokens. *Tokens* represent the basic lexical unit from which a program is composed. Compilers use lexical analyzers in the first stage of compilation to convert high-level statements into tokens for further processing. Halstead (1977) proposed a new metric based on counts of program operators and operands:

n_1 = the number of unique operators

n_2 = the number of unique operands

N_1 = the total number of operators

N_2 = the total number of operands

The vocabulary of a program (n) is defined as the sum of operators and operands $(n = n_1 + n_2)$, and the length of a program (N) is equal to the sum of the total number of operators and operands $(N_1 + N_2)$. If each line of a machine language program consists of one operator and one operand, source lines of code can be defined as $N/2$.

Software Science defines program size (volume in bits) as:

$$V = N * \log_2 n$$

This estimate may be made before a program is written The approximate size of a program can be calculated from knowledge of distinct operators and operands likely to be in the program:

$$N = n * \log_2 n_1 + n_2 * \log_2 n_2$$

Software Science, a popular complexity metric, has been criticized for the many variations in counting and classifying operators and operands, because there is no consistent method to define the most meaningful way to classify and count operators and operands. Ambiguity in counting labels also exists. This metric can be difficult to apply to modern programming languages that support data abstraction, classes, hierarchies, and so on. This could be because Software Science formulae were developed for algorithms, not programs.

Function points. The *function point* approach represents a technology-independent way of estimating system size without using lines of code. This approach has been useful for estimating system size early in the development life cycle and is used to measure productivity trends from descriptions of user specifications and requirements. Function points supposedly can be easily understood and evaluated by nontechnical users.

When function points are used, system size is based on the total amount of information being processed, together with a complexity factor that influences the size of the end product. The metric is based on these weighted items:

- Number of external inputs
- Number of external outputs
- Number of external inquiries
- Number of internal master files
- Number of external interfaces

Weights assigned to each item vary with the characteristics of the system being developed. Weights on the number of inputs can vary from four to seven, based on the complexity of the system, which is divided into low, medium, and high. The initial count is summed to obtain unadjusted function points, which are modified using 14 factors. These factors include:

- Use of structured programming

- Use of high-level languages

- Use of on-line development

- Use of a software library

- Performance

- Ease of use

and so on.

The result of applying these factors is adjusted function points. Function point analysis may group problems into (a) problems in measuring unadjusted function point size, (b) problems with system adjustments, and (c) other general problems.

Feature points. *Feature points* complement the functionality of function points by characterizing internal complexity as a weighted algorithm count. This approach is helpful in systems containing a high degree of internal algorithmic complexity, and it allows the metric to be more widely applied.

Object-oriented applications. During detailed design, a good estimate of class size could be obtained using the number of attributes and the number of metrics. The count of classes in a system can provide a basic estimate of system size. The number of methods could be related to function points or to this modification of function points created by Henderson-Sellers (1991):

$$S = \sum_{i=1}^{n} (AW_A + MO_M)_i$$

where

A = number of attributes
W_A = low attribute weighting

M = number of methods
O_M = method weighting
N = number of object classes

Work is needed to evaluate appropriate weights for attributes and methods likely to be language dependent. Object-oriented programming strongly supports high external and internal modularization, so the variance of method lengths should be lower than that for a function point implementation in a traditional procedural language.

Object development supports reuse, the easiest kind being use of a library class. Another very common way to reuse classes is by subclassing. With subclassing, part (l) of the existing code is used and part ($1 - l$) is written for the new class. So if there are k classes reused as is, l classes partially reused, and m classes fully developed anew (N is the total number of classes = $k + l + m$):

$$S = \sum_{i = k+1+1}^{k+1} [(AW_A + MW_M)_i(1 - 1) + W_{Ri}]$$

where W_{Ri} is the weighting/cost of library reuse with regard to the cost of locating and obtaining a single library class, independent of the degree of reuse of that class.

Along with the measures equivalent to standard metrics, some measures are needed that are very specific to object-oriented development (from Jacobson et al. 1992):

- Width and height of inheritance hierarchies

- Number of classes inheriting a specific operation

- Number of collaborating classes

- A measure of the proportion of the system that measures the costs of reused code

Lorenz (1993) suggests measuring 11 items:

Metric	Item Being Measured
1. Average method size	Size
2. Average number of methods per class	Size
3. Average number of instance variables per class	Coupling
4. Class hierarchy nesting level	Size

Metric	Item Being Measured
5. Number of subsystem-subsystem relationships	Coupling
6. Number of class-class relationships within each subsystem	Cohesion and coupling
7. Instance variable usage	Semantic complexity
8. Average number of comment lines	Cognitive complexity
9. Number of problem reports per class	Process
10. Number of times a class is reused	Process
11. Number of classes and methods thrown away	Process

Chidamber and Kemerer (1991) recommend six items:

Metric	Item Being Measured
1. Weighted methods per class	Size and complexity
2. Depth of inheritance tree	Size
3. Number of children	Size/coupling/cohesion
4. Coupling between objects	Coupling
5. Response for class	Communication/complexity
6. Lack of cohesion in methods	Internal cohesion

Lorenz suggests a maximum method size for SmallTalk of eight SLOC and 24 LOC for C++. The average number of methods per class should not exceed 20 in general, but examine the semantic cohesion of a class. Weighted methods per class focuses on the class rather than on the system level, and weights used represent static complexity of methods not defined by Chidamber and Kemerer.

Inheritance structures may be evaluated in terms of depth and node density, measured by maximum depth, because depth affects node distribution. Another depth measure is the average inheritance depth, calculated as:

$$\frac{\Sigma \text{ Depth of class}}{\text{Number of classes}}$$

The average depth of inheritance indicates the general level of abstraction in a hierarchy. Chidamber and Kemerer introduce NOC as the number of children. Two similar measures for evaluating the level of reuse possible within hierarchies are introduced by Yap and Henderson-Sellers (1993). The reuse ratio, U, is defined as:

$$U = \frac{\text{Number of superclasses}}{\text{Total number of classes}}$$

This ratio indicates the degree to which class library implementers have inherited from their own classes. The specialization ratio, S, is defined as:

$$S = \frac{\text{Number of subclasses}}{\text{Number of superclasses}}$$

This ratio measures the degree to which a superclass models the abstraction; a large value indicates a high degree of reuse via subclassing.

Logic structure metrics. Perhaps the best known measure of module complexity is McCabe's cyclomatic complexity. The measure describes a connected graph, whose cyclomatic number, v, is calculated as:

$$v = e - n + 1$$

and for a graph with p components:

$$v = e - n + p$$

where

e = the number of edges
n = the number of nodes

A connected graph has all nodes reachable from every other node; a disconnected graph has p components that are disjoint but which could, with the addition of $(p - 1)$ additional edges, be converted into a connected graph. The cyclomatic complexity (cycle rank) is given for a single, strongly connected directed acyclic graph by:

$$V(G) = e - n + 2$$

Henderson-Sellers (1992) suggests using:

$$V_{LI}(G) = e - n + P + 1$$

where *LI* represents "linearly independent." This equation has these properties:

1. Modularization (before removal of repetitive code) has no effect on $V_{LI}(G)$.

2. The value of $V_{LI}(G)$ for the full program is equal to the total number of decisions, *D*, plus one:

$$V_{LI}(G) = \sum_{i=1}^{p} d_i + 1 = D + 1$$

3. The value of $V_{LI}(G)$ is unchanged when subroutines are merged back into the program either by nesting or sequence.

4. The value of $V_{LI}(G)$ provides a basis set for testing.

The third point above supports the argument that the testing procedures are unchanged by modularization.

Application of McCabe's metric to object-oriented systems has been limited. A class provides services to external clients. Each service must be implemented inside the class as an algorithm, represented as a directed acyclic graph. This graph may be self-contained or may reference other algorithms within the class. Any change in complexity of an external class should not alter the complexity of another class (except a subclass).

An average complexity measure could be expressed across all features of a class using an arithmetic average and standard deviation, or variance, that could then be used to highlight complex structures. This could be referred to as class method complexity and class method variance (see Henderson-Sellers and Edwards 1994, p. 497).

Other procedural complexity measures.   Data structure metrics (Conte et al. 1986) include:

- The number of variables

- Which variables are locally live

- What the span of each variable is

- Whether the variable is ever referenced

The number of variables can be easily obtained from compiler reports, but which variables are live and what the variable span is can be difficult to obtain. Still, the scope of variables can help one understand and maintain code. Also, the existence of non-referenced variables does not harm software operation, although it can mislead someone trying to modify and test the code.

Internal cohesion can be viewed as syntactic cohesion determined by examining the code of each module. It is closely related to the manner in which large programs are modularized. The components of a module should somehow fit together to provide a single function.

Chidamber and Kemerer (1991) have suggested a metric for evaluating the internal cohesion by considering the number of disjoint sets formed by the intersection of n sets created by taking all instance variables used by each of n methods. A high resulting value indicates that the methods in the class are not really related to each other or to a single overall abstraction. The class should probably be split into two or more classes.

Another measure of cohesion (Emerson 1984) is:

$$r_c = \frac{|M_i| dimM_i}{|VF - \{T\}| dimVF}$$

where VF is the set of nodes in a directed graph, F, containing a subset $\{M_i\}$, and T is the terminal vertex. The dimension of A equals $1 + V_G(A)$. The metric r_c provides the cohesion of this module to the average cohesion of the reference sets.

Fenton (1991) suggests a system measure of cohesion:

$$\text{cohesion ratio} = \frac{\text{number of modules having (functional) cohesion}}{\text{total number of modules}}$$

The word "functional" could be replaced with "abstract" for object-oriented systems.

Composite Metrics

We need to combine various module and intermodule metrics into the overall structural or document complexity. Some people try to create a single composite metric by adding components, sometimes without regard to the dimensional analysis considerations. Others argue that a single number cannot capture all aspects of full system complexity, so they suggest a vector notation (but without proper accommodation of orthogonality of components).

Myers (1977) suggested use of two versions of cyclomatic complexity, Hansen (1978) a cyclomatic number and operation count, Baker and Zweben (1980) Software Science E and $V(G)$, and Oviedo (1980) control flow complexity and data flow complexity. These metrics will not be discussed here.

Cognitive Complexity Model

A cognitive complexity model by Cant et al. (1992) provides an approach to complexity metrics by analyzing cognitive models for programmer comprehension of code and the code development process. This model is described as a "landscape model" encapsulated quantitatively by a set of equations. It is based on the idea of programmers "chunking" code into logical groupings. Effects of code chunking and tracing difficulty on complexity can be graphically depicted as "landscapes."

The difficulty of solving a programming inquiry focused on the ith chunk can be described as:

$$C_i = R_i + \Sigma_{j \in N} C_j + \Sigma_{j \in N} T_j$$

where R_i represents the difficulty of understanding the immediate (the ith) chunk, N the set of chunks on which the ith chunk is directly dependent, and T_j the difficulty of tracing a particular dependency. Functional dependencies of R and T are:

$$R = R(R_S, R_C, R_E, R_R, R_V, R_D, R_F)$$

and

$$T = T(T_L, T_A, T_S, T_C, T_F)$$

where

$$
\begin{aligned}
C_i &= \text{complexity if } i\text{th chunk} \\
N &= \text{set of chunks on which } i\text{th chunk depends} \\
R_i &= \text{difficulty of understanding } i\text{th chunk}
\end{aligned}
$$

R_C = difficulty of comprehending control structure
R_D = disruption effect from other dependencies
R_E = difficulty of comprehending Boolean expressions
R_F = difficulty contributed by familiarity
R_S = difficulty contributed by size
R_V = difficulty contributed by visual layout
T = difficulty of tracing
T_j = difficulty of tracing jth chunk
T_A = ambiguity of dependency
T_C = level of cueing in dependency
T_F = familiarity
T_L = localization effect on tracing
T_S = spatial dependency

Each of these measures should be quantified using standard measures (Conte et al. 1986).

Object-oriented systems reduce complexity via data encapsulation, limiting the complexity of backward tracing to resolve variable dependencies or forward tracing to follow ripple effects. Inheritance may have varying effects on complexity. An object-oriented program should have a shallower landscape (fewer levels of comprehension) than a traditional structured program. This is because much less tracing is required to determine how to use variables in particular roles and because of the high degree of location and encapsulation with objects.

Building a general variable plan for a class if often not enough. Occasionally, a programmer needs to trace the exact determinants of a variable or data structure referred to in an assignment statement or needs to trace the impact of an assignment on the remainder of the program. This requires following the execution flow of the program to determine which classes in the system influence values of a particular data structure.

Process Metrics

Cost estimation for software development involves these stages:

- Size estimation
- Cost calculation
- Schedule development

- Performance monitoring

Software sizing is perhaps the most difficult of these stages to deal with. Component size and complexity have been linked in terms of productivity at a given point in the development life cycle or integrated over the total life cycle:

Effort = fn(Productivity, Size)

There are numerous cost estimation models being used today. Most of these models estimate effort and schedule in terms of source lines of code expected in the target system. If we consider E as the effort in developer months and L as the estimated number of lines of code (in thousands), most cost estimation models would use an equation similar to this:

$$e = \alpha * L^{\beta}$$

where α and β are constants derived by regression analysis. A small error in estimating lines of code will likely result in a large error in estimated effort.

Once overall cost estimates are established, staff allocation is determined, along with the schedule. Optimum time to completion is given by Card and Glass (1990) as approximated by:

$$t* = 2.5E^{0.4}$$

where $t*$ is represented in months when E is in staff months.

Object-Oriented Application

It is initially very difficult to transfer a management and measurement strategy from a traditional systems development environment to an object-oriented one. Consider, for example, the evaluation of the regular mean effort/productivity metric in lines of code delivered per unit of effort. The mean productivity may be calculated as:

$$\text{Mean Productivity} = \frac{\text{Product Size}}{\text{Total Effort}}$$

This could be calculated at the end of a project, when the product is ready to be placed in production. In an object-oriented environment, on the other hand, it is likely that developers would continue to work on the product to generalize the component classes, actually reducing the lines of code. This results in fewer lines of code and more effort, bringing down the ratio of lines of code per unit of effort. One would think that object orientation brings with it enhanced productivity, but a short-term estimation of productivity such as mean productivity is not a useful metric for object projects. Generalization costs and a reuse strategy must be factored into any productivity measures for object projects.

Thomsett (1990) describes a way to fit an equation to a curve depicting effort for each phase of development such that it is more applicable to object technology. Unfortunately, there is no causal, quantifiable relationship underlying this curve. Rather, what is required is development of an entirely new model. Jacobson et al. (1992) suggest collection of the following process metrics for object-oriented projects:

- Total development time

- Development time in each process and subprocess

- Time spent modifying reused components

- Fault counts

- Quality assurance costs

and any other costs to introduce new technology. Lorenz (1993) suggests collecting data on:

- Time per application class

- Fault counts

- Extent and difficulty of reuse

Lorenz supports the counting numbers of classes and methods thrown away during the process as an indicator of increasing quality of object-oriented code as object technology is increasingly used. A detailed discussion of the object-oriented metrics of Lorenz and Kidd (1994) is included in "Project Metrics" and Design Metrics," later in this chapter.

Cost-Benefit Metrics

A cost-benefit analysis for object projects requires an additional return on investment metric of:

$$R = \frac{\text{Reuse Savings}}{\text{Generalization Costs}}$$

This measure should be calculated to assess the usefulness of object technology on a project, but no productivity enhancements will be realized if the generalization costs exceed long-term reuse benefits (as you can see from the ratio calculation). If this is the case, you cannot recommend object technology on the basis of reuse alone. Also, object project life cycle models include at least part of the acceptance (after system delivery) phase of the life cycle, whereas traditional metrics tend to include phases only through system delivery. Traditional metrics may thus be ignoring up to 70 percent of all software costs related to postacceptance phase activities (e.g., Meyer 1988). It is likely that development could take much longer with objects, since generalization and code reuse take extra effort (with savings later on, perhaps on other projects). Another difference between traditional and object-oriented development is that testing tends to be incorporated into object development approaches, not necessarily as a separate phase.

Any cost-benefit metrics for object projects need to allow for costs of code reuse, creating generalized classes for future use, and locating and managing stored library classes. New metrics are needed that are aimed at size and productivity for overall project estimates and dynamic allocation of personnel at various points during the development life cycle. The major difference is in code reuse to achieve equivalent functions and the additional effort on any project to achieve code reuse benefits on a future project.

Generalization and Reuse

If the cost of finding and understanding any class in a reuse library is F, then the cost of reusing k classes with no modification is:

$$C_R = \sum_{I=1}^{k} F = kF$$

The cost of reusing l classes with modification is:

$$C_M = \sum_{i=k+1}^{k+1} [s_i(1-1)_i + F]$$

where F is the fixed cost of finding a class, modified or not. The total cost may be estimated as:

$$C = C_R + C_M + C_D$$

The cost of the project without reuse would be S, and the reuse savings for a project with no generalization costs are $S - C$.

To calculate net savings and return on investment completely, generalization costs need to be evaluated. If a project of size N produces P reusable classes ($P \leq N$), which requires extra costs of generalization of g, the cost with generalization becomes:

$$CG = \sum_{I=1}^{p} g_i$$

The cost of generalization, g, depends upon the class size, s_i. We can then express return on investment as:

$$R = \frac{S - (C + C_g)}{C_G} = \frac{S - C}{C_G} - 1$$

Reuse is beneficial if the reuse savings ($S - C$) exceed the generalization costs (C_G). This discussion of cost estimation has focused on project costs. To get a better picture of costs over time, you should consider averaging the return on investment over several projects.

Simulation of ROI over Multiple Projects

Henderson-Sellers and Edwards (1994) present a simple illustration of return on investment estimation over a number of projects. In their model, it is necessary to assume values for k, l, m, and P as well as an initial value for the size of the library. Consider for simplicity a set of Q projects, each of which contains 100 classes. A fraction, say 50 percent, of these classes is available as library classes (assume that $l = 0$). Also assume that in each project a fraction (10 percent) of the new classes can be generalized and added to the library. If there is no disparity between classes, the total cost is:

$$C = kF + (100 - k)s + gP$$

Reuse savings are:

$$100s - kF + (100 - k)s + gP$$

Project return on investment is:

$$\frac{100s - (kF + (100 - k)s + gP)}{gP}$$

In the simulation, project costs fall as savings increase. The rate of return on successive projects is positive for all projects if there are no library classes available initially; the return on investment becomes greater than zero for the third project. In a reuse environment, a project gets a head start over nonobject environments. The savings from reuse may not start until the second or third project.

You could run a similar simulation, changing the values to be more pessimistic in the costs for reuse where fewer classes are available in the class library. This would move the break-even point out so that more projects are required in order to profit from reuse. In real-life projects, Humphrys (1991) found that the initial investment was recovered after three projects, and that each subsequent project experienced a 50 percent savings.

Object-Specific Metrics

Project Metrics

Application size metrics.

Number of scenario steps. Number of scenario scripts indicates the size of an application to be developed. Script steps must relate to the public responsibilities of subsystems and classes to be developed and to the number of test cases to be written.

Number of key classes. Key classes are fundamental to a business domain. They are usually discovered early in analysis, providing an indication of the amount of total work on a project. Key classes form a foundation for reuse on future projects.

The number of key classes counts classes determined to be central to a business model. This count indicates the volume of work needed to develop an application, as well as an indicator of the amount of long-term reusable objects to be developed as part of an application.

Number of support classes. A support class is not central to a business model but provides functions that support key classes, which are central to a business model. Support classes provide help in estimating the size of development effort.

The number of support classes indicates the volume of work needed in order to develop an application. These classes are usually discovered later in development than key classes.

Average number of support classes per key class. This metric is used to find useful correlations between key and support classes in order to better estimate early in a project.

The average number of support classes per key class indicates the total volume of classes for a project. It can be used to estimate the total number of classes for a project based on results from a previous project.

Number of subsystems. For our purposes, a subsystem is a collection of classes that supports a set of business functions. Partitioning a system into relatively independent subsystems assists in dividing development work among separate teams. The size of subsystems may vary greatly and is not usually identified until after analysis work is done.

The number of subsystems affects scheduling, each being developed as a black box. A system's architecture can be controlled by using interfaces between subsystems. Subsystems are abstractions that assist developers to understand a large, complex system.

Staffing size metrics.

Average person-days per class. Once you have an estimate of the number of classes for a project, a good indicator of work required on the project is the amount of effort spent on a single class.

Scheduling, staffing, and funding a project requires (at a minimum) an estimate of the amount of effort required to complete the project. Average person-days per class predicts development effort based on estimated numbers of key and support classes.

Average number of classes per developer.   Average number of classes per developer uses the numbers of key and support classes to estimate the staffing required for a project.

Scheduling metrics

Number of major iterations.   For large projects, iterative development is almost required due to the size and complexity. Iterations allow for early validation of results and making quick adjustments.

Number of contracts completed.   Completion of major public system and class interfaces is a good indicator of project completion. Contracts between classes comprise the public protocols of a system, providing a good way to measure progress in system function delivery.

Design Metrics

Method size metrics.

Number of message sends.   Number of message sends indicates the number of messages sent from a method, grouped by message type:

* Unary
* Binary
* Keyword

This metric measures the size of a method, relatively independently of coding style and other variations among methods.

Number of statements.   This metric depends heavily on the language used to construct a program. For SmallTalk, you can use an expression series, as defined by the SmallTalk Backus-Naur Format, as a statement for this metric. A statement in C++ is the same as a statement for this metric.

The number of statements metric measures method code size in a fairly unbiased way (for a given programming language).

Lines of code. The lines of code metric measures physical lines of active code in a method. It measures the size of a method without accounting for coding style.

Average method size. Methods should be small, but by examining methods across a system, you can determine to a degree the system's design quality. The average method size is one indicator of design quality, with large numbers indicating a more nonobject code structure. A growing average method size indicates that a design could probably be improved. Large individual methods are not as much of a concern as is a large average method size.

Method internals metrics.

Method complexity. Much work has been done in the area of code complexity (as discussed earlier). The bulk of this work emphasizes factors such as the number of decision points in a function. Basic differences in object code make these measurements less useful: Object methods tend to be short, use few CASE statements, and use fewer IF statements.

Object designs (the good ones) lessen the usefulness of historical measures of program complexity. What is needed is a complexity metric that examines the number and types of message sends in a method as a basic measure of complexity.

Strings of message sends. Stringing messages together can decrease the amount of intelligent error handling that can be performed, because the results of each individual message cannot easily be tested in a calling method. Well-designed systems can usually do a good job of detecting and handling errors. The strings of message sends metric examines lengths of strings of message sends.

Class size metrics.

Number of public instance methods in a class. Public methods are available to other classes and provide a good way to judge the amount of work performed by a class. The number of public instance methods in a class measures the amount of responsibility for a class, with public methods consisting of the contracts tested during verification.

Number of instance methods in a class. The total number of instance methods in a class measures all methods defined for instances of a class. This metric relates to the amount of collaboration existing for a class. Larger classes might do too much work themselves instead of delegating some portion of the work to other supporting classes. Large classes are more difficult to construct and maintain and thus are less reusable than smaller classes that are more cohesive.

Average number of instance methods per class. A very high number of methods in one class could indicate that too much responsibility is being placed in one object type. This metric examines the public methods that relate to the amount of work a class must perform. Private methods simply support the public methods.

The number of instance methods in a class should relate strongly to the amount of responsibility in a class. Good object designs tend to distribute class responsibilities among many cooperating objects.

Number of instance variables in a class. The number of instance variables in a class is a measure of class size. A class with a lot of instance variables tends to have more relationships to other objects.

Average number of instance variables in a class. The average number of instance variables per class, when measured across a project, provides an indication of class size. The existence of more instance variables indicates that classes may be doing more work than they should; classes may have too many relationships to other objects.

Number of class methods in a class. The number of methods available to a class (and not its instances) affects class size. Usually, the number of class methods should be small compared with the number of instance methods. This metric can indicate the degree of generality being handled for all instances of a class and can indicate poor design if services handled by the class should be handled by instances instead. This may be occurring if there is a large amount of condition logic based on data values.

Number of class variables in a class. Class variables, being localized global variables, provide objects to all instances of a class. Usually, we expect to find a fairly low number of class variables, compared to the number of instance variables. The average number of class variables should be low; there generally should be fewer class variables than instance variables.

Class inheritance metrics.

Class hierarchy nesting level.
The further down from the root of a hierarchy a class is, the greater is its nesting level. The deeper a class is in an inheritance hierarchy, the more public and protected methods there are available to the class and thus more chances for method overrides or extensions. This makes testing deeply nested classes difficult.

Large numbers for class hierarchy nesting level indicate a design problem. This often results in subclasses that are not really specializations of the superclasses. A subclass (as with a subtype) should extend the functionality of superclasses (as with a supertype) so that the subclass is really a "kind of" the subclass. Avoid inheriting simply to reuse functionality in superclasses—keep the inheritance meaningful.

Number of abstract classes.
A superclass does not need to be abstract, but in practice some abstract classes exist in successful systems. The number of abstract classes indicates the successful use of inheritance and the degree of discovery of general concepts during problem domain analysis. Although a large number of abstract classes may make models more difficult to read (due to deeper hierarchies), they do make generality explicit. This means that abstract classes can make a class hierarchy more understandable and usable across many projects.

Use of multiple inheritance.
When a programming language allows for multiple inheritance, some complications may occur from use of this feature. Name collisions must be resolved when inheriting from multiple superclasses, and understanding a class fully requires tracing up through two or more inheritance levels. Thus system maintenance will likely be greater with extensive use of multiple inheritance.

Some experts preach that multiple inheritance is simply not necessary; there are many ways to model a problem domain. If your systems do incorporate multiple inheritance, use it sparingly and deliberately. Use this metric to identify possible problem areas where multiple inheritance may not be needed at all.

Method inheritance metrics.

Number of methods overridden by a class.
A subclass may redefine a method in one of its superclasses, but a large number of overridden methods may indicate design problems. A subclass should be a specialization of its superclasses, extending inherited services when needed.

These extended services should use unique names. A large number of overridden methods indicate use of subclasses for ease of programming when a new subclass is not a specialized type of the superclasses.

Number of methods inherited by a subclass. Subclasses inherit behavior via methods and states via instance variables. The number of methods inherited indicates the strength of inheritance by specialization. Generally, most methods should be inherited from superclasses.

Number of methods added by a subclass. Normally, the methods introduced in a subclass should be new ones, not overridden ones. Subclasses should define new methods that extend the behavior of superclasses. If a class has no methods added at all, we should question why it is a separate class. The number of new methods should usually decrease as the nesting level of a class increases.

Specialization index. Specialization via subclasses can be accomplished in several ways:

- Adding new methods

- Adding behavior to existing methods, invoking the superclass method

- Overriding methods with totally new behavior

- Deleting methods by overriding with no behavior

Specialization extends the capabilities of superclasses and is the most desirable form of inheritance, resulting in:

- Low numbers of method overrides

- Decreasing numbers of added methods

- Few or no deleted methods

Implementation inheritance involves use of some portion of the behavior or state data of one or more superclasses simply for programming convenience. The subclass is not of the same object type as the superclasses. This kind of inheritance makes systems less adaptable to change and difficult to understand.

Class internals metrics.

Class cohesion. Message connections within a class, and the use of instance variables, are a kind of cohesion. Thus we can measure the amount of cohesion within a class to evaluate its design qualities. In object systems, we allocate behavior to objects using human intervention. To fund measurements that can be mechanized, we need other metrics for cohesion. The interrelationships among the methods of a class and patterns of variable usage by methods relate to the cohesion of the class.

Global variable usage. Global variables can be considered as system global variables, class variables, or pool dictionaries. Generally, global variable usage should be minimized. Extensive use of global variables indicates poor object design.

Average number of parameters per method. Use of parameter passing versus instance variable usage may have to do with how object relationships are maintained (perhaps via pointers). Other times, it may be due to how much client code responsibility is expected for some functions. Parameters require more effort on the part of clients.

Use of friend functions. In languages such as C++, you can write code that violates class encapsulation. The friend function of C++ allows you to do this and may be required in rare cases. You should justify each and every use of the friend function (or its equivalent).

Percentage of function-oriented code. Languages such as C++ allow you to write some program code outside of any class. Nonobject code should in and of itself raise questions of design quality; it may indicate a trend toward nonobject coding in general.

Average number of comment lines per method. Generally, methods in a class should have at least one comment line. Looking at method comment percentages can help indicate whether enough comments are being written to explain the workings of the methods. Be sure not to include in this metric any system-generated comment lines, except those that were entered by a developer in a design model used to generate the program code.

Average number of commented methods. This metric examines the degree of overall comment documentation in methods, including any comments at all. On average, methods should have at least one comment line. Do not include system-generated comment lines, except those that were entered by a developer in a design model used to generate the program code.

Number of problem reports per class or contract. Classes with a lot of problem reports should be carefully examined for additional unplanned requirements or poor design. Use of the number of problem reports per class or contract metric can allow designers to more easily focus on areas of a system that require rework.

Class externals metrics.

Class coupling. Message connections between classes should be examined as a measure of class coupling. You can use the number of other classes collaborated with and the amount of collaboration with other classes.

We should strive to leverage other class services but use them at the correct level; we should know about only a limited number of objects and their services at any given point in a system. It is often much better to delegate responsibilities so that objects are accessed directly for their services rather than indirectly through other objects. If an object needs to interact with a lot of indirectly related objects, a complicated web of interdependencies results, along with increased maintenance effort.

Number of times a class is reused. Software components may be reused in a variety of ways. White box reuse involves examination of the internals of a candidate reuse component. Black box reuse involves examination only of the defined public interface of a candidate reuse component.

The number of times a class is reused refers to the number of applications using a class. Proper planning for future use of a class during its development helps one develop more reusable classes and frameworks the first time. This metric helps measure actual reuse once a component is available for incorporation into multiple applications.

Number of classes/methods thrown away. Iterative design necessarily involves some throwing away of developed system components, but as someone once said, we throw away a system at least once. Hopefully, this throwaway is during early stages of development, not during system maintenance.

This metric has value in detecting whether or not a development team is moving fast enough. If nothing is being thrown away, then the team may be stuck with "analysis paralysis." Developers cannot get all designs perfected on the first try, no matter how good they are at design work. Iteration involves learning about the problem domain and technology. This learning helps developers "build it better the next time" while still constructing a system.

SOMA Metrics

Ian Graham (1995) has suggested metrics for both the Business Object Model and the Task Object Model. These metrics are based on MOSES (Henderson-Sellers and Edwards 1994), the work of Chidamber and Kemerer (1991), and the original contribution of SOMA itself. Graham argues that weighted methods per class are not quite sufficient to capture the complexity of an object, since they do not allow for complexity due to rulesets. SOMA metrics allow for this but do not measure the effect of assertions where they are used (true, some assertions stand for rules and should be counted). Graham proposes metrics that should be collected by all object-oriented projects.

For the Business Object Model, the metrics are:

$BM1$ The weighted complexity, WC_C, of each class C, defined as:

$$WC_C = W_A * A + W_M * L_M * M + W_R * N_R * R$$

where

A = the number of attributes
M = the number of operations/methods
R = the number of rulesets
N_R = the number of rules per ruleset * the average number of antecedent clauses per rule
L_M = the proportional excess of SLOCs per method over an agreed, language-dependent standard (say, 17 lines)

$BM2$ The fan-outs and fan-ins for all structures together with their averages

*BM*3 The structure depths for the two acyclic structures: Dclass and Dcomp. This generalizes DIT.

*BM*4 The numbers of abstract and concrete classes

*BM*5 The numbers of interface, domain, and application objects incorporated into a project

For the Task Object Model, the metrics are:

*TM*1 The number of external objects in the context model

*TM*2 The weighted complexity, WC_T, of each task T, defined as:

$$WC_T = W_I * I + W_E * E + W_R * N_R * R$$

where

I = the number of indirect objects per task
E = the number of exceptions
R = the number of rulesets
N_R = the number of rules per ruleset * the average number of antecedent clauses per rule

W_E and W_R are empirically discovered weights, which may be zero if empirical study shows that a factor such as I has no effect.

*TM*3 The fan-outs and fan-ins for all structures in the task object model together with their averages

*TM*4 The structure depths for the two acyclic structures: Dsub and Dcomp. This generalizes DIT.

*TM*5 The number of atomic tasks (those with no component tasks) and the leaf nodes of the task tree (task points)

The last metric is unique to SOMA, offering a potential replacement for function points as a measure of overall complexity. It has the added benefit of automated collection and can be collected earlier in the development life cycle (at requirements capture). It requires skill and consistency on the part of developers to identify when the atomic task level is reached.

Graham goes on to propose that once sufficient data have been collected, effort estimation will be based on this model:

$$E = a + pT^K$$

where

E is effort in person-hours
T is the task point count
p is the inverse of productivity in task points per person-hour
k and a are constants (a the start-up and constant overhead costs)

Productivity itself is a function of the level of reuse and can depend on the ratio of domain to application objects in the Business Object Model and on the complexity of the Business Object Model on weighted class complexity, fan measures, and so on. Work still needs to be done on this, and, theoretically, function points can be computed directly from task points using these two estimating functions.

References

Baker, A. L., and S. H. Zweben. "A Comparison of Measures of Control Flow Complexity." *IEEE Transactions on Software Engineering* SE-6(6) (1980): 506–512.

Booch, G. *Object-Oriented Design with Applications*. Menlo Park, CA: Benjamin/Cummings, 1991.

Cant, S. N., D. R. Jeffrey, and B. Henderson-Sellers. "A Conceptual Model of Cognitive Complexity of Elements of the Programming Process." *CITR Report No. 57*. Australia: University of New South Wales, 1992.

Card, D. N., and R. L. Glass. *Measuring Software Design Quality*. Englewood Cliffs, NJ: Prentice Hall, 1990.

Chidamber, S., and C. Kemerer. "Towards a Metric Suite for Object-Oriented Design." In *Proceedings of OOPSLA '91, Sigplan Notices* 26(11) (1991): 197–211.

Conte, S. D., H. E. Dunsmore, and V. Y. Shen. *Software Engineering Metrics and Models*. Menlo Park, CA: Benjamin/Cummings, 1986.

Emerson, T. J. "A Discriminant Metric for Module Cohesion." In *International Conference on Software Engineering* (1984): 294–303.

Fenton, N. E. *Software Metrics: A Rigorous Approach*. London: Chapman and Hall, 1991.

Graham, I. *Migrating to Object Technology*. Wokingham, England: Addison-Wesley, 1994.

Halstead, M. H. *Elements of Software Science*. Amsterdam: Elsevier Scientific Publishing, 1977.

Hansen, W. J. "Measurement of Program Complexity by the Pair (Cyclomatic Number, Operator Count)." *ACM SIGPLAN Notices* (April 1978): 29–33.

Henderson-Sellers, B. "Modularization and McCabe's Cyclomatic Complexity." *Communications of the ACM: Technical Correspondence* 35(12) (1992): 17–19.

— — —. "Some Metrics for Object-Oriented Software Engineering." In *Technology of Object-Oriented Languages and Systems: TOOLS6*, edited by B. Meyer, J. Potter, and M. Tokoro. Sydney, Australia: Prentice Hall, 1991, 131–139.

Henderson-Sellers, B., and J. Edwards. *Book Two of Object-Oriented Knowledge: The Working Object*. Sydney, Australia: Prentice Hall, 1994.

Henry, S., and D. Kafura. "Software Structure Metrics Based on Information Flow," in *IEEE Transactions on Software Engineering*, 1981, 7(5), 510–518.

Humphrys, M. "The Object Evidence: A Real-Life Comparison of Procedural and Object-Oriented Programming." In *IISL Innovative Solutions Project*. Ireland: IBM Ireland Information Services Ltd (IISL), 1994.

Jacobson, I., M. Christerson, P. Johnsson, and G. Overgaard. *Object-Oriented Software Engineering: A Use Case Driven Approach*. Reading, MA: Addison-Wesley, 1992.

Lorenz, M. *Object-Oriented Systems Development: A Practical Guide*. Englewood Cliffs, NJ: Prentice Hall, 1993.

Lorenz, M., and J. Kidd. *Object-Oriented Software Metrics*. Englewood Cliffs, NJ: Prentice Hall, 1994.

McCabe, T. J. "A Complexity Measure," in *IEEE Transactions on Software Engineering*, vol. 2 (1976) 308–20.

Meyer, B. *Object-Oriented Software Construction*. Hemel Hempstead, England: Prentice Hall, 1988.

Myers, G. J. *Composite Structured Design*. Wokingham, England: Van Nostrand Reinhold, 1978.

— — —. "An Extension to the Cyclomatic Measure of Program Complexity." *SIGPLAN Notices* (October 1977): 61–64.

Oviedo, E. I. "Control Flow, Data Flow, and Program Complexity." In *Proceedings of COMPSAC 80* (1980): 146–152.

Sharble, R. C., and S. S. Cohen. "The Object-Oriented Brewery: A Comparison of Two Object-Oriented Development Methods." *ACM SIGSOFT Software Engineering Notes* 18(2) (1993): 60–73.

Sheetz, S. D., D. P. Teegarden, and D. E. Monarchi. "Measuring Object-Oriented System Complexity." In *Proceedings of the First Workshop on Information Technologies and Systems*. Cambridge, MA: MIT Sloan School of Management, December 1991.

Tegarden, D. P., S. D. Sheetz, and D. E. Monarchi. "A Software Complexity Model of Object-Oriented Systems." *Decision Support Systems* (1992).

Thomsett, R. "Management Implications of Object-Oriented Development." *ACS Newsletter* (October 5–7, 1990): 10–12.

Tsai, W. T., M. A. Lopez, V. Rodriguez, and D. Volovik. "An Approach Measuring Data Structure Complexity." In *COMPSAC 86* (1986): 240–246.

Yap, L-M., and B. Henderson-Sellers. "A Semantic Model for Inheritance in Object-Oriented Systems." In *Proceedings of ASWEC93*. Sydney, Australia: IREE, 1993, 28–35.

Zuse, H. *Software Complexity: Measures and Methods*. Berlin: Walter de Gruyter, 1990.

Formal Specification

Why Mathematics Is Useful for Specifying Systems

Current object-oriented development techniques, such as those discussed in this book, have been used successfully to develop a wide variety of object-oriented systems. The benefits include the ability to capture requirements in a more intuitive manner, facilitating communication of system descriptions to people not skilled in either software development or mathematics. Also, the use of separate but related models (e.g., structure, behavior, and function models) provides a way to ensure internal consistency and completeness checking.

Unfortunately, these object notations are based primarily on diagrams or natural language, so they cannot capture semantic details with the same precision as formal specification languages can. This imprecision implies that ambiguities in the meanings of certain notational constructs exist when interpreting diagrams—for instance, various object modeling notations depict events as either queued or ignored in state-transition diagrams (state charts) if they occur in a state for which there is no corresponding transition.

For critical systems (systems for which there is a possibility of loss of human life or severe environmental or economic damage), standards increasingly require a way of verifying development steps, such as for formally proving that a portion of constructed software meets its specification. This kind of proof may only be performed if the specification is provided in a mathematics-based language.

Generally, critical systems developed using formal specifications have been successful, with some evidence that use of formal techniques can result in lower costs than many other development approaches for these systems. This reduction in costs occurs because redevelopment and rework costs are reduced in spite of the increased analysis and specification costs. Some tools for formal methods support animation of specifications, allowing performance of testing and validation earlier in development.

For development of object-oriented software, some additional benefits may be obtained:

- To demonstrate that a class D is truly a subtype of a class C (instances of D may always be used as if they were instances of C), we need a precise definition of subtyping and a language in which to establish subtyping relations.

- Mathematical descriptions of classes at the boundary of a system, or that are reused from a library, provide a concise, abstract, yet complete description of services provided by each class and the meaning of their features.

- The need to implement requirements may be separated into a precise definition of what is required, independent of the way they are implemented, and defining how these formal requirements may be implemented in software.

- The precise semantics of diagramming notations may be defined.

Formal Methods for Software Development

The decision of whether to introduce formal methods into the software development process, and how this is to be done, depends on how software development is currently performed in an organization. If current practice does not meet requirements, formal methods might help, but if software development is not already systematic and disciplined, then introduction of formal techniques will not likely help but rather might make things worse.

An approach to formal methods that has seemed to work well is the introduction of structured diagrammatic methods with formal specification methods. This approach leverages existing software development expertise rather than replacing it. The various ways that these two disciplines have been integrated range from a highly focused use of formal techniques to verify a security-critical or safety-critical system kernel to extensive combination at several stages of system development.

Kevin Lano (1995) has developed a "degree of formality" scale that includes the rigor of the correspondence between formal and diagrammatic notations (whether a precise translation may be conducted or whether the mapping is intuitive). Lano discusses work in the security field, where a dual-team approach has been used to support formal specification and proof of security-critical parts of an application within an overall design using structured methods. He then mentions that the Fusion and SAZ methods aim to support the combined use of formal specifications and diagrammatic notations at several life cycle stages. Yourdon's structured techniques were used at Rolls Royce and Associates to give an architectural specification of a system, and the VDM formal notation was used to specify the semantics of operations. This is also the approach used with the Syntropy methods, wherein formal notation can be added to the data model or used in place of it and can be used to define preconditions and postconditions on state charts to describe the effects of events. Finally, the methods described in Lano's book could be used for an integration approach called OOFM (Object-Oriented Formal Methods).

A formal specification is a very precise description of the possible effects of a software component. A list of the requirements of a specification technique should include:

- It must be possible to construct specifications with reasonable effort.

- It must be possible, with some training, to read and understand specifications.

- A specification must be minimal.

- A specification technique should allow the capture of the correct type of information in a natural way.

TABLE 11.1   Ways That Formal Methods Support System Assessment

Consistency	There should be no contradictions within the specifications; consistency may be ensured by mathematical proof that the initial facts can be formally mapped into later statements within a specification.
Completeness	The goal is to ensure that all aspects of a proposed system are described, but this is difficult to achieve, even with formal methods.
Correctness	This may be achieved if there is a complete mapping between analysis and design.
Precision	There should be no ambiguity within any specifications.

Table 11.1 lists ways that a formal method should provide as a means to specify a system so that consistency, completeness, and correctness may be assessed systematically.

The properties required for an effective specification include:

- Expressiveness

- Semantic soundness

- Programming language independence

- Machine manipulation ability

- Combinability

The main components of a specification language include those listed in Table 11.2.

TABLE 11.2   Specification Language—Main Components

Syntax	Defines the specific notation with which to represent a specification, possibly based on set theory and predicated calculus
Semantics	Defines how representations describe system requirements; must be able to express noncomputable concepts and system behavior
Relations	Defines rules for indicating which objects correctly satisfy a specification

TABLE 11.3   Characteristics of Languages Used to Specify System Requirements

Language	Expressiveness	Semantic Soundness	Independence	Manipulation Ability	Combinability
Natural Language	Very capable of representing types of components	Vague	Yes	No	No theory exists to support combination of text fragments
Programming Language	Can only represent computable functions, but good for describing algorithms	Yes	No	Yes	Yes
Formal Grammar	Not very expressive	Yes	Yes	Somewhat	Yes
Logical Formalisms	Can be used to represent many different types of behavior, but not good at describing algorithms	Yes	Yes	Good	Yes

Table 11.3 lists characteristics of languages used to specify system requirements.

Table 11.4 summarizes the types of specification techniques.

TABLE 11.4   Types of Specification Techniques

Informal	Expressed in Natural Language or Pictures
Specification by Preconditions and Postconditions	Establish what should hold before and after execution of a procedure, which transforms preconditions into postconditions
Model Oriented	Provide a direct means to describe a system's behavior in terms of mathematical structures (VDM and Z)
Property Oriented	Use indirect means to specify behavior by stating the properties (the constraints) that the system must satisfy (Eiffel, OBJ, and AFFIRM)

Some arguments against the use of formal methods in software development include:

- Formal methods are difficult
- Only highly critical systems benefit from formal methods
- Formal methods involve complex mathematics
- Formal methods increase development costs
- Formal methods are incomprehensible to clients
- No one uses formal methods for real projects

Types of Formal Specification Languages

Model Oriented

These specification languages construct a mathematical model of a system. A model-oriented language describes the state of the system, together with a number of operations (transitions) over that state. An operation is a function that maps a value of the state, together with values of parameters to the operation, onto a new state value. A model-oriented language is used to describe specific mathematical objects (such as functions or data structures) that are structurally similar to the required software. These mathematical objects are then transformed during analysis and design. Examples of model-oriented languages include VDM-SL and Z.

Algebraic

Algebraic specification languages specify information systems using methods derived from abstract algebra or category theory. Abstract algebra studies certain kinds or aspects of structure abstracted from other features of objects being studied. Algebraic methods are helpful in describing information systems without prejudicing questions that will be answered later on in development. The OBJ language is a well-known algebraic specification language.

Process Model

Specification languages used to describe concurrent systems are sometimes based on a specific model for concurrency. Within these languages, expressions represent processes and are constructed from elementary expressions that describe simple processes by operations that combine processes to yield new, potentially more complex processes. CSP and CCS are examples of process modeling languages.

Logic Oriented

Logic-oriented specification languages are closest to logical languages. Some people advocate that a formal logic be used for specification in a fairly unrestrained, axiomatic manner. Others advocate that specifications be constructed using only conservative extensions of a sufficiently rich mathematical basis. With the former approach, weaker constraints on the means of specifications result in a logical system that does not fully provide a foundation for mathematics. With the latter approach, the kind of logical system adopted as baseline needs to amount to a logical foundation for mathematics.

First-order logic is a traditional example of the first kind of logic specification. First-order set theory has also been adapted for the second approach, but usually some kind of logical typed set theory (such as HOL) has been used. The Z specification language is a typed set theory that could be used as a foundational specification language, but no rules have been defined to permit specification by conservative extension.

Constructive

The field of constructive mathematics is concerned with realizability. Classical mathematics supports the idea of functions in a very broad sense, including many functions that could never be evaluated by a computer. Constructive mathematics is concerned only with functions that are effectively computable.

Constructive logic demonstrates the existence of functions satisfying some property but in a restricted number of ways. This means that, from any proof of a specification's consistency, a value satisfying the specification may be extracted. In principle, then, the post hoc verification paradigm of specify, implement, and verify may be modified when using a constructive logic to specify, verify consistency, and extract implementation, with the last stage being automatic. Proof tools for constructive logics such as the NUPRL system have demonstrated this capability.

Cross-Life Cycle

A cross-life cycle specification language is suitable for use at all stages in information system development, from concept through requirements specification, design, implementation, and verification. Included here are languages that are hybrids. Examples of hybrid notations include RSL, the specification language associated with the RAISE development methods, and LOTOS, a specification notation originally intended for specification of communication protocols. RAISE synthesizes model oriented, process model, and algebraic methods; LOTOS combines process model and algebraic paradigms.

Formal Methods and Object Orientation

Formal techniques have not been combined with object-oriented techniques until fairly recently. There are two main parts of this practice:

1. Use of object-oriented structuring to enhance formal notations and methods

2. Use of formal methods to analyze the semantics of object-oriented notations or to enhance these notations

Object Technology Applied to Formal Methods

The Z and VDM formal specification languages are limited when used to specify large systems in a modular manner. Several researchers and practitioners have worked to extend these languages to support object concepts, because the objects seemed to complement model-based specification languages (Goldsack and Kent 1996):

- Object orientation encourages creation of abstractions, and formal techniques provide the means to precisely describe such abstractions.

- Object orientation provides the structuring mechanisms and development disciplines needed to scale up formal techniques to large systems.

- Formal techniques allow a precise meaning to be given to complex object-oriented mechanisms such as aggregation or state charts.

The Z language was extended by Carrington and others with object concepts to form Object-Z, which featured key aspects of object-oriented structuring:

- Encapsulation of data and operations on that data into named modules, which also define types

- The possibility of creating subclasses of classes via inheritance and the ability to use operations polymorphically between a subclass and its superclasses containing a particular operation

- The ability to use instances of a class within another class (the concept of class composition)

Other object extensions of Z include Z++, MooZ, OOZE, and ZEST. OOZE is the only one of these languages that is based on algebraic specification approach (using OBJ and FOOPS as its foundation but with a Z-like syntax). The Fresco language was developed to provide formal specification and verification for SmallTalk development.

Formal Methods Applied to Object Technology

Experts in both formal methods and object technology have examined how formal methods can be used to augment object-oriented development or to help clarify the semantics of object notations and concepts. Examples of these efforts include:

- Formalization of the Object Management Group's core object model using the Z specification

- The Fusion method

- The Syntropy method

Methods integration has demonstrated definite advantages in minimizing disruption to existing software development practices. Two main approaches to methods integration have been used:

1. Use of mathematical notation to enhance diagramming notation, with development conducted primarily using diagrams

2. Use of a transition from diagram-based analysis methods into formal notations, with development conducted primarily using formal notations

Diagramming notations do not support proof or verification, so the first approach is rigorous but not fully formal. Examples of this use of formal methods include the Fusion and Syntropy methods. The second approach is more appropriate for highly critical systems. Examples of this approach include using B AMN or LOTOS as formal languages.

Fusion. This modeling method was begun by Coleman, Dolling, and others working at Hewlett-Packard. It provides semiformal notations (in structured English) for operation preconditions, postconditions, and invariants using the OMT object notation and Booch object interaction diagrams, as well as other notations. It uses basic concepts of formal specification without mathematical notation:

• Abstraction

• Refinement by model exclusion

• Operation specification using preconditions and postconditions

Fusion provides techniques for specifying required operations at a system level without forcing development to prematurely place operations as methods in classes.

Syntropy. A similar object modeling method, Syntropy, combines state charts and object model notations of OMT with object interaction diagrams, allowing use of Z notations on these diagrams for specifying preconditions and postconditions, invariants, and constraints. This method emphasizes events for modeling system requirements rather than message passing. Synchronization between objects may be implemented by a method call. Unlike Fusion, Syntropy covers concurrency modeling.

Z++

The Z++ language was originally used to describe abstracted specifications of legacy systems for the purpose of reengineering. It has since been extended to include object reference semantics and real-time logic. Systematic translations of OMT diagrams into Z++ have been defined. This language has been applied to a variety of systems, from artificial intelligence and reverse-engineering to reactive systems.

VDM++

VDM++ is an object-oriented extension of the VDM-SL language, an ISO standard. It extends VDM by class declarations and types and replaces VDM operation definitions by specification statements or hybrid method definitions involving method invocations, procedural code constructs, and specification statements. It adds mechanisms for definition of dynamic and concurrent behavior, including real-time properties.

Formalizing Diagramming Methods

Two procedures have been used to integrate diagrams and formal methods (Lano 1995):

1. Covert formality—a mathematical notation and an explicitly formal specification language may be avoided, but with mathematical semantics being provided for structured English or diagram specification forms.

2. Overt formality—a translation process from a diagram notation into formal notation, sometimes in the reverse direction, and use of development steps within the formal specification and design language.

The Fusion method follows the first approach, and Z++ and VDM++ follow the second approach. Fusion consists of elements of Booch and OMT methods (now merged into UML by Booch and Rumbaugh of Rational Software) and extends them with operation specifications using informal preconditions, postconditions, and logical invariants. The covert approach is more readily acceptable and usable in most organizations but does not provide a correct way to reason about formally refined system models; mathematical notation cannot be avoided if a proof is used. Complex mathematical notation is used in engineering disciplines, but in cases where only a small increase in rigor and formality is needed, and where formal refinement and proof is not necessary, a covert formality approach to integrating diagrams and formal methods may be preferable.

Problems in Verifying or Validating Object-Oriented Software

Lano (1995) lists some aspects of object orientation that may be harmful to the possibility of verifying or validating object-oriented software:

- The ambiguity of concepts such as aggregation and other aspects of diagrammatic object-oriented methods
- Polymorphism and dynamic binding, because these make it difficult to control which version of a method is actually to be executed for a particular invocation of the method
- Inheritance, because this can be used to fragment the definition of a method across many classes (making it difficult to determine)
- Clientship, due to the use of aliasing and interconnected networks of objects

Formality can help alleviate these problems. Precise definitions may be given to particular forms of aggregation and to concepts such as subtype migration. Mathematical notation can more precisely express the intent of operations and semantics in data models that cannot be expressed in diagrams. A meaningful definition of subtyping provides a means to infer results about subtype objects on the basis of theorems provided about a subtype. Once we can prove that S is a subtype of T, for example, we do not need to reprove properties about programs that rely on T, since, by definition, these cannot be invalidated by instances of S. This means that dynamic binding becomes less of a problem in verification. Inheritance may be restricted to a purely syntactic role (code reuse and sharing and module importation). This means that long chains of inheritance would not exist.

Finally, aliasing is a big problem for preventing modular reasoning about a class. When class A depends on class S, we have to account for other classes that refer to S in their text that can share instances of S with instances of A. We can't easily solve this problem, but we can use specification languages that are expressive enough to assert properties about object identifiers and the set of existing objects in a system, in addition to interdependencies between objects.

References

Coleman, D., P. Arnold, S. Bodoff, C. Dollin, H. Gilchrist, and F. Hayes. *Object-Oriented Development: the Fusion Method.* Englewood Cliffs, NJ: Prentice Hall, 1994.

Goldsack, S. J., and S. J. H. Kent, eds. *Formal Methods and Object Technology.* London: Springer Verlag, 1996, 24.

Harrington, H. J. *Business Process Improvement.* New York: McGraw-Hill, 1991.

Lano, K. *Formal Object-Oriented Development.* London: Springer Verlag, 1995, 4, 12, 13.

12

Patterns

What Is a Pattern?

Patterns help us take advantage of work done previously either by ourselves or others when constructing something new. When working with systems requirements and software specifications, patterns deal with specific, recurring problems and can be used to develop software architectures with specific characteristics.

When an experienced person begins work on a particular problem, he or she rarely invents a totally new solution. Usually, this person remembers a similar situation where a problem was solved and is able to reuse the basic ideas in that solution to solve the problem at hand. This kind of reuse of ideas occurs not only in software development but in architecture, economics, and various engineering fields.

Whenever we abstract ideas from specific problems and their solutions and draw out the common characteristics, we are dealing with some sort of pattern. Building a system with adequate flexibility to remain viable for the long-term future is difficult and error-prone if user interfaces are tightly coupled with the functional core of the system.

When an expert works on a particular problem, he or she usually attacks it by recalling a similar problem encountered and solved earlier, reusing the essence of the solution to solve the new problem. Abstracting from specific combinations of problem-solution pairs, extracting common factors, often leads to patterns. Christopher Alexander describes a pattern this way: Each pattern is a three-part rule, which expresses a relation between a certain context, a problem, and a solution. As an element in the world, each pattern is a relationship between a certain context, a certain system of forces that occurs repeatedly in that context, and a certain spatial configuration that allows these forces to resolve themselves. As an element of language, a pattern is an instruction, which shows how this spatial configuration can be used, over and over again, to resolve the given system of forces, wherever the context makes it relevant. The pattern is, in short, at the same time a thing, which happens in the world, and the rule that tells us how to create that thing, and when we must create it. It is both a process and a thing; both a description of a thing that is alive and a description of the process that will generate that thing.

Of course, patterns occur in business processes and the software that implements those processes. System developers recognize these patterns from their work experiences and follow them when analyzing, designing, and developing software applications. Buschmann et al. (1996) describe several properties of patterns for software architecture:

- A pattern addresses a recurring design problem that occurs in specific design situations and presents a solution to it.

- Patterns document existing, well-proven design experience.

- Patterns identify and specify abstractions that are above the level of single classes and instances, or of components.

- Patterns provide a common vocabulary and understanding for design principles.

- Patterns are a means of documenting software architectures.

- Patterns support the construction of software with defined properties.

- Patterns help you build complex and heterogeneous software architectures.

- Patterns help you to manage software complexity.

These authors go on to offer this definition of a pattern: A pattern for software architecture describes a particular recurring design problem that occurs in specific design contexts and presents a well-proven generic scheme for its solution. The solution scheme is specified by describing its constituent components, their responsibilities and relationships, and the ways in which they collaborate.

What Constitutes a Pattern?

Buschmann et al. (1996) suggest a three-part schema, which underlies every pattern:

1. Context—a situation giving rise to a problem
2. Problem—the recurring problem in that context
3. Solution—a proven resolution of the problem

Such a schema provides a rule that sets up an association between a particular context, a certain problem appearing in that context, and an appropriate solution to the problem. These components of a pattern schema are tightly coupled.

Context

The context of a pattern is the situation causing a problem. It extends the ordinary problem and solution pair by describing situations where a problem might occur. A context might be general or could tie specific patterns together.

Problem

The problem part of a pattern describes the problem that occurs repeatedly in the particular context. It contains a general problem specification describing the design issue that must be solved. Christopher Alexander uses the term force to describe any aspect of a problem that should be considered when solving it:

• Requirements the solution must fulfill

- Constraints that must be considered

- Desirable properties that the solution should have

The forces idea discusses a problem from various viewpoints and helps us understand its details. It may complement or contract other forces, but, most importantly, it provides a key to solving a problem. Some problem categories from Buschmann et al. are listed in Figure 12.1 and described in detail later in this chapter.

Solution

The solution part of a pattern describes how to solve the recurring problem, balancing the forces associated with it. This includes two aspects:

1. Every pattern specifies a certain structure—a spatial configuration of elements. This structure addresses the static aspects of the solution, consisting of both components and their relationships. The components act as building blocks, each having a defined responsibility; relationships between components determine their placement.

From Mud to Structure—support a suitable decomposition of an overall system task into cooperating subtasks

Distributed Systems—provide infrastructures for systems that have components located in different processes or in several subsystems and components

Interactive Systems—help to structure systems with human-computer interaction

Structural Decomposition—support a suitable decomposition of subsystems and complex components into cooperating parts

Organization of Work—define how components collaborate to provide a complex service

Access Control—guard and control access to services or components

Management—handle homogenous collections of objects, services, and components in their entirety

Communication—help to organize communication between components

Resource Handling—help to manage shared components and objects

---

Figure 12.1   Pattern problem categories.

2. Every pattern specifies run-time behavior—addressing the dynamic aspects of the solution. It describes how the participants of the pattern collaborate, how work is organized among them, and how they communicate with each other.

A pattern provides a solution schema, not a fully specified blueprint. The solution should be reusable across multiple implementations. The pattern is a conceptual building block.

Types of Patterns

Architectural Patterns

According to Buschmann et al., an architectural pattern expresses a fundamental structural organization schema for software systems. It provides a set of predefined subsystems, specifies their responsibilities, and includes rules and guidelines for organizing the relationships among them.

This kind of pattern can be used as templates for building software architectures that specify system-wide structural aspects of applications. They impact the architecture of subsystems.

Design Patterns

Software architectural subsystems may consist of smaller architectural units, which can be described using design patterns. Gamma et al. describe a design pattern this way: A design pattern provides a scheme for refining the subsystems or components of a software system or the relationships between them. It describes a commonly recurring structure of communicating components that solves a general design problem within a particular context.

This kind of pattern is a medium-scale pattern, smaller in scale than the architectural patterns but rather independent of programming languages or approaches. Ideally, use of a design pattern will not affect the basic structure of a system but will influence the architecture of subsystems. Design patterns often provide structures for subdividing complex services or components.

Idioms

An idiom can be described as a low-level pattern specific to a programming language, describing how to implement specific parts of components or the relationships among them using language features. These patterns address both design and implementation and are usually specific to a particular language. Idioms are the lowest-level patterns that deal with implementation of particular design issues by addressing both design and implementation.

The above paragraphs have described a classification schema for patterns defined by Buschmann et al. (1995). Another well-known schema is described by Gamma et al. This schema has two dimensions: purpose and scope. The first criterion, called *purpose*, reflects what a pattern does. Patterns can have either creational, structural, or behavioral purposes:

- Creational patterns involve the process of creating objects.

- Structural patterns involve composition of classes or objects.

- Behavioral patterns characterize ways that classes or objects may interact and distribute responsibility.

The Composite and Whole-Part patterns are structural object patterns. The Interpreter pattern is a behavioral class pattern.

What Patterns Provide for Systems Developers

Consistent Terminology

Systems development knowledge and experience involve much more than syntax: It consists of algorithms, data structures, and idioms, as well as plans for fulfilling specific goals. Notations are not nearly as important as attempting to match current business analysis and software design situations against plans, algorithms, data structures, and idioms used in the past. Patterns provide a common terminology for use in communicating, documenting, and exploring business modeling and design concepts. They can make systems seem simpler by allowing discussions to be conducted at higher levels of abstraction than those of a simple business modeling or design notation or a programming language.

Better Communication

When you read the various books about patterns listed in the references, you will no doubt discover that you are familiar with many of the patterns discussed. Many large systems have these patterns in them, and most large object-oriented systems these days use analysis and design patterns. Object-oriented software can often be complicated to work with when inheritance mechanisms are difficult to follow and understand. It has been said that this is because the design patterns in the system have not been formally documented by designers or understood by developers. Using patterns can help analysts and designers better by providing consistent descriptions of problems and solutions to these problems.

Using patterns to describe a complex system makes the system much easier to comprehend. Without these patterns, it is necessary to reverse-engineer the design to discover the patterns within it. A common terminology set allows us to refer to an entire pattern just by naming it—the details are easily accessed somewhere else when needed. Many authors listed in the references have described "catalogs" of patterns.

A Supplement to Existing Methods

Any method used to analyze and design object-oriented systems should, of course, promote good techniques, teach analysts and designers to build better models, and standardize the development process. Development methods define sets of notations for modeling various aspects of a system, including rules to govern how and when to use each notation. These methods are extremely useful, but they do not capture the experience of expert analysts, designers, and developers. Patterns can help to address this shortcoming.

Patterns show us how to use fundamental concepts such as objects, inheritance, and polymorphism. They describe how to make systems more generalized through the use of parameters that refer to algorithms, behavior, state, or type of object. Patterns describe the philosophy (why a particular system model is being explored), not just what decisions were made.

Many times it has been said that object designs may be easily derived from object analysis models. Anyone working with complex system designs knows that this transition from analysis to design is not usually smooth. Designs built for flexibility almost always contain objects that don't exist in an analysis model. This is because the analysis model captures business (or other real-world domain) concepts and should not refer to technology concepts. Designs, on the other hand, necessarily must begin to address specific technology options used to implement analysis model concepts. This often means that analysis models must be restructured to make them reusable, even when they were modeled with reuse in mind. Analysis and design models serve different purposes. Many design patterns listed in the various pattern references address this transition problem. Ideally, any development method includes many more patterns than just design patterns:

- Analysis patterns

- User-interface design patterns

- Network-interface patterns

- Performance-tuning patterns

Help in Reorganizing Systems

Reusable software often must be reorganized (or "refactored"). Analysis and design patterns help us determine when and how to reorganize models and designs in order to reduce the amount of rework needed later on. Constructing prototypes of parts of complex systems has been very successful, especially when accompanied by some reasonably formal modeling of the evolving architecture as prototypes develop into evolutionary systems (building screen mockups without business object and database object layer modeling can result in *more* rework, not less, when systems are complex).

When a system has been placed into production, its further development must balance conflicting needs. The system must, at the same time, both satisfy more requirements and be more reusable. Any new requirements usually add new classes and operations—indeed, entire class hierarchies. Thus as new requirements are added, the system tends to expand, with the risk that its architecture becomes too rigid to support additional changes. To address this problem, software must be periodically reorganized. Of course, modeling the breadth of the system early on and building in key architectural elements from the beginning helps a lot, but there is still a transition problem that exists when moving from analysis to design that requires reorganization.

During the system reorganization process, frameworks can be discovered. As classes are split into special-purpose and general-purpose components, operations are moved up and down class hierarchies and the class interfaces adjusted accordingly. As this work is done, many new object types may be discovered. The best designers know that changes to the system requirements can result in major restructuring, but they also know of class and object structures that can alleviate restructuring problems. As mentioned earlier, one key element in preparing to adapt to change is to examine the requirements in their entirety, highlighting areas that will cause software restructuring. The designs will be adjusted to provide a more flexible architecture that supports change. Design patterns, when used early in the design process, can help to prevent later restructuring. They are even useful after the system has been built, because some restructuring will be required eventually and the patterns provide a guide for this restructuring.

Selecting a Pattern

The procedure for selecting a specific pattern could follow the one listed by Buschmann et al.:

1. Specify the problem.

2. Select the pattern category that corresponds to the design activity being performed.

3. Select the problem category that corresponds to the general nature of the design problem.

4. Compare the problem descriptions.

5. Compare benefits and liabilities.

6. Select the variant that best implements the solution to the design problem.

7. Select an alternative problem category.

If steps 2, 3, and 4 bring you no results, stop searching. You may need to examine other pattern languages, systems, or catalogs for patterns you can use. When implementing or refining a pattern already selected, this search procedure is not necessary.

Developing Systems Using Patterns

Patterns do not, by themselves, define a new method for developing software systems. Rather, they complement general but problem-independent analysis and design methods with aids for solving specific, concrete problems. When preparing to develop systems using patterns, use any method to define an overall software development process and detailed activities to be performed in each development phase. Then use an appropriate pattern system to guide the design and development of solutions to particular problems.

When a pattern system includes a pattern that addresses one of your design problems, follow the implementation steps for that pattern to solve the problem. When this involves reference to other patterns, apply those patterns and their associated implementation steps to complement your development of the original pattern. If a pattern system does not include a pattern for your problem, try to discover a pattern from other known pattern sources. If no pattern is available, apply guidelines from your chosen development method.

When there is not an appropriate pattern for solving a concrete design problem, you may want to "mine" patterns that address these problems (Buschmann et al. 1996). Steps for mining patterns are outlined in the following list:

1. Find at least three examples where a particular recurring design or implementation problem is solved effectively by using the same solution schema.

2. Extract the solution schema from the specific details of its concrete applications.

3. Declare the solution schema to be a pattern candidate.

4. Run a writer's workshop to improve the description of the candidate pattern and to share it.

5. Apply the candidate pattern in a real-world project.

6. Declare the candidate pattern to be a pattern if its application is successful, and integrate it into your pattern system.

When it comes time to integrate a new pattern into your pattern system, you should specify the relationships of the new pattern to other patterns in the system, as well as all relationships from existing patterns to the new one. Also, classify the pattern, assigning it to pattern and problem categories, or extend your schema as necessary. New problem categories may be needed to extend your pattern system, as suggested by Gamma et al. (1995):

- Creation patterns help with instantiating objects and recursive object structures.

- Service variation patterns support changing the behavior of an object or component.

- Service extension patterns help to add new services to an object or object structure dynamically.

- Adaptation patterns help with interface and data conversion.

The "Gang of Four" Design Patterns

Erich Gamma, Richard Helm, Ralph Johnson, and John Vlissides, the "Gang of Four," have described a catalog, consisting of 23 design patterns. This section provides an overview of these important patterns.

1. *Abstract Factory*—provides an interface for creating families of related or dependent objects without specifying their concrete classes.

2. *Adapter*—converts the interface of a class into another interface that clients expect. An adapter allows classes that otherwise couldn't work together, due to incompatible interfaces, to do so.

3. *Bridge*—decouples an abstraction from its implementation, so that the two can vary independently.

4. *Builder*—separates the construction of a complex object from its representation, so that the same construction process can create different representations.

5. *Chain of Responsibility*—avoids coupling the sender of a request to the receiver, by giving more than one object a chance to handle the request. Chains the receiving object and passes the request along the chain until an object handles it.

6. *Command*—encapsulates a request as an object, thereby letting you parameterize clients with different requests, queue or log requests, and support undoable operations.

7. *Composite*—composes objects into tree structures to represent part-whole hierarchies. Composite allows clients to treat individual objects and compositions of objects uniformly.

8. *Decorator*—attaches additional responsibilities to an object dynamically. Decorators provide a flexible alternative to subclassing for extending functionality.

9. *Facade*—provides a unified interface to a set of interfaces in a subsystem. Facade defines a higher-level interface, which makes the subsystem easier to use.

10. *Factory Method*—defines an interface for creating an object, but lets subclasses decide which class to instantiate. Factory Method allows a class to defer instantiation to subclasses.

11. *Flyweight*—uses sharing to support large numbers of fine-grained objects efficiently.

12. *Interpreter*—given a language, defines a representation for its grammar along with an interpreter that uses the representation to interpret sentences in the language.

13. *Iterator*—provides a way to access the elements of an aggregate object sequentially, without exposing its underlying representation.

14. *Mediator*—defines an object that encapsulates how a set of objects interact. Mediator promotes loose coupling by keeping objects from referring to each other explicitly and allows you to vary their interaction independently.

15. *Memento*—without violating encapsulation, captures and externalizes an object's internal state, so that the object can be restored to this state later.

16. *Observer*—defines a one-to-many dependency between objects, so that when one object changes state, all its dependents are notified and updated automatically.

17. *Prototype*—specifies the kinds of objects to create using a prototypical instance and creates new objects by copying this prototype.

18. *Proxy*—provides a surrogate or placeholder for another object to control access to it.

19. *Singleton*—ensures that a class has only one instance and provides a global point of access to it.

20. *State* — allows an object to alter its behavior when its internal state changes. The object will appear to change its class.

21. *Strategy* — defines a family of algorithms, encapsulates each one, and makes them interchangeable. Strategy allows the algorithm to vary independently from clients using it.

22. *Template Method* — defines the skeleton of an algorithm in an operation, deferring some steps to subclasses. Template Method allows subclasses to redefine certain steps of an algorithm without changing the algorithm's structure.

23. *Visitor* — represents an operation to be performed on the elements of an object structure. Visitor allows you to define a new operation without changing the classes of the elements upon which it operates.

The Architectural Patterns of Buschmann et al.

From Mud to Structure Patterns

Layers — help to structure applications that can be decomposed into groups of subtasks in which each group of subtasks is at a particular level of abstraction.

Pipes and Filters — provide a structure for systems that process a stream of data. Each processing step is encapsulated in a filter component. Data are passed through pipes between adjacent filters. Recombining filters allows you to build families of related systems.

Blackboard — is useful for problems for which no deterministic solution strategies are known. In Blackboard, several specialized subsystems assemble their knowledge to build a possibly partial or approximate solution.

Distributed Systems Patterns

Broker — can be used to structure distributed software systems with decoupled components that interact by remote service invocations. A broker component is responsible for coordinating communication, such as forwarding requests, as well as for transmitting results and exceptions.

Interactive Systems

Model-View-Controller—divides an interactive application into three components. The model contains the core functionality and data. Views display information to the user. Controllers handle user input. Views and controllers together comprise the user interface. A change-propagation mechanism ensures consistency between the user interface and the model.

Presentation-Abstraction-Control—defines a structure for interactive software systems in the form of a hierarchy of cooperating agents. Every agent is responsible for a specific aspect of the application's functionality and consists of the three components: presentation, abstraction, and control. This subdivision separates the human-computer interaction aspects of the agent from its functional core and its communication with other agents.

Adaptable Systems

Microkernel—applies to software systems that must be able to adapt to changing system requirements. It separates a minimal functional core from extended functionality and customer-specific parts. The microkernel also serves as a socket for plugging in such extensions and coordinating their collaboration.

Reflection—provides a mechanism for changing structure and behavior of software systems dynamically. It supports the modification of fundamental aspects, such as type structures and function call mechanisms. In this pattern, an application is split into two parts. A metalevel provides information about selected system properties and makes the software self-aware. A base level includes the application logic. Its implementation builds on the metalevel. Changes to information kept in the metalevel affect subsequent base-level behavior.

The Design Patterns of Buschman et al.

Structural Decomposition

Whole-Part—helps with the aggregation of components that together form a semantic unit. An aggregate component, the whole, encapsulates its constituent components, the parts, organizes their collaboration, and provides a common interface to its functionality. Direct access to the parts is not possible.

Composite—organizes objects into tree structures that represent part-whole hierarchies. Composite allows clients to interact with individual objects and compositions of objects uniformly.

Organization of Work

Master-Slave—supports fault tolerance, parallel computation, and computational accuracy. A master component distributes work to identical slave components and computes a final result from the results these slaves return.

Access Control

Proxy—makes the clients of a component communicate with a representative rather than with the component itself. Introducing such a placeholder can serve many purposes, including enhanced efficiency, easier access, and protection from unauthorized access.

Facade—provides a uniform interface to a set of interfaces in a subsystem. Facade defines a higher-level interface, which makes the subsystem easier to use.

Iterator—provides a way to access the elements of an aggregate object sequentially, without exposing its underlying representation.

Management

Command Processor—separates the request for a service from its execution. A command processor component manages requests as separate objects, schedules their execution, and provides additional services, such as the storing of request objects for later undo.

View Handler—helps to manage views in a software system. A view handler component allows clients to open, manipulate, and dispose of views; coordinates dependencies between views; and organizes their update.

Memento—allows the capture and externalization of an object's internal state without violating encapsulation, so that its state can be restored later.

Communication

Forwarder-Receiver—provides transparent interprocess communication for software systems with a peer-to-peer interaction model. It introduces forwarders and receivers to decouple peers from the underlying communication mechanisms.

Client-Dispatcher-Server—introduces an intermediate layer between clients and servers, the dispatcher service, and hides the details of the establishment of the communication connection between clients and servers.

Publisher-Subscriber—helps to keep the state of cooperating components synchronized. To achieve this, it enables one-way propagation of changes: One publisher notifies any number of subscribers about changes to its state.

Design Pattern Approaches

Object-Oriented Patterns

According to Peter Coad (1992; 1995), patterns can be identified by examining classes and objects and relationships established between them. A general scheme is proposed for describing a particular pattern:

- A brief introduction and discussion of the typical problem that a pattern helps to solve, including an analogy, if suitable

- An informal textual description of the pattern, accompanied by a graphical representation

- Guidelines about when (and when not) to use a pattern and about which patterns are suited for combination with a particular pattern

Wolfgang Pree (1995) categorizes Coad's patterns into:

- Basic inheritance and interaction patterns
- Patterns for structuring object-oriented software systems
- Patterns related to the Model-View-Controller framework

The inheritance and interaction patterns include basic modeling capabilities of object-oriented programming languages. These languages provide ways of overriding methods, adding instance variables, and adding methods in subclasses. Abstract classes are also discussed as a pattern. This category of patterns also covers message sending if more than two objects are involved.

Patterns for structuring object-oriented software describe how a small group of classes supports structuring of systems if certain conditions hold. Examples of this kind of pattern include:

- Item descriptions
- Changing roles
- Object collections

Patterns dealing with the Model-View-Controller (MVC) framework incorporate the idea of user-interface applications consisting of three components: a model, a view, and a controller. The *model* stores application-specific data, such as a text processing application storing text characters or a graphical application storing drawings. The *view* presents a model on a display device. Multiple view components might present a model in different ways, with each view having access to model information. The *controller* handles input events from the user interface. A controller is associated with each view, serving to connect that view with appropriate input devices. A model may have many associated view-controller pairings. Views and controllers can access models and can inform themselves about data stored in the model; they are allowed to change model data. Models may not access controllers or views.

There are some deficiencies the MVC framework presents for user-interface programming: A strict separation of three components is too rigid, and the update mechanism of views is inefficient due to inaccurate information about necessary updates. Still, the MVC framework did influence later frameworks. Coad refers to MVC as the Publisher-Subscriber framework.

Coding Patterns

Coding patterns are close to the programming language level of abstraction. This kind of pattern helps to solve specific programming tasks. James Coplien (1992) states the goals of coding patterns:

- To demonstrate useful ways of combining basic language concepts

- To form the basis for standardizing source code structure and names

- To avoid pitfalls and to weed out deficiencies of object-oriented programming languages

Coplien describes in detail some coding patterns for C++. Coding patterns often depend on a particular programming language and/or class library, giving basic hints on how to structure software from a syntactical perspective. These patterns do not help much for class design. They do not help a programmer to adapt or develop a framework.

Framework Adaptation Patterns

This kind of pattern allows a programmer to use a framework as a basis for application development, with a particular framework adapted to specific needs. These patterns are sometimes referred to as "cookbook" recipes and usually do not explain the internal design and implementation details of a framework. A cookbook may exist for various frameworks: for the MVC framework, for the GUI application framework MacApp, and for the HotDraw framework for implementing graphical editors.

Recipes are fairly informal documents but are structured to include purpose, procedure, and source code examples. A programmer finds the recipe for a certain framework adaptation and then follows the steps that describe how to perform a particular task. Wolfgang Pree (1995) describes a sample recipe for creating documents in the GUI application framework ET++.

Cookbook recipes incorporate hypertext structures via their references to other recipes. Since a hypertext system allows creation of links and navigation through a directed graph of links between parts of documents, cookbooks written with a hypertext system can contain recipes as links. The parts of the recipes are separated from the actual recipes, simplifying the presentation of recipe information. Still, some problems must be considered with use of this approach when adapting application frameworks. Cookbooks must cover a broad range of framework adaptations and are rarely complete. Cookbooks need to be written by people with a good understanding of a framework, preferably the framework developers themselves.

Formal Contracts

The formal approach of Helm et al. (1990) is important for the study of design patterns, because contracts are aimed at frameworks and the few elements of the notation are not too difficult to group. A contract is an alternative term for class interface, but Helm et al. (1990) expand this to include groups of interdependent objects cooperating to accomplish tasks. They refer to contracts as a construct for the explicit specification of behavioral compositions. Bertrand Meyer (1988) uses the term contract in conjunction with preconditions and postconditions supported by the Eiffel programming language.

The Publisher-Subscriber pattern is an example of a contract whereby a Publisher object notifies its dependent Subscriber objects whenever changes occur (by invoking the Update method for each Subscriber object). Participants in a contract are the Publisher and a set of Subscriber participants. For each participant, the contractual obligations must be defined, consisting of type obligations (corresponding to instance variables and methods) and causal obligations (describing actions and conditions associated with type obligations).

Some advantages of formal notations for contracts include (Pree 1995):

- The suggested notation consists of few elements. The concepts introduced mirror those of object-oriented programming languages (e.g., participants are close to objects).

- Formal contracts account for the fact that complex behavioral compositions are built of simpler ones. Operations contract refinement and contract inclusion support the adaptation of contracts and contribute to the flexibility of this approach.

Disadvantages of formal notations for contracts include:

- Formal contracts can be difficult to apply in certain situations. Introducing new notational elements can help, but the formal notation becomes more complex.

- Formal notation imposes a sense of exactness that may mask flaws in specifications.

- Essential aspects become cluttered with too many details. The abstraction level of a formal notation appears to be too close to object-oriented programming languages.

Summary

Analysis and design patterns try to describe concepts at higher levels of abstraction than the code that implements a system. Modern pattern approaches aim to select frameworks that are not too domain-specific, so that models and designs may be applied to development of other patterns and frameworks. The various catalogs of patterns appearing in the literature are useful for building new frameworks, but more advanced abstractions are helpful. Newer research involves the concept of *metapatterns*, sets of patterns that describe how to construct frameworks independent of a specific domain. Metapatterns can be an elegant and powerful approach for categorizing and describing any pattern on a *metalevel*; thus, metapatterns do not replace pattern approaches but complement them. See Wolfgang Pree (1995) for a good discussion of metapatterns.

References

Alexander, C., S. Ishikawa, M. Silverstein, M. Jacobson, I. Fiksdahl-King, and S. Angel. *A Pattern Language*. New York: Oxford University Press, 1977.

Buschmann, F., R. Meunier, H. Rohnert, P. Sommerlad, and M. Stal. *Pattern-Oriented Software Architecture: A System of Patterns*. Chichester, England: John Wiley & Sons, 1996, 5–8, 364, 365, 368–370, 376, 377.

Coad, P. "Object-Oriented Patterns." *Communications of the ACM* 33(9) (1992).

Coad, P., D. North, and M. Mayfield. *Object Models: Strategies, Patterns, and Applications*. Englewood Cliffs, NJ: Yourdon Press, 1995.

Coplien, J. O. *Advanced C++ Progamming Styles and Idoms*. Reading, MA: Addison-Wesley, 1992.

Gamma, E., R. Helm, R. Johnson, and J. Vlissides. *Design Patterns: Elements of Reusable Object-Oriented Software*. Reading, MA: Addison-Wesley, 1995.

Helm, R., I. M. Holland, and K. D. Gangopadhyay. "Contracts: Specifying Behavioral Compositions in Object-Oriented Systems." In *Proceedings of OOPSLA '90*, Ottawa, Canada, 1990.

Meyer, B. *Object-Oriented Software Construction*. Englewood Cliffs, NJ: Prentice Hall, 1988.

Pree, W. *Design Patterns for Object-Oriented Software Development*. Wokingham, England: Addison-Wesley, 1995, 65, 80–82.

13

Reuse

Analysis Considerations— Development for Reuse

Guideline

Gather information from as many different sources as possible.

Capture all requirements as parts of the analysis models.

Use a notation that is easy to understand.

Present the models in a clearly visible way to all project members.

Reuse Aspects

It's more likely that all requirements can be found and dealt with if several sources are used.

The complete understanding of requirements is essential in order to capture invisible and nonfunctional requirements—those that are difficult to easily state in words.

It is essential that models are easy to comprehend for the reuser.

Try to keep all project members motivated and contributing to the project. Make it easy for members to discuss and refer to the models to promote quality and reusability of a component.

Guideline	Reuse Aspects
Refine and formalize the analysis models.	Higher abstraction levels are likely to be found during refinement. Try to use several conceptual models as the basis for validation of reuse components.
Conduct a formal review of the outputs from the analysis phase.	A thorough examination of analysis output may result in new, previously undiscovered requirements that need to be dealt with to obtain a fully reusable component. Review of abstractions can result in new, even higher abstractions, enhancing reusability.
Use inheritance to express specialization on types.	Inheritance structures identified early on are likely to be problem domain specific, contrary to solution-specific structures that are likely to be identified later on (and likely to remain unchanged).
Analyze existing applications within the domain and identify commonalities.	Proper abstractions are found more easily if existing applications are examined. Abstractions common to several applications may remain stable over time.
Generalize so that future alterations are supported.	Abstractions at a high level facilitate alterations of the component without restructuring the architecture merely by creating subclasses from it.
Pinpoint variants among existing and future systems within the domain.	Use inheritance to point out differences between systems, forcing analysis to focus on finding established, stable abstractions.

Architectural Design Considerations— Development for Reuse

Guideline	Reuse Aspect
Model optional parts of a system as subsystems.	Possible combinations of optional functionality or behavior should be supported by reusable components associated with a family of software products.
Distribute system intelligence evenly.	A very intelligent object, class, or subsystem will be hard to subclass or otherwise adapt. Distributing intelligence allows objects to know about fewer things. The simpler objects will be easier to modify.

Guideline	Reuse Aspect
Make subsystems of strongly coupled classes that implement one unit of functionality.	Classes in a subsystem are likely to be affected at the same time and by the same changes in requirements.
Factor common responsibilities as high as possible in the inheritance hierarchy.	This helps find the most suitable abstraction so that no inadequate responsibilities are inherited—a few must be added and redefined.
State responsibilities as generally as possible.	This helps you find the most suitable abstraction for reuse by inheritance.
Minimize the number of collaborations a class has with other classes or subsystems.	This implies that a class is less likely to be affected by changes in other parts of the system.
Minimize the number of subsystems.	This implies that only minor changes of the subsystem may be necessary when other parts of the system are changed. Only a few parts are dependent on parts outside the subsystem.
Make subsystems out of classes that are likely to be affected by the same minor change in requirements.	Such objects or classes should be grouped together to minimize the effect of the new requirements.
Create as many abstract classes as possible.	This helps you find the most suitable abstraction. Defining many abstract classes means that you have factored out much common behavior.
Introduce subsystems late in the architectural design phase.	As more detailed class and object designs develop, a better division into subsystems is possible. Subsystems may also be introduced to streamline communications between design objects, achieving low coupling.

Detailed Design Considerations— Development for Reuse

Guideline	Reuse Aspects
View general properties of some classes as making up a generalization or abstraction of the class via a superclass.	Reusers can find the most suitable abstraction easier if common properties are identified, and modifications are easier to make.
Use multiple inheritance sparingly.	Inheritance structure will be simpler if multiple inheritance is avoided.
Name similar operations the same.	A more limited set of method names and protocols needs to be managed.

Guideline	Reuse Aspects
Each method should perform only one task.	The protocol of the class will be easier to understand and reuse.
Subclasses should be specializations.	Use inheritance to implement specialization, but not other uses, in order to avoid confusion. Try not to use inheritance for code reuse.
The top of a class hierarchy should be abstract.	A concrete class must provide a definition for its data representation, and some subclasses may need different representations. Abstract superclasses allow for any data representation in subclasses.
Keep a small total protocol for each class.	It is difficult to reuse large classes.
Keep classes small, avoiding too many methods.	It is difficult to reuse large classes.
Use abstract classes as far as possible in inheritance hierarchies.	It is often better to inherit from an abstract class than from a concrete one. Abstract superclasses allow maximum flexibility in subclasses.
Class hierarchies should be fairly deep and narrow.	Capturing commonalities in superclasses allows subclasses to focus on differences. Reusers can find the most suitable abstraction easier and need to make fewer redefinitions in subclasses.
Factor implementation differences into new abstractions.	Too deep and large an inheritance hierarchy can be difficult to understand, so try to identify abstractions to separate implementation differences.
Favor uniformity over specificity in naming conventions.	Reuses only need to manage a limited set of method names and protocols and can focus on function and/or performance aspects of similar components.
Keep method signatures consistent.	This better supports standard protocols and polymorphism and makes maintenance easier.

Implementation Considerations— Development for Reuse

Guideline	Reuse Aspects
Do not use multiple inheritance just to minimize code.	The structure will confuse reusers, and ambiguous inheritance may be introduced. Multiple inheritance increases complexity.

Guideline	Reuse Aspects
All methods intended to be overloaded or redefined in subclasses must be declared as virtual.	This tells a reuse which methods are intended to be redefined, making reuse safer.
Do not cast down the inheritance hierarchy unnecessarily.	Don't call methods lower in a class hierarchy if it can be avoided. If a component uses a number of base class pointers and uses downcasting, a reuser must continue to use downcasting if new subclasses are used in the component.
Try to avoid inheritance with cancellation.	This occurs when there are restrictions to inheritance made by a subclass; this contradicts specialization relationships. This creates an unclear interface for subclasses.
Do not use private inheritance.	This is not an object-oriented concept and may confuse reusers. It is difficult to examine what is inherited and therefore what is reused.
Keep classes small.	It is difficult to reuse a large class.
Keep the number of method arguments small.	Methods with many (more than five) arguments are difficult to read and reuse.
Keep methods small.	It is easier to reuse by subclassing if superclasses have small methods. Smaller methods are easier to understand and modify, and common behavior is easier to identify with smaller methods.
Declare parameters constant when possible.	This clearly shows a reuser that the parameters (pointers to parameters) are not changed in the method's implementation, so there is no risk in passing a parameter that is not intended to be changed.
Always make destructors virtual in the base classes.	If a component is reused by subclassing and base class pointers are used, there may be memory allocation problems when an object is deleted. If destructors are declared virtual in the base classes, the amount of work is decreased for subclassing.
Eliminate switch statements in object types.	When checking object types, unnecessary dependencies on other object types are created. Use polymorphism instead for greater adaptability.
Specify attributes as private.	Reusers need not worry about the implementation. The interface for a reuser is the public and protected methods so that the component is reused correctly.

Guideline	Reuse Aspects
Use protected methods instead of protected attributes in base classes.	If a component can be reused using inheritance, the developer can control how it is reused via a well-defined interface. If the component is replaced with a new version with a different data representation, the reuse interface is the same.
Avoid using friends if possible.	Using friends violates encapsulation and makes reuse difficult. A friend relation is difficult to follow and handle by a reuser.
Avoid implicit implementation and code in header files.	Use of the in-line keyword violates encapsulation and shows the implementation to the reuser. The reuser should not have to care about the implementation.
Inhibit classes intended to be abstract from being instantiated.	Making methods that should not be instantiated virtual instead forces subclasses to contain a uniform protocol. This prevents misuse.
When copying or assignment makes no sense, hide the copy constructor and assignment operator in the private part of the class specification.	This inhibits reusers from performing unintentional operations with the component, preventing misuse.

Developing Reusable Components

Development for reuse is independent of component size and life cycle phase. A component may have different degrees of generality, so we should try to identify the steps in a general development framework for reuse independent of where the component is in the system structure and what kind of development model is used to represent the requirements and solution.

Below are listed some steps useful in developing components for reuse:

1. Capture the initial requirements, collecting the set of requirements to make an initial solution.

2. Define an initial solution or identify previous solutions to the same set of requirements.

3. Identify possible generalizations.

4. Identify potential reusers and collect their requirements.

5. Estimate the cost and benefit of added functionality.

6. Analyze the added requirements with respect to invariants and variation.

7. Propose a generalized solution with specializations and cost estimates.

8. Present the solution to reusers and reuse experts for validation and approval.

9. Develop and document the solution.

Apply these steps at any point during development and system structure. Iterate over the steps as necessary. The search for a general solution and study of other potential reusers can sometimes uncover hidden requirements for the current system from the original customer, lead to an improved solution, and avoid costly changes later in development.

Developing with Reusable Components

Some generic activities in developing with reuse can be identified, independent of component, model, or type of component being reused:

1. Identify components needed to build the application with reuse and that could be reused, derived, or adapted from existing reusable components.

2. Formalize the requirements for these components in terms of search conditions, and search for candidate components.

3. Evaluate the retrieved components.

4. Choose the best candidate and investigate the chosen component thoroughly.

5. Adapt the component if necessary, and integrate it into the application.

Repeat steps 2 through 4 until you find a suitable component.

Documenting a Reusable Component

Proper documentation allows a producer of a reusable component to communicate with potential consumers. This documentation should be tailored to development with reuse. Three different forms of such documentation can be considered:

1. *Engineering documentation*—Produced during all development stages and is usually not part of the product documentation (includes project plans, test plans, etc.).

2. *Product documentation*—Accompanies the product and contains information for those who will use the product after its release (users, system administrators, sales staff, and installers).

3. *Maintenance documentation*—Contains information (such as requirements and design specifications) for those who will maintain or evolve the product.

To best position a component for reuse, some maintenance documentation should be converted to product documentation. Engineering documentation should also be accessible to later projects. With reuse, the distinctions between types of documentation decrease. The need for specific reuse documentation includes:

Searching—A reuse repository must be organized to support retrieval of a suitable set of candidate components.

Evaluation—When a set of candidate components is retrieved, you need to evaluate them to select one to try for reuse.

Investigation—When a component is selected for the purpose of reuse, you need to understand how to use it.

Adaptation—Many components developed for reuse are intended to be adapted before being reused.

Integration—You need to incorporate the documentation of the reused component into that of the current system.

Testing a Reusable Component

Both producers and consumers of reusable components need to test these components. A producer must check that the component is adaptable as intended and test the correctness of its functions. A reuser must test the adapted and integrated component. Good documentation reduces the effort required to reuse a component.

Some ideas for preparing tests for different adaptation techniques:

Widening — Identify a set of requirements that are not contradictory, and then make a general component that satisfies all of them Tests can be prepared as for a component reused as is.

Narrowing — Identify functions common to several customers that can be represented by an abstract component. Tests can be prepared by allocating general test cases to general components.

Isolation — Isolate different requirements to a small part of the system, and construct the rest of the system relatively independently of whatever specialization is chosen. Just the test cases for the adaptations are isolated.

Configurability — Make a set of smaller components that can be configured or composed in different ways to satisfy different requirements. Provide guidelines and standards for testing the system that contain the component.

Incorporating Reuse into a Development Process

Existing development processes may be adapted to development for and with reuse by application of general concepts presented earlier. For our purposes, a development process can be viewed as having these facets:

- Models used to analyze a problem and express the solution

- Processes performed when working with models

- Documents and components where information about models is stored

- Roles involved in the processes

Components

Opportunities for finding reusable components exist almost everywhere in a system structure. You need to analyze what system structure is used and, based on that structure, identify component types. Also, you need to ensure that the information provided along with the components is useful. Do you have an appropriate abstraction for each component? Are the reusable component types properly isolated? You also need to evaluate whether the component type already in use is appropriate for the kind of reuse desired.

Reusers

Types of reusers must be identified at each level in a system structure. Identify potential reusers and what kind of components they may require. Identify the capabilities of reusers who will adapt and integrate components in new applications. Also, note the experience level of the reusers.

Models

Generally, three different kinds of models are used in development:

1. *Requirements (analysis) models* — Capture and explain customer requirements (the problem domain).

2. *Intermediate (design) models* — Transform requirements into a general solution model.

3. *Implementation (construction) models* — The final result of system development.

The models you choose for a particular purpose must fit with your analysis of component types, customers, and reusers — not just the development process model.

Activities

Once you have identified reusable components, who the reusers are, and how, in general, the components will be represented in models, you can begin to adapt the development process to directly address development for and with reuse. Then you need to identify where in the development process reuse activities should be inserted to achieve development for and with reuse.

Strategies for Reusing a Component

- Choose to reuse a component in a discontinuous way in each development phase, focusing on part of the component associated with the current phase and reporting adaptations for later phases.
- Select a component and choose to adapt all its associated parts at once.
- Employ a mix of these approaches.

Your choice of reuse strategy depends upon:

Reuse process mapping — Reuse activities need to be divided between different phases, depending upon availability of requirements for selection of a component and necessary adaptations of the component.

Reuse efficiency — It may be most efficient to reuse and adapt the design of a subsystem and reimplement it entirely than to reuse some implementation parts of a component.

Distribution of work — Each worker on a system needs to thoroughly understand a reuse component to properly integrate it into the phase he or she is working on.

Scheduling and time interval — Knowledge about a component rapidly fades in the time between two adaptations of the same component.

Identifying Requirements for Reusable Components

Guideline	Description
Use different abstraction levels for the requirements, depending upon the phase of development.	Earlier development stages require more general requirements.
	For the analysis phase, requirements must be as general as possible.
	For design and implementation, it is easier to identify low-level components from very specific requirements.

Searching for Reusable Components

Guideline	Description
Enlarge the scope of the search as widely as possible within the organization; do not ignore external sources of reusable components.	The success of a search for components depends on their accessibility. This requires efficient communications and inventory procedures.
	The external market for software components tends to be limited to general-purpose components or general components in a number of specific domains.
Use the taxonomy put in place by the organization.	The search-term space used by search tools must fit the taxonomy defined for each application domain of the organization.
	The taxonomy is constructed after analyzing the domains and promotes use of a common vocabulary for the domain.

Understanding Retrieved Components

Guideline	Description
Use the appropriate view of a component to understand it.	The understanding of a component varies greatly among different individuals.
	A combination of views is a powerful way to enhance software understandability.
Use domain analysis results, if available, to understand the characteristics of the component.	Domain analysis results are a good support for understanding the purpose of available components and the context of their use in an application domain.
	The *classification* of a component provides a broad view of its functional and nonfunctional requirements.
	The *generic requirements* provide information on the context of use of a component—the functional and nonfunctional constraints on the component within an application domain.
	The *object model* describes the structure of the component and its relationships with other components.
	The *functional model* provides information on the behavior of the component.

Guideline	Description
Use domain analysis results, if available, to understand the characteristics of the component. *(cont.)*	The *dynamic model* describes the control and sequencing associated with the component.
	The *architecture* describes the place of the component in the system structure.
Consult experienced people.	Domain experts
	Developers of a component
	Previous reusers

Exploring Possible Adaptations of Reusable Components

Guideline	Description
Study the technical solutions for implementing adaptations based on your chosen mode of reuse.	As is (black box reuse)
	Few changes—(gray box reuse)
	Major changes—(white box reuse)
Determine the appropriate level of investigation of components, depending upon the component type and requirements to be fulfilled.	This provides the necessary information for selecting appropriate alternatives between components.
	It can be very costly depending upon level of detail.
	The level of information necessary to select a component varies, depending upon component and requirement types.
Evaluate the distance between candidate components and requirements.	The *functional distance* corresponds to the gap between required functions and those the component provides.
	The *nonfunctional distance* includes gaps in portability, efficiency, understandability, and reliability, as well as platform considerations.
When using evaluation models on metrics, consider different evaluation levels of metrics, criteria, factors.	*Factors*—used in analysis to fit to customer requirements.
	Criteria—used in design.
	Metrics—used in implementation and documentation.
Do not forget to study the adaptations needed to integrate a component into application development.	Integration of a complete reusable component for more limited needs
	Redundancy of functions
	Conflicts (object names, communications, etc.)

Selecting a Component for Reuse

Guideline	Description
When selecting components, choose standardized ones in the absence of any other decision criteria.	Standardization helps keep systems understandable and maintainable, so usually costs less in the long run.

Adapting and Integrating Reusable Components

Guideline	Description
Use a project-wide or module-wide prefix for each outstanding global name.	Longer prefixes reduce clashes with other prefixes.
Define a standard communication protocol.	If the communication protocol is not fixed for the application being developed, you should use the same one as is used in existing reusable components.
When adapting a component in a given phase, do not forget to carry this information forward to subsequent phases.	For high-level components with information about each phase of the life cycle, carry forward to all subsequent phases: analysis > design > coding > testing (if this represents your development process).

A

Common Object Request Broker Architecture (CORBA)

The Object Management Group

The Object Management Group (OMG) is an industry-sponsored consortium established to develop object technology standards for distributed computing. It was founded in 1989 by Hewlett-Packard, Sun Microsystems, and nine other companies; it now has over 500 corporate members. OMG's mission is to:

- Maximize software portability, reusability, and interoperability

- Provide a reference architecture for specifications and create industry object standards

- Provide an open forum for discussion, education, and promotion of sponsored object technology

Standards developed by OMG support distributed applications, distributed services, and common facilities for distributed object computing.

Object Management Architecture

OMG has developed an object management architecture guide that outlines an object model and a reference model for object standards. The Core Object Model defines common semantics for specifying standard and implementation-independent object behavior. This model is used by other OMG specifications, such as CORBA. The Object Management Architecture Reference Model is a conceptual architecture for distributed systems of objects and is extended by other OMG specifications. The Reference Model describes a high-level architecture (see Figure A.1), which can accommodate a variety of designs. CORBA is a design solution for the communication core of the Reference Model.

Within the Object Management Architecture, the Object Request Broker (ORB) allows objects to send requests transparently and receive responses in a distributed computing environment, acting as a software bus that supports interoperation of objects. An ORB supplies sockets into which objects can be plugged and then shared across a distributed network of objects. Major architectural components that can be shared using an ORB include:

- Application objects
- Object services
- Common facilities

Application objects collaborate to provide application-specific functions. *Object services* provide a set of basic services for implementing and using distributed objects. These services are independent of appli-

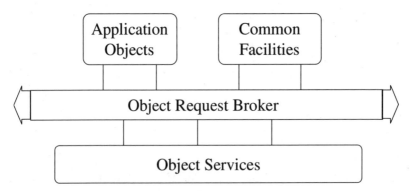

Figure A.1   The object management architecture.

cations and must be implemented for each ORB in a network. The following services have been adopted:

- Event notification
- Life cycle
- Naming
- Persistence
- Concurrency
- Externalization
- Relationships
- Transaction services

Other proposed services include:

- Security
- Time
- Licensing
- Properties
- Query services

Common facilities are services that applications may share and are sometimes referred to as application frameworks designed to promote software reuse. Common facilities include horizontal, application-independent utilities, and application-dependent utilities. Object services must be implemented for each ORB, but common facilities are optional.

Application objects and common facilities are concerned with applications, while ORB and object services are involved with the distributed object computing infrastructure. In practice, common facilities provide high-level services that access features in the object services.

Common Object Request Broker Architecture (CORBA)

OMG's publication, *The Common Object Request Broker: Architecture and Specification*, defines a framework for ORB implementations so that common ORB services and interfaces are provided for distributed object computing. CORBA defines a framework for different interoperating ORB implementations to provide common services interfaces. It specifies an object model and an architecture based on the OMG Core Object Model and the Object Management Architecture Reference Model.

The Object Model

CORBA defines a concrete object model based on the abstract Core Object Model. CORBA refines and extends that model for detailed ORB specification. An object system is described as a collection of collaborating client and server objects. Client objects send requests for services to server objects (object implementations).

Objects. An object is an identifiable, encapsulated entity that provides one or more services to clients. Objects encapsulate state and behavior, usually as attributes and operations. Each object has a unique identity, used to distinguish it from other objects, even if another object has the same state and behavior (is equivalent). An object can model any kind of entity.

Requests. Clients issue requests for services to server objects—a request is an event that invokes an operation. A request usually consists of an operation name and, optionally, actual parameters and a request context. An actual parameter is a value, and if it refers to a specific object it is called an object reference. Object references provide unique identities for ORB messaging. These references allow clients to maintain references to server objects as long as the server objects are active. They can be converted into strings for permanent storage if necessary.

Types and object types. A type is an identifiable entity associated with a Boolean condition (a predicate) defined over a range of values. A value is said to satisfy a type if the type condition is true for that value. When a value satisfies a type, it is a member of that type. Types can be used to restrict input parameters and specify returned results for operations.

An object type is a type whose members are values identifying objects; only values that identify objects can satisfy an object type condition. Object types form a type hierarchy, which forms a directed acyclic graph (with one-way edges and no cycles) with object as the root. Applications build new types by subtyping from the object root.

In the OMG Object Model, subtyping is different from inheritance. Subtyping represents a generalization/specialization relationship between types based on their interfaces. Inheritance represents a generalization/specialization relationship between types that includes not only interfaces but also implementations. The Object Model specifies interface inheritance but does not specify implementation inheritance, which includes operations.

Interfaces.   An object interface describes operations and attributes that the object provides to clients; it includes operation signatures and attribute types. An object satisfies an interface if it can be specified as a target object for requests that use the interface. An object may also have other operations reserved for internal operations (private operations), not defined by its public interface. Interface inheritance allows objects to support multiple interfaces. Object interfaces are specified using an interface definition language that supports interface inheritance.

Operations.   An object operation is a service that can be requested as a unit; it implements the behavior of an object and is identified by an operation identifier. An operation's signature describes its input request parameters and returned results. Operations may be generic, so that a single operation may be uniformly requested on objects with different implementations and possibly different behavior. The ability of a language to provide parameterized modules or types is affected by interface inheritance in OMG's Interface Definition Language (IDL) and by separating interface and implementation specifications. Thus the Object Model supports polymorphism.

Attributes.   An object attribute associates an object variable with a value; an object's state is maintained by its attributes. An attribute is equivalent to declaring an access function to set an attribute value and another to retrieve the attribute value. Read-only access permissions are supported, and, if an attribute is designated as read-only, only a retrieval accessor function is defined.

Object implementation. An object's implementation defines the various activities needed to execute the behavior required of requested services. An object implementation consists of an execution model and a construction model. The *execution model* defines how services are performed. Requested services are performed by executing code that operates on data. In CORBA, the code that is executed to perform a service is called a method. Method execution is called activation. When a client request is executed, a method in a target object is invoked with the actual parameters of the request, and the return value (or exception) is sent back to the requester. The *construction model* describes how services are defined. An object implementation usually includes definitions of object state, methods, and an infrastructure for selecting methods for execution and selecting parts of object state for external access.

Object Request Broker Architecture

An Object Request Broker (ORB) is a mechanism that transports a request from a client to the appropriate object implementation. The client issues the request and the implementation is the code and data that implement the requested service. An ORB is used to:

- Find an object implementation to receive a request

- Prepare the object implementation to receive the request

- Communicate the requested data

The ORB interface is independent of any object's physical location and implementation. See Figure A.2 for an illustration of moving a request from a client to the appropriate object implementation.

CORBA specifies an application-level communication infrastructure, providing communication facilities to applications through static interfaces and the Dynamic Invocation Interface. An Interface Repository stores on-line descriptions of Interface Definition Language interfaces. The Basic Object Adapter is a set of ORB interfaces for object implementations. CORBA represents a peer-to-peer distributed computing infrastructure, where all applications are objects that can play the role of both clients and servers. More flexible architectures may be implemented using CORBA than pure client/server architectures using remote procedure calls.

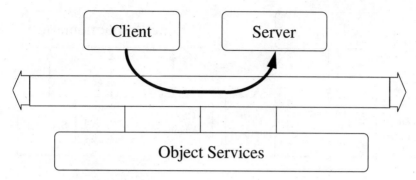

Figure A.2   An ORB request.

ORB structure. An ORB's structure (Figure A.3) allows a client to send a request through three interfaces:

1. A *Dynamic Invocation Interface*, which provides a dynamic interface for object services that determine the method to be invoked at run time.

2. *Interface Definition Language* stubs, which provide static interfaces for object services that determine the method to be invoked at compile time.

3. An *ORB Interface*, which directly accesses basic ORB services that are independent of an object's interfaces or object adapter.

An object implementation can receive a request through four interfaces:

1. A Dynamic Skeleton Interface

2. An IDL Skeleton

3. An Object Adapter

4. An ORB Interface

A *Dynamic Skeleton Interface* provides a dynamic binding mechanism for object implementations that lack IDL skeletons; it is able to process both static and dynamic requests. An *IDL Skeleton* provides static interfaces for each object service exported by an object implementation. Object services are defined using an IDL. The IDL skeleton pro-

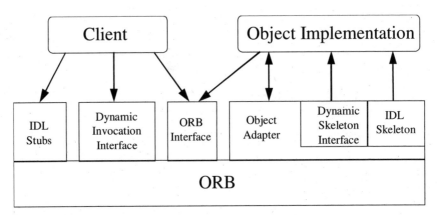

Figure A.3   ORB structure.

vides a server IDL stub. An *Object Adapter* is the primary way that an object implementation accesses core ORB communication services. An *ORB Interface* allows an object implementation to directly access basic ORB services. These interfaces are identical to the client ones.

ORB components.   The ORB core is the component primarily responsible for transferring requests from clients to the appropriate object adapters associated with object implementations. CORBA specifies interfaces above the core, but does not specify the core itself, because it is implementation specific. Differences among vendor implementations are hidden. CORBA 2.0 defines General Interoperability Protocols for interoperability. Only the Internet Inter-ORB Protocol on TCP/IP networks, the Dynamic Interaction Interface, the Dynamic Skeleton Interface, IDL stubs, IDL skeletons, object adapters, and the ORB Interface are used to access the ORB.

Clients.   A client is an entity that issues requests to an implementation object via the ORB. Clients have access to the unique identity of implementation objects by their object references and know their logical structure by their interfaces. A client first builds a request, with one request defined for each operation that an object implementation supports via its interface. A client request consists of the operation name, zero or more actual parameters, and, optionally, a request context. Clients can invoke three kinds of service requests:

1. Synchronous

2. Deferred synchronous

3. One-way

A *synchronous* request is one where the client waits for completion of the request. With a *deferred synchronous* request, the client does not wait for completion of the request but intends to accept request results later. A *one-way* request is one with a client not waiting for request completion and not intending to accept request results at a later time. Deferred synchronous and one-way requests are really asynchronous messages, and are required to support a high degree of concurrency with distributed objects.

Clients can use two invocation interface types: an IDL stub interface for compile-time request definition and the Dynamic Invocation Interface for run-time request definition. Synchronous and one-way requests can be made with either interface. Deferred synchronous requests can only be made using the Dynamic Invocation Interface. Either way, the object implementation sees the request as the same.

A client accesses the implementation object using a language-dependent object reference (see Figure A.4). This object reference is a token invoked directly or passed as a parameter to an invocation on an-

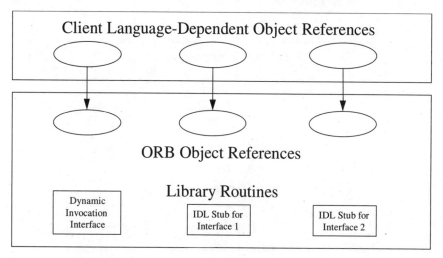

Figure A.4 Client structure.

other implementation object. Invocation of an object involves specification of its object reference and the operation and parameters for the request. The ORB coordinates control and data transfers to the object implementation and back to the client. Usually, a client calls a routine to execute the invocation request and return when completed. If the ORB cannot complete the invocation request, an exception is generated.

Clients access interface stubs as library routines in programs. With static invocations, the client passes object reference to stub routines to initiate requests. These stubs interact with the ORB to execute the invocation. A set of library routines is available for execution of dynamic invocations via the Dynamic Invocation Interface. Clients usually view objects and ORB interfaces via program language bindings associated with a program-level abstraction.

Object implementations.   An object implementation is used to specify semantics for a server object, usually defining code for the server object operations and data for attributes. Also, the object implementation typically defines procedures for object activation and deactivation and for using other objects to make an object persistent, control access, and implement methods. Physical object implementation locations are transparent to clients issuing requests. Object implementation service requests are received through either the Dynamic Skeleton Interface or the IDL skeleton interface.

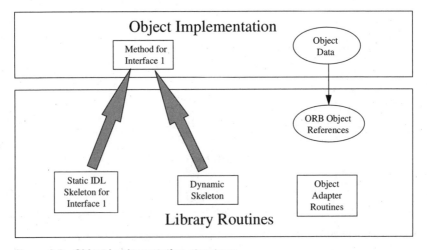

Figure A.5   Object implementation structure.

Object implementation structuring can be accomplished variously, with client requests transferred from dynamic and IDL skeletons to object implementation methods. An object implementation interacts with an ORB to establish its identity, create objects, and obtain ORB services. An object adapter provides an interface to ORB services pertinent to a specific object implementation. Figure A.5 shows a typical object implementation structure.

Dynamic invocation interface. The Dynamic Invocation Interface allows clients to issue requests dynamically at run time. While the result is the same as issuing a static request using IDL stubs, the dynamic approach has the advantage that it eliminates the need for clients to issue specific requests to object implementation-specific stubs. The disadvantage of the dynamic approach is that it often involves significant performance overhead costs.

Dynamic invocation is usually more complex than static invocation via stubs and involves these steps:

1. Retrieve interface definitions from the interface repository.

2. Obtain object references.

3. Build a request to include arguments and optional context.

4. Invoke the request.

5. Obtain the results (if appropriate).

6. Delete the request (if appropriate).

The Dynamic Invocation Interface varies among programming language bindings. The Dynamic Skeleton Interface provides dynamic binding for object implementations lacking IDL skeletons. The Dynamic Invocation Interface can process both static and dynamic service requests.

IDL stubs and skeletons. IDL stubs allow clients to define compile-time requests. These stubs provide access to IDL-defined operations on an object in a straightforward manner. Stubs call the ORB core using interfaces private to specific ORBs; if more than one ORB is being used, there may be different stubs for the different ORBs.

IDL skeletons provide an object implementation equivalent of an IDL stub. They provide, for each programming language binding, interfaces to the methods that implement object types. Client requests received by the ORB core are forwarded to a skeleton, which relays the request to the appropriate object implementation. The IDL compiler generates IDL stubs for object clients and IDL skeletons for object implementations.

Object adapters. An object adapter is the main way that an object implementation accesses core ORB communication services, providing a dynamic environment for:

- Generating and interpreting object references
- Mapping object references to object implementations
- Registering object implementations
- Activating and deactivating objects and implementations
- Invoking implementation methods
- Interaction security

The object adapter (see Figure A.6) is indirectly involved in method invocation; the direct interface is via skeletons. An object adapter may be involved with implementation activation or request authentication.

Each ORB must support a standard object adapter, the Basic Object Adapter. Object implementations must depend upon object adapters. Other useful adapters include a Library Object Adapter (for objects implemented as libraries) and an Object-Oriented Database Adapter (for objects persistently stored in an object database).

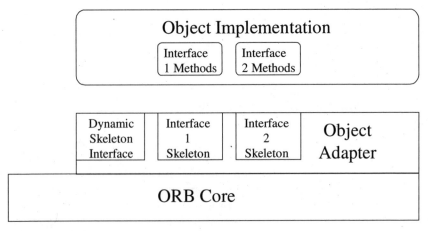

Figure A.6   Object adapter structure.

ORB interface. The ORB interface for clients is the same as for object implementations. It directly accesses basic ORB services not dependent on object interfaces or object adapters. The ORB interface does not provide many operations because other interfaces provide such functionality. Figure A.7 describes the various CORBA interfaces.

Interface and implementation repositories. An interface repository stores interface information needed by clients. It contains information similar to that stored in IDL stubs for static invocations. The interface repository provides interface descriptions for dynamic invocation requests. The implementation repository stores information needed by object implementations, allowing the ORB to locate and activate object implementations. This repository is similar to the interface repository, but it is only for object implementations. It relates object references with object implementations in a manner similar to how the interface repository relates object references with interfaces.

Interface definition language. OMG has defined a language, Interface Definition Language (IDL), which defines interfaces that client objects call and that implementation objects provide. This language defines object types via their interfaces. Each interface consists of named operations, parameters, and exception conditions for each operation. IDL is used to specify interfaces and data formats, not implementations. The syntax is a subset of ANSI C++, supporting encapsulation, inheritance, and polymorphism. It follows the same syntax rules as C++ but with

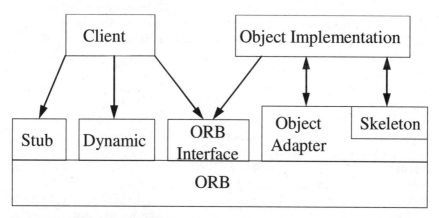

Figure A.7   CORBA interfaces.

new keywords for distributed objects. See Appendix B for a brief intro-duction to the IDL syntax and semantics.

IDL is a technology-independent syntax for describing object encap-sulations, serving as a universal notation for defining software inter-faces. Interfaces that have attributes and operation signatures may be defined, with IDL supporting inheritance between interface descrip-tions to facilitate reuse. Specifications are compiled into header files and stub programs. Mappings from IDL to any programming language could be supported, with C, C++, and SmallTalk already supported; other language mappings are being developed (several ORB vendors claim to support Java as of this writing).

IDL is independent of programming language, with specific lan-guage bindings that have a programming interface and a programming stub interface for each interface. The subs provide interfaces to IDL-de-fined operations. Object services are also defined using IDL. The IDL compiler generates IDL stubs for object clients and IDL skeletons for object implementations. Client programs link directly to IDL stubs, with stubs acting as local function calls. A stub provides a transparent interface to the ORB that performs marshaling to encode and decode an operation's parameters into communication formats for transmis-sion. IDL skeleton programs provide server-side implementation of IDL interfaces. When an ORB receives a request, a skeleton provides a callback to a server-supplied function implementation. When the serv-er completes request processing, the skeleton and stub return results to the client program along with any exception information.

Using IDL specifications.   OMG's Interface Definition Language is a specification language and can be used as built-in library interfaces, ORB interfaces, or Remote Procedure Call (RPC) interfaces. An IDL in-terface need not be used with an ORB product or vice versa. The lan-guage may be used by itself to specify Application Programming Interfaces (APIs) implemented with CORBA or non-CORBA tools. IDL provides a technology-independent interface, but an application is not distributed. Clients and servers are compiled and linked as a single program. An ORB or RPC mechanism provides the means for distribu-tion of system components. A client still makes local function calls, but a stub call is sent using an ORB or RPC to a remote skeleton function, which, in turn, activates a server implementation (see Figure A.8).

When IDL is mapped to a programming language, three arguments (object handle, environment, and context) are generated automatically along with optional user-defined parameters. The object handle speci-

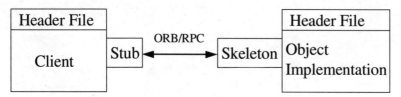

Figure A.8   ORB/RPC Distribution (see Mowbray, p. 42).

fies the handle of the server to be activated. The context contains system- or user-specific properties not suitable for argument passing, and context objects contain properties consisting of a name and a string value. These properties provide information about the client, environment, or a request. Clients pass this information to the server, which can use it for policy and binding decisions. CORBA defines operations for creating, deleting setting values, and obtaining property values.

References

Mowbray, T. J., and R. Zahavi. *The Essential CORBA: Systems Integration Using Distributed Objects*. New York: John Wiley & Sons, 1994.

OMG. *The Common Object Request Broker: Architecture and Specification*. Revision 2.0. Framingham, MA: OMG, July 1995 (updated July 1996).

B

OMG Interface Definition Language Syntax and Semantics

The OMG Interface Definition Language (IDL) is the language used to describe the interfaces that client objects call and object implementations provide. An interface definition written in OMG IDL completely defines the interface and fully specifies each operation's parameters. An OMG IDL interface provides the information needed to develop clients that use the interface's operations. Clients are not written in OMG IDL, which is purely a descriptive language, but in languages for which mappings from OMG IDL concepts have been defined. The mapping of an OMG IDL concept to a client language construct will depend on the facilities available in the client language. For example, an OMG IDL exception might be mapped to a structure in a language that has no notion of exception or to an exception in a language that does. The binding of OMG IDL concepts to the C, C++, and SmallTalk languages are described in the OMG manual. Bindings from OMG IDL to additional programming languages will be added to future versions of *Cobra*.

OMG IDL obeys the same lexical rules as C++1, although new keywords are introduced to support distribution concepts. It also provides full support for standard C++ preprocessing features. The OMG IDL specification is expected to track relevant changes to C++ introduced by the ANSI standardization effort.

This appendix provides only a sample of the comprehensive coverage of the CORBA specification and only a small portion of the IDL section (Chapter 3 of the CORBA specification) is addressed here. Please refer to the OMG publications for current and complete information on OMG's evolving object standards.

OMG IDL Grammar

```
(1) <specification> ::= <definition>?

(2) <definition>      ::= <type_dcl> ";"
                        | <const_dcl> ";"
                        | <except_dcl> ";"
                        | <interface> ";"
                        | <module> ";"

(3) <module>          ::= "module" <identifier> "{" <definition> + "}"

(4) <interface>       ::= <interface_dcl>
                        | <forward_dcl>
(5) <interface_dcl> ::= <interface_header> "{" <interface_body> "}"

(6) <forward_dcl>     ::= "interface" <identifier>

(7) <interface_header>::= "interface" <identifier> [
<inheritance_spec> ]

(8) <interface_body>::= <export> *

(9) <export>          ::= <type_dcl> ";"
                        | <const_dcl> ";"
                        | <except_dcl> ";"
                        | <attr_dcl> ";"
                        | <op_dcl> ";"

(10) <inheritance_spec>::= ":" <scoped_name> { "," <scoped_name> } ?

(11) <scoped_name>    ::= <identifier>
                        | "::" <identifier>
                        | <scoped_name> "::" <identifier>

(12) <const_dcl>      ::= "const" <const_type> <identifier> "="
<const_exp>
```

```
(13) <const_type>    ::= <integer_type>
                      | <char_type>
                      | <boolean_type>
                      | <floating_pt_type>
                      | <string_type>
                      | <scoped_name>

(14) <const_exp>     ::= <or_expr>

(15) <or_expr>       ::= <xor_expr>
                      | <or_expr> "|" <xor_expr>

(16) <xor_expr>      ::= <and_expr>
                      | <xor_expr> "^" <and_expr>

(17) <and_expr>      ::= <shift_expr>
                      | <and_expr> "&" <shift_expr>

(18) <shift_expr>    ::= <add_expr>
                      | <shift_expr> ">>" <add_expr>
                      | <shift_expr> "<<" <add_expr>

(19) <add_expr>      ::= <mult_expr>
                      | <add_expr> "+" <mult_expr>
                      | <add_expr> "-" <mult_expr>

(20) <mult_expr>     ::= <unary_expr>
            <mult_expr> "*" <unary_expr>
                      | <mult_expr> "/" <unary_expr>
                      | <mult_expr> "%" <unary_expr>

(21) <unary_expr>    ::= <unary_operator> <primary_expr>
                      | <primary_expr>

(22) <unary_operator> ::= "-"
                       | "+"
                       | "~"

(23) <primary_expr>::= <scoped_name>
                      | <literal>
                      | "(" <const_exp> ")"

(24) <literal>       ::= <integer_literal>
                      | <string_literal>
                      | <character_literal>
                      | <floating_pt_literal>
                      | <boolean_literal>

(25) <boolean_literal> ::= "TRUE"
                        | "FALSE"
```

```
(26)  <positive_int_const>::=<const_exp>

(27)  <type_dcl>     ::= "typedef" <type_declarator>
                       | <struct_type>
                       | <union_type>
                       | <enum_type>

(28)  <type_declarator> ::= <type_spec> <declarators>

(29)  <type_spec>    ::= <simple_type_spec>
                       | <constr_type_spec>

(30)  <simple_type_spec>::=<base_type_spec>
                       | <template_type_spec>
                       | <scoped_name>

(31)  <base_type_spec>::= <floating_pt_type>
                       | <integer_type>
                       | <char_type>
                       | <boolean_type>
                       | <octet_type>
                       | <any_type>

(32)  <template_type_spec>::=<sequence_type>
                       | <string_type>

(33)  <constr_type_spec>::=<struct_type>
                       | <union_type>
                       | <enum_type>

(34)  <declarators> ::= <declarator> { "," <declarator> } ?

(35)  <declarator>   ::= <simple_declarator>
                       | <complex_declarator>

(36)  <simple_declarator>::=<identifier>

(37)  <complex_declarator>::=<array_declarator>

(38)  <floating_pt_type>::= "float"
                       | "double"

(39)  <integer_type>::= <signed_int>
                       | <unsigned_int>

(40)  <signed_int>   ::= <signed_long_int>
                       | <signed_short_int>

(41)  <signed_long_int> ::= "long"

(42)  <signed_short_int>::= "short"
```

```
(43) <unsigned_int>::= <unsigned_long_int>
                     | <unsigned_short_int>

(44) <unsigned_long_int>::="unsigned" "long"

(45) <unsigned_short_int>::="unsigned" "short"

(46) <char_type>      ::= "char"

(47) <boolean_type>   ::= "boolean"

(48) <octet_type>     ::= "octet"

(49) <any_type>       ::= "any"

(50) <struct_type>    ::= "struct" <identifier> "{" <member_list>
"}"

(51) <member_list>    ::= <member>?

(52) <member>     ::= <type_spec> <declarators> ";"

(53) <union_type>     ::= "union" <identifier> "switch" "("
<switch_type_spec> ")"
             "{" <switch_body> "}"

(54) <switch_type_spec>::=<integer_type>
                       | <char_type>
                       | <boolean_type>
                       | <enum_type>
                       | <scoped_name>

(55) <switch_body>    ::= <case>?

(56) <case>       ::= <case_label>??<element_spec> ";"

(57) <case_label>    ::= "case" <const_exp> ":"
                     | "default" ":"

(58) <element_spec>   ::= <type_spec> <declarator>

(59) <enum_type>     ::= "enum" <identifier> "{" <enumerator> { ","
<enumerator> } ??"}"

(60) <enumerator>    ::= <identifier>

(61) <sequence_type> ::= "sequence" "<" <simple_type_spec>
","<positive_int_const>">"
                       | "sequence" "<" <simple_type_spec> ">"
```

```
(62) <string_type>       ::= "string" "<" <positive_int_const> ">"
                           | "string"

(63) <array_declarator>::= <identifier> <fixed_array_size>?

(64) <fixed_array_size>::= "[" <positive_int_const> "]"

(65) <attr_dcl>          ::= [ "readonly" ] "attribute"
<param_type_spec>
             <simple_declarator> { "," <simple_declarator> }*

(66) <except_dcl>        ::= "exception" <identifier> "{" <member>*
"}"

(67) <op_dcl>            ::= [ <op_attribute> ] <op_type_spec>
<identifier>
             <parameter_dcls>
         [ <raises_expr> ] [ <context_expr> ]

(68) <op_attribute>      ::= "oneway"

(69) <op_type_spec>      ::= <param_type_spec>
                           | "void"

(70) <parameter_dcls>    ::= "(" <param_dcl> { "," <param_dcl> }
??")"
                           | "(" ")"

(71) <param_dcl>    ::= <param_attribute> <param_type_spec>
<simple_declarator>

(72) <param_attribute> ::= "in"
                         | "out"
                         | "inout"

(73) <raises_expr>       ::= "raises" "(" <scoped_name> { ","
<scoped_name> } ??")"

(74) <context_expr>      ::= "context" "(" <string_literal> { ","
<string_literal> } ??")"

(75) <param_type_spec> ::=<base_type_spec>
                         | <string_type>
                         | <scoped_name>
```

OMG IDL Specification

An OMG IDL specification consists of one or more type definitions, constant definitions, exception definitions, or module definitions. The syntax is:

```
<specification>    ::= <definition>?
<definition>       ::= <type_dcl> ";"
                    | <const_dcl> ";"
                    | <except_dcl> ";"
                    | <interface> ";"
                    | <module> ";"
```

See "Constant Declaration," "Type Declaration," and "Exception Declaration," respectively, in the CORBA specification for details of `<const_dcl>`, `<type_dcl>`, and `<except_dcl>`.

Module Declaration

A module definition satisfies the following syntax:.

```
<module>    ::= "module" <identifier> "{" <definition> + "}"
```

The module construct is used to scope OMG IDL identifiers; see "CORBA Module" in the CORBA specification for details.

Interface Declaration

An interface definition satisfies the following syntax:.

```
<interface>        ::= <interface_dcl>
                    | <forward_dcl>

<interface_dcl>    ::= <interface_header> "{" <interface_body> "}"

<forward_dcl>      ::= "interface" <identifier>

<interface_header> ::="interface" <identifier> [
<inheritance_spec> ]
```

```
<interface_body>   ::=<export> *

<export>        ::= <type_dcl> ";"
                | <const_dcl> ";"
                | <except_dcl> ";"
                | <attr_dcl> ";"
                | <op_dcl> ";"
```

Interface Header

The interface header consists of two elements:

1. The interface name—The name must be preceded by the keyword `interface` and consists of an identifier that names the interface.

2. An optional inheritance specification—The inheritance specification is described in the next section.

The `<identifier>` that names an interface defines a legal type name. Such a type name may be used anywhere an `<identifier>` is legal in the grammar, subject to semantic constraints as described in the following sections. Since one can only hold references to an object, the meaning of a parameter or structure member that is an interface type is as a *reference* to an object supporting that interface. Each language binding describes how the programmer must represent such interface references.

Inheritance Specification

The syntax for inheritance is as follows:

```
<inheritance_spec>::= ":" <scoped_name> {"," <scoped_name>}*
<scoped_name>      ::= <identifier>
                   | "::" <identifier>
                   | <scoped_name> "::" <identifier>
```

Each `<scoped_name>` in an `<inheritance_spec>` must denote a previously defined interface. See "Inheritance" in the CORBA specification for the description of inheritance.

Interface Body

The interface body contains the following kinds of declarations:

- Constant declarations, which specify the constants that the interface exports; constant declaration syntax is described in "Constant Declaration" in the CORBA specification.

- Type declarations, which specify the type definitions that the interface exports; type declaration syntax is described in "Type Declaration" in the CORBA specification.

- Exception declarations, which specify the exception structures that the interface exports; exception declaration syntax is described in "Exception Declaration" in the CORBA specification.

- Attribute declarations, which specify the associated attributes exported by the interface; attribute declaration syntax is described in "Attribute Declaration" in the CORBA specification.

- Operation declarations, which specify the operations that the interface exports and the format of each, including operation name, the type of data returned, the types of all parameters of an operation, legal exceptions that may be returned as a result of an invocation, and contextual information that may affect method dispatch; operation declaration syntax is described in "Operation Declaration" in the CORBA specification.

Empty interfaces are permitted (that is, those containing no declarations). Some implementations may require interface-specific pragmas to precede the interface body.

Forward Declaration

A forward declaration declares the name of an interface without defining it. This permits the definition of interfaces that refer to each other. The syntax consists simply of the keyword `interface` followed by an `<identifier>` that names the interface. The actual definition must follow later in the specification. Multiple forward declarations of the same interface name are legal.

Differences from C++

The OMG IDL grammar, while attempting to conform to the C++ syntax, is somewhat more restrictive. The current restrictions are as follows:

- A function return type is mandatory.

- A name must be supplied with each formal parameter to an operation declaration.

- A parameter list consisting of the single token `void` is *not* permitted as a synonym for an empty parameter list.

- Tags are required for structures, discriminated unions, and enumerations.

- Integer types cannot be defined as simply int or unsigned; they must be declared explicitly as `short` or `long`.

- `char` cannot be qualified by `signed` or `unsigned` keywords.

Reference

OMG. *The Common Object Request Broker: Architecture and Specification.* Revision 2.0. Framingham, MA: OMG, July 1995 (updated July 1996).

UML Summary

Introduction

The Unified Modeling Language (UML) is a language for specifying, visualizing, constructing, and documenting the artifacts of software systems, as well as for business modeling and other nonsoftware systems. The UML represents a collection of best engineering practices that have proven successful in the modeling of large and complex systems. The UML definition consists of the following documents:

UML Semantics—defines the rich semantics and expressive syntax of the Unified Modeling Language. The UML is layered architecturally and organized by package. Within each package, the model elements are defined in terms of their abstract syntax (using the UML class diagram notation), well-formedness rules (using text and Object Constraint Language expressions), and semantics (using precise text). Two appendices are included: UML Glossary and Standard Elements.

UML Notation Guide—defines notion and provides supporting examples. The UML notation represents the graphic syntax for expressing the semantics described by the UML metamodel.

UML Extension for the Objectory Process for Software Engineeering and *UML Extension for Business Modeling*—These UML extensions includes process- and domain-specific extensions to the UML, in terms of its extension mechanisms and process-specific diagram icons.

The UML uses OCL, defined separately in the *Object Constraint Language Specification* document.

Intended Audience

This document set is intended primarily as a precise and self-consistent definition of the UML's semantics and notation. The primary audience of this document set consists of the Object Management Group, standards organizations, book authors, trainers, and tool builders. The authors assume familiarity with object-oriented analysis and design methods. These documents are not written as an introductory text on building object models for complex systems, although they could be used in conjunction with other materials or instruction. This set of documents will become more approachable to a broader audience as additional books, training courses, and tools that apply the UML become available.

Motivation to Define the UML

This section describes several factors motivating the UML. We discuss why modeling is essential, highlight a few key trends in the software industry, and describe the issues caused by divergence of modeling approaches.

Why We Model

Developing a model for an industrial-strength software system prior to its construction or renovation is as essential as having a blueprint for large building. Good models are essential for communication among project teams and to assure architectural soundness. We build models of complex systems because we cannot comprehend any such system in its entirety. As the complexity of systems increase, so does the importance of good modeling techniques. There are many additional factors of a project's success, but having a rigorous *modeling language* standard is one essential factor. A modeling language must include:

- Model elements—fundamental modeling concepts and semantics

- Notation—visual rendering of model elements

- Guidelines—idioms of usage within the trade

In the face of increasingly complex systems, visualization and modeling become essential. The UML is a well-defined and widely accepted response to that need. It is the visual modeling language of choice for building object-oriented and component-based systems.

Industry Trends In Software

As the strategic value of software increases for many companies, the industry looks for techniques to automate the production of software. We look for techniques to improve quality and reduce cost and time-to-market. These techniques include component technology, visual programming, patterns, and frameworks. We also seek techniques to manage the complexity of systems as they increase in scope and scale. In particular, we recognize the need to solve recurring architectural problems, such as physical distribution, concurrency, replication, security, load balancing, and fault tolerance. Development for the worldwide web makes some things simpler, but exacerbates these architectural problems.

Complexity will vary by application domain and process phase. One of the key motivations in the minds of the UML developers was to create a set of semantics and notation that adequately addresses all scales of architectural complexity, across all domains.

Prior To Industry Convergence

Prior to the UML, there was no clearly leading modeling language. Users had to choose from among many similar modeling languages with minor difference in overall expressive power. Most of the modeling languages shared a set of commonly accepted concepts that are expressed slightly differently in different languages. This lack of agreement discouraged new users from entering the OO market and from doing OO modeling, without greatly expanding the power of modeling. Users longed for the industry to adopt one, or a very few, broadly supported modeling languages suitable for general-purpose usage. They wanted a *lingua franca* for modeling.

Some vendors were discouraged from entering the OO modeling area because of the need to support many similar, but slightly different, modeling languages. In particular, the supply of add-on tools has been depressed because small vendors cannot afford to support many different formats from many different front-end modeling tools. It is important to the entire OO industry to encourage broadly based tools and vendors, as well as niche products that cater to the needs of specialized groups.

The perpetual cost of using and supporting many modeling languages motivated many companies producing or using OO technology to endorse and support the development of the UML.

While the UML does not guarantee project success, it does improve many things. For example, it significantly lowers the perpetual cost of training and retooling when changing between projects or organizations. It provides the opportunity for new integration between tools, processes, and domains. But most importantly, it enables developers to focus on delivering business value and provides them a paradigm to accomplish this.

Goals of the UML

The primary goals in the design of the UML were as follow:

1. Provide users a ready-to-use, expressive visual modeling language so they can develop and exchange meaningful models.

2. Provide extensibility and specialization mechanisms to extend the core concepts.

3. Be independent of particular programming languages and development processes.

4. Provide a formal basis for understanding the modeling language.

5. Encourage the growth of the OO tools market.

6. Support higher-level development concepts such as collaborations, frameworks, patterns, and components.

7. Integrate best practices.

These goals are discussed, below.

Provide users a ready-to-use, expressive visual modeling language so they can develop and exchange meaningful models. It is important that the OOAD standard support a modeling language that can be used "out of the box" to do normal general-purpose modeling tasks. If the standard merely provides a meta-meta-description that requires tailoring to a particular set of modeling concepts, then it will not achieve the purpose of allowing users to exchange models without losing information or without imposing excessive work to map their models to a very abstract form. The UML consolidates a set of core modeling concepts that are generally accepted across many current methods and modeling tools. These concepts are needed in many or most large applications, although not every concept is needed in every part of every application. Specifying a meta-meta-level format for the concepts is not sufficient for model users, because the concepts must be made concrete for real modeling to occur. If the concepts in different application areas were substantially different, then such an approach might work, but the core concepts needed by most application areas are similar and should therefore be supported directly by he standard without the need for another layer.

Provide extensibility and specialization mechanisms to extend the core concepts. We expect that the UML will be tailored as new needs are discovered and for specific domains. At the same time, we do not want to force the common core concepts to be redefined or re-implemented for each tailored area. Therefore we believe that the extension mechanisms should support deviations from the common case, rather than being required to implement the core OOA&D concepts themselves. The core concepts should not be changed more than necessary. Users need to be able to 1) build models using core concepts without using extension mechanisms for most normal applications; 2) add new concepts and notations for issues not covered by the core; 3) choose among variant interpretations of existing concepts, when there is no clear consensus; and 4) specialize the concepts, notations, and constraints for particular application domains.

Be independent of particular programming languages and development processes. The UML must and can support all reasonable programming languages. It also must and can support various methods and processes of building models. The UML can support multiple programming languages and development methods without excessive difficulty.

Provide a formal basis for understanding the modeling language. Because users will use formality to help understand the language, it must be both precise and approachable; a lack of either dimension damages its usefulness. The formalisms must not require excessive levels of indirection or layering, use of low-level mathematical notations distant from the modeling domain, such as set-theoretic notation, or operational definitions that are equivalent to programming an implementation. The UML provides a formal definition of the static format of the model using a metamodel expressed in UML class diagrams. This is a popular and widely accepted formal approach for specifying the format of a model and directly leads to the implementation of interchange formats. UML expresses well-formedness constraints in precise natural language plus Object Constraint Language expressions. UML expresses the operational meaning of most constructs in precise natural language. The fully formal approach taken to specify languages such as Algol-68 was not approachable enough for most practical usage.

Encourage the growth of the OO tools market. By enabling vendors to support a standard modeling language used by most users and tools, the industry benefits. While vendors still can add value in their tool implementations, enabling interoperability is essential. Interoperability requires that models can be exchanged among users and tools without loss of information. This can only occur if the tools agree on the format and meaning of all of the relevant concepts. Using a higher meta-level is no solution unless the mapping to the user-level concepts is included in the standard.

Support higher-level development concepts such as collaborations, frameworks, patterns, and components. Clearly defined semantics of these concepts is essential to reap the full benefit of OO and reuse. Defining these within the holistic context of a modeling language is a unique contribution of the UML. *Integrate best practices.* A key motivation behind the development of the UML has been to integrate the best practices in the industry, encompassing widely varying views based on levels of abstraction, domains, architectures, life cycle stages, implementation technologies, etc. The UML is indeed such an integration of best practices.

Scope of the UML

The Unified Modeling Language (UML) is a language for specifying, constructing, visualizing, and documenting the artifacts of a software-intensive system.

First and foremost, the Unified Modeling Language fuses the concepts of Booch, OMT, and OOSE. The result is a single, common, and widely usable modeling language for users of these and other methods.

Second, the Unified Modeling Language pushes the envelope of what can be done with existing methods. As an example, the UML authors targeted the modeling of concurrent, distributed systems to assure the UML adequately addresses these domains.

Third, the Unified Modeling Language focuses on a standard modeling language, not a standard process. Although the UML must be applied in the context of a process, it is our experience that different organizations and problem domains require different processes. (For example, the a development process for shrink-wrapped software is an interesting one, but building shrink-wrapped software is vastly different from building hard-real-time avionics systems upon which lives depend.) Therefore, the efforts concentrated first on a common metamodel (which unifies semantics) and second on a common notation (which provides a human rendering of these semantics). The UML authors promote a development process that is *use-case driven, architecture centric, and iterative and incremental.*[1]

The UML specifies a modeling language that incorporates the object-oriented community's consensus on core modeling concepts. It allows deviations to be expressed in terms of its extension mechanisms. The developers of the UML had the following objectives in mind during its development:

- Provide sufficient semantics and notation to address a wide variety of contemporary modeling issues in a direct and economical fashion.

- Provide sufficient semantics to address certain expected future modeling issues, specifically related to component technology, distributed computing, frameworks, and executability.

- Provide extensibility mechanisms so individual projects can extend the metamodel for their application at low cost. We don't want users to have to need to adjust the UML metamodel itself.

---

1. The *Rational Objectory Process* is such a process. See *www.rational.com.*

- Provide extensibility mechanisms so that future modeling approaches could be grown on top of the UML

- Provide sufficient semantics to facilitate model interchange among a variety of kinds of tools.

- Provide sufficient semantics to specify the interface to repositories for the sharing and storage of model artifacts.

Primary Artifacts of the UML

What are the primary artifacts of the UML? This can be answered from two different perspectives: the UML definition itself and how it is used to produce project artifacts.

UML-defining artifacts.   To aid the understanding of the artifacts that constitute the Unified Modeling Language itself, this document set consists of the *UML Semantics, UML Notation Guide,* and *UML Extensions* documents, plus appendices. Some context for each of these is described below. In addition to these documents, books are planned that will focus on understandability, examples, and common usage idioms.

UML semantics.   The *UML Semantics* document defines the language definition using three consistent views:

Abstract syntax—UML class diagrams are used to present the UML metamodel, its concepts (metaclasses), relationships, and constraints. Definitions of the concepts are included.

Well-formedness rules—The rules and constraints on valid models are defined. Therules are expressed English prose and in a precise Object Constraint Language (OCL). OCL is a specification language that uses simple logic for specifying invariant properties of systems comprising sets and relationships between sets.

Semantics—The semantics of model usage are described in English prose.

These views constitute a formal definition of the UML. A more formal definition would involve mathematical expressions that few people could understand directly.

A metamodel is a language for specifying a model, in this case an object model. In other words, it is a model of modeling elements. The purpose of the UML metamodel was to provide a single, common, and definitive statement of the syntax and semantics of the elements of the UML. The presence of this metamodel has made it possible for its developers to agree on semantics, de-coupled from the human-factors issues of how those semantics would best be rendered. Additionally, the metamodel has made it possible for the team to explore ways to make the modeling language much simpler by, in a sense, unifying the elements of the Unified Modeling Language. (For example, commonality among the concepts of classes, patterns, and use cases was discovered.) The authors expect select individuals to express this metamodel even more precisely by describing its semantics using formal techniques.

The "level" of meta in a model is somewhat arbitrary, and the UML developers consciously chose a semantically rich level, because that level is necessary to enable the semantically rich agreement necessary for the design of complex systems, consistent use, and tool interchange.

There are two appendices: *Standard Elements* and *UML Glossary*.

UML notation guide. The *UML Notation Guide* describes the UML notation and provides examples. The graphical notation and textual syntax are the most visible part of the UML (the "outside" view), used by humans and tools to model systems. These are representations of a user-level model, which is semantically an instance of the UML metamodel. The standard diagram types are listed in section 4.1.2, below. The Notation Guide also summarizes the UML semantics; however, the UML Semantics document contains the definitions.

UML extensions. User-defined extensions of the UML are enabled through the use of stereotypes, tagged values, and constraints. Two extensions are currently defined: 1) Objectory Process and 2) Business Engineering.

The UML is broadly applicable without extension, so companies and projects should define extensions only when they find it necessary to introduce new notation and terminology. Extensions will not be as universally understood, supported, and agreed upon as the UML itself. In order to reduce potential confusion around vendor implementations, the following terms are defined:

UML Variant — a language with well-defined semantics that is built on top of the UML metamodel, as a metamodel. It can specializes the UML metamodel, without changing any of the UML semantics or redefining any of its terms. (For example, it could not reintroduce a class called State).

UML Extension — a predefined set of Stereotypes, TaggedValues, Constraints, and notation icons that collectively extend and tailor the UML for a specific domain or process, e.g., the Objectory Process extension.

Development project artifacts.   The choice of what models and diagrams one creates has a profound influence upon how a problem is attacked and how a corresponding solution is shaped. *Abstraction*, the focus on relevant details while ignoring others, is a key to learning and communicating. Because of this:

- Every complex system is best approached through a small set of nearly independent views of a model; No single view is sufficient.
- Every model may be expressed at different levels of fidelity.
- The best models are connected to reality.

In terms of the views of a model, the UML defines the following graphical diagrams:

- use case diagram
- class diagram
- behavior diagrams:
    - statechart diagram
    - activity diagram
- interaction diagrams:
    - sequence diagram
    - collaboration diagram
- implementation diagrams:
    - component diagram
    - deployment diagram

Although other names are sometimes given these diagrams, this list constitutes the canonical diagram names. These diagrams provide multiple perspectives of the system under analysis or development. The underlying model integrates these perspectives so that a self-consistent system can be analyzed and built. These diagrams, along with supporting documentation, are the primary artifacts that a modeler sees, although the UML and supporting tools will provide for a number of derivative views. These diagrams are further described in the *UML Notation Guide*.

A frequently asked question has been, "Why doesn't UML support data-flow diagrams?" Simply put, data-flow and other diagram types that were not included in the UML do not fit as cleanly into a consistent object-oriented paradigm. Activity diagrams accomplish much of what people want from DFDs, and then some; activity diagrams are also useful for modeling workflow. The authors of the UML are clearly promoting the UML diagrams above over all others for object-oriented projects, but don't necessarily condemn all other diagrams. We believe we defined a set of successful and practical techniques, fitting within a consistent paradigm.

Outside the Scope of the UML

Programming languages. The UML, a visual *modeling* language, is not intended to be a visual *programming* language, in the sense of having all the necessary visual and semantic support to replace programming languages. The UML is a language for visualizing, specifying, constructing, and documenting the artifacts of a software-intensive system, but it does draw the line as you move toward code. Some things, like complex branches and joins, are better expressed in a textual programming language. The UML does have a tight mapping to a family of OO languages, so that you can get the best of both worlds.

Tools. Standardizing a language is necessarily the foundation for tools and process. The Object Management Group's RFP (OADTF RFP-1) was a key driver in motivating the UML definition. The primary goal of the RFP was to enable tool interoperability. However, tools and their interoperability are very dependent on a solid semantic and notation definition, such as the UML provides. The UML defines a *semantic* metamodel, not an tool *interface, storage,* or *run-time* model, although these should be fairly close to one another.

The UML documents do include some tips to tool vendors on implementation choices, but do not address everything needed. For example, they don't address topics like diagram coloring, user navigation, animation, storage/implementation models, or other features.

Process. Many organizations will use the UML as a common language for its project artifacts, but will use the same UML diagram types in the context of different processes. The UML is intentionally process independent, and defining a standard process was not a goal of the UML or OMG's RFP.

The UML authors *do* recognize the importance of process. The presence of a well-defined and well-managed process is often a key discriminator between hyperproductive projects and unsuccessful ones. The reliance upon heroic programming is not a sustainable business practice. A process 1) provides guidance as to the order of a team's activities, 2) specifies what artifacts should be developed, 3) directs the tasks of individual developers and the team as a whole, and 4) offers criteria for monitoring and measuring a project's products and activities.

Processes by their very nature must be tailored to the organization, culture, and problem domain at hand. What works in one context (shrink-wrapped software development, for example) would be a disaster in another (hard-real-time, human-rated systems, for example). The selection of a particular process will vary greatly, depending on such things like problem domain, implementation technology, and skills of the team.

Booch, OMT, OOSE, and many other methods have well-defined processes, and the UML can support most methods. There has been some convergence on development process practices, but there is not yet consensus for standardization. What will likely result in the industry is general agreement on best practices and potentially the embracing of a process framework, within which individual processes can be instantiated. Although the UML does not mandate a process, its developers have recognized the value of a *use-case driven, architecture-centric, iterative, and incremental* process, so were careful to enable (but not require) this with the UML.

Comparing UML to Other Modeling Languages

It should be made clear that the Unified Modeling Language is not a radical departure from Booch, OMT, or OOSE, but rather the legitimate successor to all three. This means that if you are a Booch, OMT, or OOSE user today, your training, experience, and tools will be preserved, because the Unified Modeling Language is a natural evolutionary step. The UML will be equally easy to adopt for users of many other methods, but their authors must decide for themselves whether to embrace the UML concepts and notation underneath their methods.

The Unified Modeling Language is more expressive yet cleaner and more uniform than Booch, OMT, OOSE, and other methods. This means that there is value in moving to the Unified Modeling Language, because it will allow projects to model things they could not have done before. Users of most other methods and modeling languages will gain value by moving to the UML, since it removes the unnecessary differences in notation and terminology that obscure the underlying similarities of most of these approaches.

With respect to other visual modeling languages, including entity-relationship modeling, BPR flow charts, and state-driven languages, the UML should provide improved expressiveness and holistic integrity.

Users of existing methods will experience slight changes in notation, but this should not take much relearning and will bring a clarification of the underlying semantics. If the unification goals have been achieved, UML will be an obvious choice when beginning new projects, especially as the availability of tools, books, and training becomes widespread. Many visual modeling tools support existing notations, such as Booch, OMT, OOSE, or others, as views of an underlying model; when these tools add support for UML (as some already have) users will enjoy the benefit of switching their current models to the UML notation without loss of information.

Existing users of any OO method can expect a fairly quick learning curve to achieve the same expressiveness as they previous knew. One can quickly learn and use the basics productively. More advanced techniques, such as the use of stereotypes and properties, will require some study, since they enable very expressive and precise models, needed only when the problem at hand requires them.

New Features of the UML

The goals of the unification efforts were to keep it simple, to cast away elements of existing Booch, OMT, and OOSE that didn't work in practice, to add elements from other methods that were more effective, and to invent new only when an existing solution was not available. Because the UML authors were in effect designing a language (albeit a graphical one), they had to strike a proper balance between minimalism (everything is text and boxes) and over-engineering (having an icon for every conceivable modeling element). To that end, they were very careful about adding new things, because they didn't want to make the UML unnecessarily complex. Along the way, however, some things were found that were advantageous to add because they have proven useful in practice in other modeling.

There are several new concepts that are included in UML, including extensibility mechanisms: stereotypes, tagged values, and constraints; threads and processes; distribution and concurrency (e.g. for modeling ActiveX/DCOM and CORBA); patterns/collaborations; activity diagrams (for business process modeling); refinement (to handle relationships between levels of abstraction); interfaces and components; and a constraint language.

Many of these ideas were present in various individual methods and theories but UML brings them together into a coherent whole. In addition to these major changes, there are many other localized improvements over the Booch, OMT, and OOSE semantics and notation.

The UML is an evolution from Booch, OMT, OOSE, several other object-oriented methods, and many other sources. These various sources incorporated many different elements from many authors, including non-OO influences. The UML notation is a melding of graphical syntax from various sources, with a number of symbols removed (because they were confusing, superfluous, or little used) and with a few new symbols added. The ideas in the UML come from the community of ideas developed by many different people in the object-oriented field. The UML developers did not invent most of these ideas; rather, their role was to select and integrate the best ideas from OO and computer-science practices. The actual genealogy of the notation and underlying detailed semantics is complicated, so it is discussed here only to provide context, not to represent precise history.

Use-case diagrams are similar in appearance to those in OOSE.

Class diagrams are a melding of OMT, Booch, class diagrams of most other OO methods. Extensions (e.g., stereotypes and their corresponding icons) can be defined for various diagrams to support other modeling styles. Stereotypes, constraints, and taggedValues are concepts added in UML that did not previously exist in the major modeling languages.

Statechart diagrams are substantially based on the statecharts of David Harel with minor modifications. The Activity diagram, which shares much of the same underlying semantics, is similar to the work flow diagrams developed by many sources including many pre-OO sources. Oracle and Jim Odell were instrumental in incorporating Activity Diagrams into UML.

Sequence diagrams were found in a variety of OO methods under a variety of names (interaction, message trace, and event trace) and date to pre-OO days. Collaboration diagrams were adapted from Booch (object diagram), Fusion (object interaction graph), and a number of other sources.

Collaborations are now first-class modeling entities, and often form the basis of patterns.

The implementation diagrams (component and deployment diagrams) are derived from Booch's module and process diagrams, but they are now component-centered, rather than module-centered and are far better interconnected.

Stereotypes are one of the extension mechanisms and extend the semantics of the metamodel. User-defined icons can be associated with given stereotypes for tailoring the UML to specific processes.

Object Constraint Language is used by UML to specify the semantics and is provided as a language for expressions during modeling. OCL is an expression language having its root in the Syntropy method and has been influenced by expression languages in other methods like Catalysis. The informal navigation from OMT has the same intent, where OCL is formalized and more extensive.

Each of these concepts has further predecessors and many other influences. We realize that any brief list of influences is incomplete and we recognize that the UML is the product of a long history of ideas in the computer science and software engineering area.

UML Past, Present, and Future

The UML was developed by Rational Software and its partners (see Figure C.1). It is the successor to the modeling languages found in the Booch, OOSE/Jacobson, OMT, and other methods. Many companies are incorporating the UML as a standard into their development process and products, which cover disciplines such as business modeling, requirements management, analysis & design, programming, and testing.

UML 0.8–0.91

Precursors to UML. Identifiable object-oriented modeling languages began to appear between mid-1970 and the late 1980s as various methodologists experimented with different approaches to object-oriented

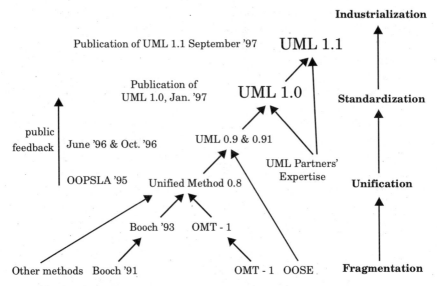

Figure C.1   UML development.

analysis and design. Several other techniques influenced these languages, including Entity-Relationship modeling, the Specification & Description Language (SDL, circa 1976, CCITT), and other techniques. The number of identified modeling languages increased from less than 10 to more than 50 during the period between 1989–1994. Many users of OO methods had trouble finding complete satisfaction in any one modeling language, fueling the "method wars." By the mid-1990s, new iterations of these methods began to appear, most notably Booch '93, the continued evolution of OMT, and Fusion. These methods began to incorporate each other's techniques, and a few clearly prominent methods emerged, including the OOSE, OMT-2, and Booch '93 methods. Each of these was a complete method, and was recognized as having certain strengths. In simple terms, OOSE was a use-case oriented approach that provided excellent support business engineering and requirements analysis. OMT-2 was especially expressive for analysis and data-intensive information systems. Booch '93 was particularly expressive during design and construction phases of projects and popular for engineering-intensive applications.

Booch, Rumbaugh, and Jacobson join forces.   The development of UML began in October of 1994 when Grady Booch and Jim Rumbaugh of Rational Software Corporation began their work on unifying the Booch and OMT (Object Modeling Technique) methods. Given that the Booch and OMT methods were already independently growing together and were collectively recognized as leading object-oriented methods worldwide, Booch and Rumbaugh joined forces to forge a complete unification of their work. A draft version 0.8 of the Unified Method, as it was then called, was released in October of 1995. In the Fall of 1995, Ivar Jacobson and his Objectory company joined Rational and this unification effort, merging in the OOSE (Object-Oriented Software Engineering) method. The Objectory name is now used within Rational primarily to describe its UML-compliant process, the Rational Objectory Process.

As the primary authors of the Booch, OMT, and OOSE methods, Grady Booch, Jim Rumbaugh, and Ivar Jacobson were motivated to create a unified modeling language for three reasons. First, these methods were already evolving toward each other independently. It made sense to continue that evolution together rather than apart, eliminating the potential for any unnecessary and gratuitous differences that would further confuse users. Second, by unifying the semantics and notation, they could bring some stability to the object-oriented marketplace, allowing projects to settle on one mature modeling language and letting tool builders focus on delivering more useful features. Third, they expected that their collaboration would yield improvements in all three earlier methods, helping them to capture lessons learned and to address problems that none of their methods previously handled well.

As they began their unification, they established four goals to focus their efforts:

- Enable the modeling of systems (and not just software) using object-oriented concepts

- Establish an explicit coupling to conceptual as well as executable artifacts

- Address the issues of scale inherent in complex, mission-critical systems

- Create a modeling language usable by both humans and machines

Devising a notation for use in object-oriented analysis and design is not unlike designing a programming language. There are tradeoffs. First, one must bound the problem: Should the notation encompass requirement specification? (Yes, partially.) Should the notation extend to the level of a visual programming language? (No.) Second, one must strike a balance between expressiveness and simplicity: Too simple a notation will limit the breadth of problems that can be solved; too complex a notation will overwhelm the mortal developer. In the case of unifying existing methods, one must also be sensitive to the installed base: Make too many changes, and you will confuse existing users. Resist advancing the notation, and you will miss the opportunity of engaging a much broader set of users. The UML definition strives to make the best tradeoffs in each of these areas.

The efforts of Booch, Rumbaugh, and Jacobson resulted in the release of the UML 0.9 and 0.91 documents in June and October of 1996. During 1996, the UML authors invited and received feedback from the general community. They incorporated this feedback, but it was clear that additional focused attention was still required.

UML 1.0–1.1 and the UML Partners

During 1996, it became clear that several organizations saw UML as strategic to their business. A Request for Proposal (RFP) issued by the Object Management Group (OMG) provided the catalyst for these organizations to join forces around producing a joint RFP response. Rational established the UML Partners consortium with several organizations willing to dedicate resources to work toward a strong UML 1.0 definition. Those contributing most to the UML 1.0 definition included: Digital Equipment Corp., HP, i-Logix, IntelliCorp, IBM, ICON Computing, MCI Systemhouse, Microsoft, Oracle, Rational Software, TI, and Unisys. This collaboration produced UML 1.0, a modeling language that was well defined, expressive, powerful, and generally applicable. This was submitted to the OMG in January 1997 as an initial RFP response.

In January 1997, IBM & ObjecTime, Platinum Technology, Ptech, Taskon & Reich Technologies, and Softeam also submitted separate RFP responses to the OMG. These companies joined the UML partners to contribute their ideas, and together the partners produced the revised UML 1.1 response. The focus of the UML 1.1 release was to improve the clarity of the UML 1.0 semantics and to incorporate contributions from the new partners. It has been submitted to the OMG for their consideration for adoption.

Focus of UML cooperation. The UML Partners contributed a variety of expert perspectives, including, but not limited to, the following: OMG and RM-ODP technology perspectives, business modeling, constraint language, state machine semantics, types, interfaces, components, collaborations, refinement, frameworks, distribution, and metamodel. The result—UML 1.1—is the result of a collaborative team effort. A list of individuals contributing to the UML is in the Acknowledgments. The UML 14 UML Summary, v1.1 partners have worked hard as a team to define UML 1.0 and 1.1. While each partner came in with their own perspective and areas of interest, the result has benefited from each of them and from the diversity of their experiences.

Hewlett-Packard provided input on the relationship between UML models and reuse issues and in the use of packages and "facades" to facilitate the construction of reusable component-based application frameworks. They advocate a layered UML structure and mechanisms to define extensible, modular method subsets for HP Fusion, reuse, and domain-specific methods. They also contributed to how inter-model relationships are modeled. They also focused on the use of patterns and the relationship to CORBA services. (See *www.hp.com*; Malan 1996; Griss 1996.)

IBM's primary contribution to the UML is the Object Constraint Language (OCL). OCL was developed at IBM as a language for business modeling within IBM and is derived from the Syntropy method. It is used within UML both to help formalize the semantics of the language itself and to provide a facility for UML users to express precise constraints on the structure of models. IBM's contributions to UML have also included fundamental concepts in the semantics of refinement and templates. (See *www.ibm.com*; Cook.)

i-Logix contributed with expertise in the definition, semantics, and use of executable behavior and the use of events and signals within the UML. The UML incorporates Harel statecharts to provide a hierarchical specification of concurrent behavior. i-Logix also focused strongly on the relation between object and behavioral models in UML. (See *www.ilogix.com*; Harel 1987; Harel 1996a; Harel 1996b.)

ICON Computing contributed in the area of precise behavior modeling of component and framework-based systems, with a clear definition of abstraction and refinement from business to code. Their primary technical areas in UML have been types, behavior specifications, refinement, collaborations, and composition of reusable frameworks, adapted from the Catalysis method. (See *www.iconcomp.com*; D'Souza 1997a; D'Souza 1997b.)

IntelliCorp contributed to business modeling aspects of the UML, activity diagrams and object flow in particular, as well as formalization for the concept of roles, and other aspects of object and dynamic modeling. (See *www.intellicorp.com*; Martin/Odell 1995; Bock/Odell 1994.)

As a leading systems integrator MCI Systemhouse has worked to ensure that the UML is applicable to a wide range of application domains. Their expertise in distributed object systems has made the UML more scalable and better able to address issues of distribution and concurrency. MCI Systemhouse played an important role in defining the metamodel and the glossary, especially in their leadership of a semantics task force during the UML 1.1 phase. They also assisted in aligning the UML with other OMG standards and RM-ODP. (See *www.systemhouse.mci.com*.)

Microsoft provided expertise with the issues of building component-based systems, including modeling components, their interfaces and their distribution. They have also focused on the relationship between UML and standards such as ActiveX and COM and use the UML with their repository technology. (See *www.microsoft.com*.)

ObjecTime contributed in the areas of formal specification, extensibility, and behavior. They played a key role in definitions for state machines, common behavior, role modeling, and refinement. They also contributed to the RM-ODP comparison. (See *www.objectime.com*.)

Oracle helped in the definition and support for modeling business processes and for describing business models in UML. They focused on support for workflow descriptions and activity diagrams as well as business objects, and have prepared stereotypes for tailoring the UML for business modeling. (See *www.oracle.com*; Ramackers 1995; Ramackers 1996.)

Platinum Technology contributed in the areas of extension mechanisms, alignment with the MetaObject Facility, metamodeling, CDIF perspectives, and tool interoperability. (See *www.platinum.com*.)

Ptech contributed expertise in metamodels, distributed systems, and other topics. (See *www.ptechinc.com*.)

Rational Software defined the original UML and led the UML 1.0 and 1.1 projects, technically and managerially. Rational's diverse experience in object-oriented, component-based, and visual modeling technology has contributed greatly to the UML. (See *www.rational.com / uml*; Booch et al.; Rumbaugh et al.; Jacobson et al.)

Reich Technologies and Taskon contributed their expertise on collaborations and role modeling. (See *www.sn.no*.)

Softeam provided detailed reviews of the UML during its evolution. (See *www.softeam.fr*.)

Sterling Software contributed with their expertise on the modeling of components and types. They focused on type models and specifications, on business modeling, and on the relationship of the UML definition to standards. Texas Instruments Software, a UML Partner, was acquired by Sterling Software during the UML 1.1 definition phase. (See *www.sterling.com*.)

Unisys has a strong interest in the meta-metamodels and their relationship to the UML, including the formalization of relationships and constraints at the meta-level and meta-meta-level consistently. Within the UML proposal they have particularly focused on the integration of the UML and the OMG's Meta-Object Facility and CORBA IDL. They were instrumental in the IDL generation for the UML CORBAfacility. (See *www.unisys.com*.)

Summary of Changes between 1.0 and 1.1

The primary changes between UML 1.0 and 1.1 include:

- Increased formalism

- Improved packaging structure

- Unification of collaboration and interaction semantics

- Simplification of the class/type/interface model

- Unification of relationship semantics

- Extension of model management semantics, including models and subsystems

- Extension of use case semantics

- Improved mapping of notation to semantics

UML Present and Future

The UML is nonproprietary and open to all. It addresses the needs of user and scientific communities, as established by experience with the underlying methods on which it is based. Many methodologists, organizations, and tool vendors have committed to use it. Since the UML builds upon similar semantics and notation from Booch, OMT, OOSE, and other leading methods and has incorporated input from the UML partners and feedback from the general public, widespread adoption of the UML should be straightforward.

There are two aspects of "unified" that the UML achieves: First, it effectively ends many of the differences, often inconsequential, between the modeling languages of previous methods. Secondly, and perhaps more importantly, it unifies the perspectives among many different kinds of systems (business versus software), development phases (requirements analysis, design, and implementation), and internal concepts.

Standardization of the UML. Many organizations have already endorsed the UML as their organization's standard, since it is based on the modeling languages of leading OO methods. The UML is ready for widespread use. These documents are suitable as the primary source for authors writing books and training materials, as well as developers implementing visual modeling tools. Additional collateral, such as articles, training courses, examples, and books, will soon make the UML very approachable for a wide audience. The UML 1.1 has been submitted to the OMG for considered technology adoption in September 1997, coincident with the publication of this document.

Industrialization. Many organizations and vendors worldwide have already embraced the UML. The number of endorsing organizations is expected to grow significantly over time. These organizations will continue to encourage the use of the Unified Modeling Language by making the definition readily available and by encouraging other methodologists, tool vendors, training organizations, and authors to adopt the UML.

The real measure of the UML's success is its use on successful projects and the increasing demand for supporting tools, books, training, and mentoring.

Future UML evolution. Although the UML defines a precise language, it is not a barrier to future improvements in modeling concepts. We have addressed many leading-edge techniques, but expect additional techniques to influence future versions of the UML. Many advanced techniques can be defined using UML as a base. The UML can be extended without redefining the UML core.

The UML, in its current form, is expected to be the basis for many tools, including those for visual modeling, simulation, and development environments. As interesting tool integrations are developed, implementation standards based on the UML will become increasingly available.

The UML has integrated many disparate ideas, so this integration will accelerate the use of OO. Component-based development is an approach worth mentioning. It is synergistic with traditional object-oriented techniques. While reuse based on components is becoming increasingly widespread, this does not mean that component-based techniques will replace object-oriented techniques. There are only subtle differences between the semantics of components and classes.

Additional Information

These documents, additional information, as well as any updates to the UML will appear on Rational Software's web site, *www.rational.com/uml*.

Acknowledgments

The UML was crafted through the dedicated efforts of individuals and companies who find UML strategic to their future. This section acknowledges the efforts of these top-notch individuals who contributed to defining UML 1.1.

UML 1.1 Core Team

- *HP*: Martin Griss

- *I-Logix*: Eran Gery, David Harel

- *ICON Computing*: Desmond D'Souza

- *IBM*: Steve Cook, Jos Warmer

- *MCI Systemhouse*: Cris Kobryn, Joaquin Miller

- *ObjecTime*: John Hogg, Bran Selic

- *IntelliCorp and James Martin & Co.*: James Odell

- *Oracle*: Guus Ramackers

- *Platinum Technology*: Dilhar DeSilva

- *Rational Software*: Grady Booch, Ed Eykholt (project lead), Ivar Jacobson, Gunnar Overgaard, Karin Palmkvist, Jim Rumbaugh

- *Taskon*: Trygve Reenskaug

- *Sterling Software*: John Cheesman, Keith Short

- *Unisys*: Sridhar Iyengar, GK Khalsa

UML 1.1 Semantics Task Force

During the 1.1 phase, a team was formed to focus on improving the formality of the UML 1.0 semantics, as well as incorporating additional ideas from the partners. Under the leadership of Cris Kobryn, this team was very instrumental in reconciling diverse viewpoints into a consistent set of semantics, as expressed in the revised *UML Semantics*. Other members of this team were Dilhar DeSilva, Martin Griss, Sridhar Iyengar, Eran Gery, Gunnar Overgaard, Karin Palmkvist, Guus Ramackers, Bran Selic, and Jos Warmer. Booch, Jacobson, and Rumbaugh provided their expertise to the team, as well.

Contributors and Supporters

We appreciate the contributions, influence, and support of the following individuals.

Jim Amsden, Hernan Astudillo, Colin Atkinson, Dave Bernstein, Philip A. Bernstein, Michael Blaha, Conrad Bock, Mike Bradley, Ray Buhr, Gary Cernosek, James Cerrato, Michael Jesse Chonoles, Magnus Christerson, Dai Clegg, Peter Coad, Derek Coleman, Ward Cunningham, Raj 18 UML Summary, v1.1 Datta, Mike Devlin, Philippe Desfray, Bruce Douglass, Staffan Ehnebom, Maria Ericsson, Johannes Ernst, Don Firesmith, Martin Fowler, Adam Frankl, Eric Gamma, Dipayan Gangopadhyay, Garth Gullekson, Rick Hargrove, Tim Harrison, Richard Helm, Brian Henderson-Sellers, Michael Hirsch, Bob Hodges, Glenn Hollowell, Yves Holvoet, Jon Hopkins, John Hsia, Ralph Johnson, Anneke Kleppe, Philippe Kruchten, Paul Kyzivat, Martin Lang, Grant Larsen, Reed Letsinger, Mary Loomis, Jeff MacKay, Robert Martin, Terrie McDaniel, Jim McGee, Bertrand

Meyer, Mike Meier, Randy Messer, Greg Meyers, Fred Mol, Luis Montero, Paul Moskowitz, Andy Moss, Jan Pachl, Paul Patrick, Woody Pidcock, Bill Premerlani, Jeff Price, Jerri Pries, Terry Quatrani, Mats Rahm, George Reich, Rich Reitman, Rudolf M. Riess, Erick Rivas, Kenny Rubin, Jim Rye, Danny Sabbah, Tom Schultz, Ed Seidewitz, Gregson Siu, Jeff Sutherland, Dan Tasker, Dave Tropeano, Andy Trice, Dan Uhlar, John Vlissides, Larry Wall, Paul Ward, Alan Wills, Rebecca Wirfs-Brock, Bryan Wood, Ed Yourdon, and Steve Zeigler.

References

Bock, C., and J. Odell. "A Foundation For Composition," *Journal of Object-Oriented Programming*, October 1994.

Booch, G., J. Rumbaugh, and I. Jacobson. *Unified Modeling Language User Guide*. Reading, MA: Addison-Wesley, 1998. See *www.awl.com / cp / uml / uml.html*.

Cook, S., and J. Daniels. *Designing Object Systems: Object-Oriented Modelling with Syntropy*. Hemel Hempstead, UK: Prentice Hall, 1994.

D'Souza, D., and A. Wills. "Input for the OMG Submission." See *www.iconcomp.com / catalysis*.

D'Souza, D., and A. Wills. "Catalysis: Component- and Framework-based Development." See *www.iconcomp.com / catalysis*.

Fowler, M., and K. Scott. *UML Distilled: Applying the Standard Object Modeling Language*. Reading, MA: Addison-Wesley, 1997. See *http: / / www.awl.com / cp / uml / uml.html*.

Griss, M. "Domain Engineering and Variability In the Reuse-Driven Software Engineering Business," *Object Magazine*. Dec. 1996. See *www.hpl.hp.com / reuse*.

Harel, D. "Statecharts: A Visual Formalism for Complex Systems," *Science of Computer Programming*. 8 (1987) 231–274.

Harel, D., and E. Gery. "Executable Object Modeling with Statecharts," *Proc. 18th Int. Conf. Soft. Eng.*, Berlin: IEEE Press, March 1996, 246–257.

Harel, D., and A. Naamad. "The STATEMATE Semantics of Statecharts," *ACM Trans. Soft. Eng. Method*. 5:4 (Oct. 1996).

Jacobson, I., G. Booch, and J. Rumbaugh. *The Objectory SoftwareDevelopment Process*. Reading, MA: Addison-Wesley, 1998. See *www.awl.com / cp / uml / uml.html* and the "Rational Objectory Process" on *www.rational.com*.

Malan, R., D. Coleman, R. Letsinger, et al. "The Next Generation of Fusion," *Fusion Newsletter*, Oct. 1996. (See *www.hpl.hp.com / fusion*.)

Martin, J., and J. Odell, *Object-oriented Methods, A Foundation*. Englewood Cliffs, NJ: Prentice Hall, 1995.

Ramackers, G., and Clegg, D. "Object Business Modelling, Requirements and Approach," in *Business Object Design and Implementation: OOPSLA '95 Workshop Proceedings* 16 October 1995, Austin, Texas. London: Springer Verlag, 1997. See *www.amazon.com* or OOPSLA's Web site *http://www.tiac.net/users/jsuth/oopsla/oo95wrkf.html*.

Ramackers, G., and Clegg, D. "Extended Use Cases and Business Objects for BPR," *ObjectWorld* UK '96, London, June 18–21, 1996.

Rumbaugh, J., I. Jacobson, and G. Booch. *Unified Modeling Language Reference Manual.* Reading, MA: Addison-Wesley, 1998. See *www.awl.com/cp/uml/uml.html*.

UML Web Site. See *http://www.rational.com/uml*.

UML Extension for Business Modeling

Introduction

This document defines the UML Extension for the Business Modeling, defined in terms of the UML's extension mechanisms, namely Stereotypes, TaggedValues, and Constraints.

See the UML Semantics document for a full description of the UML extension mechanisms.

This section describes stereotypes that can be used to tailor the use of UML for business modeling. All of the UML concepts can be used for business modeling, but providing business stereotypes for some common situations provides a common terminology for this domain. Note that UML can be used to model different kinds of systems: software systems, hardware systems, and real-world organizations. Business modeling models real-world organizations.

This document is not meant to be a complete definition of business modeling concepts and how to apply them, but it serves the purpose of registering this extension, including its icons.

Summary of Extension

Stereotypes

Metamodel	Class Stereotype Name
Model	use case model
Package	use case system
Package	use case package
Model	object model
Subsystem	object system
Subsystem	organization unit
Subsystem	work unit
Class	worker
Class	case worker
Class	internal worker
Class	entity
Collaboration	use case realization
Association	subscribes

TaggedValues

This extension does not currently introduce any new TaggedValues.

Constraints

This extension does not currently introduce any new Constraints, other than those associated with the well-formedness semantics of the stereotypes introduced.

Prerequisite Extensions

This extension requires no other extensions to the UML for its definition.

Stereotypes and Notation

Model, Package, and Subsystem Stereotypes

A business system comprises several different but related models. The models are characterized by being exterior or interior to the business system they represent. Exterior models are use case models and interior models are object models. A large business system may be partitioned into subordinate business systems. The following are the model stereotypes:

Use case. A *Use Case Model* is a model that describes the business processes of a business and their interactions with extenal parties like customers and partners.
A use case model describes:

* the businesses modeled as use cases.

* parties exterior to the business (e.g., customers and other businesses) modeled as actors.

* the relationships between the external parties and the business processes.

A *Use Case System* is the top-level package in a use case model. A use case system contains use case packages, use cases, actors, and relationships.
A *Use Case Package* is a package containing use cases and actors with relationships. A use case is not partitioned over several use case packages.

Object. An *Object Model* is a model in which the top-level package is an object system. These models describe the things interior to the business system itself.
An *Object System* is the top-level subsystem in an object model. An object system contains organization units, classes (workers, work units, and entities), and relationships.

Organization unit. *Organization Unit* is a subsystem corresponding to an organization unit of the actual business. An organization unit subsystem contains organization units, work units, classes (workers and entities), and relationships.

Work unit. A *Work Unit* is a subsystem that contains one or more entities.
A work unit is a task-oriented set of objects that form a recognizable whole to the end user. It may have a facade defining the view of the work unit's entities relevant to the task.

Notation. Package stereotypes are indicated with stereotype keywords in guillemets («stereotype name»). There are no special stereotyped icons for packages.

Class Stereotypes

Business objects come in the following kinds:

- actor (defined in the UML)
- worker
- case worker
- internal worker
- entity

Worker. A *Worker* is a class that represents an abstraction of a human that acts within the system. A worker interacts with other workers and manipulates entities while participating in use case realizations.

Case worker. A *Case worker* is a worker who interacts directly with actors outside the system.

Internal worker. An *Internal worker* is a worker that interacts with other workers and entities inside the system.

Entity. An *Entity* is class that is passive; that is, it does not initiate interactions on its own. An entity object may participate in many different use case realizations and usually outlives any single interaction. In business modeling entities represent objects that workers access, inspect, manipulate, produce, and so on. Entity objects provide the basis for sharing among workers participating in different use case realizations.

Notation. Class stereotypes can be shown with keywords in guillemets within the normal class symbol. They can also be shown with the following special icons:

The icons shown in Figure D.1 represent common concepts useful in most business models.

Example of alternate notations. Tools and users are free to add additional icons to represent more specific concepts. Examples of such icons include icons for documents and actions, as shown in Figure D.2.

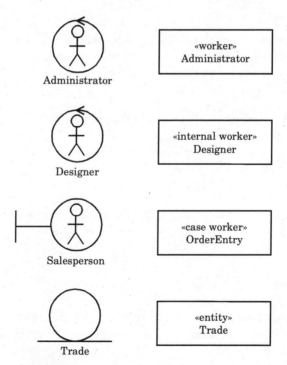

Figure D.1   Class stereotypes.

Trade   Client   Trade
[requested]   Trading   [traded]

Figure D.2   Example of special icons for entities and actions.

In this example, "Trade [requested]" and "Trade [traded]" represent an entity in two states, where the Trade is the dominant entity of a Trade Document work unit. Client Trading is an action. The icons are designed to be meaningful in the particular problem domain.

Association Stereotypes

The following are special business modeling associations between classes:

Communicates. *Communicates* is an association used by two instances to interact. This may be one-way or two-way navigation. The direction of communication is the same as the navigability of the association.

Subscribes. *Subscribes* is a association whose source is a class (called the subscriber) and whose target is a class (called the publisher). The subscriber specifies a set of events. The subscriber is notified when one of those events occurs in the target.

Notation. Association stereotypes are indicated by keywords in guillemets. There are no special stereotype icons.

Well-Formedness Rules

Stereotyped model elements are subject to certain constraints in addition to the constraints imposed on all elements of their kind.

Generalization

All the modeling elements in a generalization must be of the same stereotype.

Association

Apart from standard UML combinations the combinations shown in Table D.1 are allowed for each stereotype.

TABLE D.1 Valid Association Stereotype Combinations

To : From:	Actor	Case Worker	Entity	Work Unit	Internal Worker
Actor		Communicates		Communicates subscribes	
Case Worker	Communicates	Communicates	Communicates subscribes	Communicates subscribes	Communicates
Entity			Communicates subscribes	communicates	
Work Unit	Communicates	Communicates	Communicates subscribes	Communicates subscribes	Communicates
Internal Worker		Communicates	Communicates subscribes	Communicates subscribes	Communicates

Index

A

Abstract factory pattern, 273
Abstraction, Object Definition
    Language (ODL), 108
Abstraction test suite, 209
Access, optimization of, 131–132
Access control patterns, 277
Access paths, navigation of, 63
Active constraint, 97
Active object storage, 157–158
Actors, 5
    in business process modeling,
    1–2
    identification of, 7–8
    triggers for events, 7
Adapter pattern, 273
Agents, quality checks, 181

Algebraic specification languages,
    254
Aperiodic trigger, 100
Application classes, sources of, 46
Application objects, 300
Architectural patterns, 267,
    275–276
Arrays, 88, 93–94
    operations supported by, 93
Assertions
    conditional test suite, 205–206
    conversion of rules to, 79
Associations, 56–60, 88, 94–97
    cardinality, 58–59
    and classes, 47, 57
    constraints related to, 95–97
    functions of, 56–57
    identification of, 57–58